# Sand Dance

## BY CAMEL ACROSS
## ARABIA'S GREAT SOUTHERN DESERT

# BRUCE KIRKBY
*Foreword by Sir Wilfred Thesiger*

M&S

Cloth edition published 2000
Trade paperback edition published 2001

**Canadian Cataloguing in Publication Data**

Kirkby, Bruce, 1968-
   Sand dance : by camel across Arabia's great southern desert

ISBN 0-7710-9564-3 (bound)   ISBN 0-7710-9565-1 (pbk.)

1. Kirkby, Bruce, 1968-   - Journeys – Rub'al Khāli. 2. Thesiger, Wilfred, 1910-   –
Journeys – Rub'al Khāli. 3. Rub'al Khāli – Description and travel. 4. Bedouins –
Rub'al Khāli. I. Title.

DS247.R82K57 2000          915.38          C00-930510-6

We acknowledge the financial support of the Government of Canada through the Book Publishing Industry Development Program for our publishing activities. We further acknowledge the support of the Canada Council for the Arts and the Ontario Arts Council for our publishing program.

Photograph of Sir Wilfred Thesiger in Bedu dress. (p.viii) © Sir Wilfred Thesiger/Pitt Rivers Museum, University of Oxford. Permission granted by Curtis Brown Group Ltd.

Excerpts from *Arabian Sands* on pages 1, 91, 113, 147, 159, 203 © Wilfred Thesiger, 1959. Permission granted by Curtis Brown Group Ltd. on behalf of Wilfred Thesiger.

Typeset in Minion by M&S, Toronto
Text design by Sari Ginsberg

Printed and bound in Canada

McClelland & Stewart Ltd.
*The Canadian Publishers*
481 University Avenue
Toronto, Ontario
M5G 2E9
www.mcclelland.com

1 2 3 4 5   05 04 03 02 01

# For Dad

My father's unexpected death five years ago was a terrible shock for me and my family. Time, the great healer, has brought understanding, acceptance, and a grateful appreciation for our precious days together. Yet on occasion I still feel saddened that I can no longer share stories of my adventures with Dad. I know he would have been so interested. In the past I always returned home to relive with him the challenges, exhilarations, frustrations, achievements, and failures I had faced.

Nine months after I began planning and preparing for this expedition, I discovered my father had had a faded copy of *Arabian Sands*, the book that inspired this journey, tucked in a bedside shelf. He received it as a Christmas present from my grandparents in 1959. My mother recalled how the book had both moved and impressed my father, becoming one of his favourites. Until then I never even knew he had read it.

I have since had the privilege to cross that same desert, to follow in Wilfred Thesiger's footsteps, and to become friends with the great explorer. In that worn copy of *Arabian Sands* Sir Wilfred's signature now lies beside my father's handwritten name.

I do not want to hypothesize on what happens after death. Perhaps my father knows of my journey, perhaps not. The fact that he once read of this great land, and found a special meaning in Sir Wilfred's crossing of the Empty Quarter, has helped close that gap of unshared adventures.

I know Dad had always planned to write a book. He never got that chance. With love I dedicate this book to him.

*With Dad, California, 1971*

# Table of Contents

*Sir Wilfred Thesiger, the legendary Arabian explorer,
in 1949, after his second crossing of the Empty Quarter.*

# FOREWORD

BY SIR WILFRED THESIGER

*F*rom 1945 to 1950, I lived and travelled with the Bedu in Arabia. Those were the most memorable five years of my life.

Twice I crossed the great southern desert, that vast, desolate area of almost half a million square miles, which the Arabs call the Rub al-Khali, or "the Empty Quarter." My small party was always hungry and thirsty; sometimes our lives were threatened by fanatical tribes hostile to my presence as a Christian.

During those years, I wanted no concessions. What mattered to me was that my companions should accept me as one of them. Indeed, I have written in *Arabian Sands* that, without the comradeship of bin Kabina, bin Ghabaisha, and other Bedu who came with me, the hardships involved with my journeys would have been a meaningless penance.

Now, more than fifty years later, three adventurous young Canadians, Bruce Kirkby and brothers Jamie and Leigh Clarke, decided to retrace my first journey across the Empty Quarter. They travelled as I had done, using camels for transport, with traditional tribesmen akin to the ones who had travelled with me in 1946-47; however, at first they had difficulty persuading them to use camels instead of the four-wheel-drive vehicles which have almost entirely replaced the camels as transport.

While much of the Bedu way of life has changed dramatically since I left Arabia, Bruce Kirkby and his friends found the Empty Quarter as I described it in *Arabian Sands*.

I very much enjoyed meeting Bruce, Jamie, and Leigh when they visited me in England, before and after their journey across the Empty Quarter. I have been moved by their enthusiasm and their modest sense of achievement now that their journey is over.

Turning the pages of this book, looking at its illustrations, once again I have felt the desert come alive for me.

NOTES ON USAGE

*I* have used the word *Bedu* in reference to the nomads of southern Arabia. The familiar form found in English, Bedouin, is actually a double plural, which would never be found in proper Arabic. The Arabs refer to themselves as Bedu, from the ancient word *Badawi*, meaning "unsettled people," or "desert dwellers." The correct singular form of Bedu is *Bedui*. Thesiger and later authors used the term *Bedu* for both singular and plural, and to avoid confusion I have chosen to do the same.

The words "Arabia" and "Saudi Arabia" appear frequently in the text, and have distinct meanings. "Arabia" refers to the entire Arabian Peninsula, including the land covered by Yemen, Oman, Saudi Arabia, the United Arab Emirates, and other Gulf states. "Saudi Arabia" refers only to the Kingdom of Saudi Arabia, one of the three countries we travelled through on our journey.

Bedu names, although appearing long and difficult to our Western eyes, confer a great deal of information about the bearer, and usually include references to two generations of male ancestry, a sub-tribe or family, and then the main tribal group. For example, the full name of our young Bedu companion Ali was "Ali bin Salim bin Amir al-Musalli al-Kathiri." Named Ali at birth, he is the son of Salim (*bin* and *ibn* both meaning "son of"), who was the son of Amir, belonging to the Musalli family, part of the Bait Kathir tribe. Bedu rarely call each other by their full and proper names except in formal situations. A confusing number of variations for a single individual are often heard, including, in the case of our young companion, "Ali," "Ali Salim," and "Ali bin Salim."

The non-hereditary title "Sheikh," held by many characters in the book, confers a sign of respect, with varying connotations throughout Arabia. Its Arabic root means "elder," and it traditionally has been synonymous with the leader of a tribe or tribal sub-group. Today it is often used when referring to anyone from business managers and public figures to religious leaders and heads of state.

ربع الخالي

Measurements of distance, weight, and volume in the text have been standardized to the metric system, and conversions to imperial included in parentheses. With conversions of volume, gallon refers to a U.S. gallon (3.785 litres), not an imperial gallon (4.546 litres).

All dates in the text have been standardized to Christian years AD. It should be noted that Arabia follows the Islamic, or *hijra*, calendar, which begins in the Christian year 622 AD with the flight of the Prophet Mohammed from Mecca to Medina. The *hijra* calendar is based on the lunar cycle, and each month begins only with the actual sighting of the new moon (astronomical predictions are not acceptable). Thus each Islamic year is roughly 354 days long, and events such as Ramadan and the *Haj* cycle through the Christian calendar, occurring approximately 11 days earlier each succeeding year. For reference, on April 28, 1998, just over a month after we finished our journey, the Islamic world began the year 1419 AH (Anno Hegirae).

صحراء

The majority of Bedu we met spoke little English, and our communication was mostly in simple Arabic. Although most of the conversations are translated, I have included short sections and selected phrases of Arabic dialogue in the text, as they are essential to properly convey the spirit of the journey. These I hope will help transport the reader back to Arabia, conveying an intangible essence of the Bedu and their strong beliefs that would otherwise be lost in translation.

I have denoted Arabic using italics, and have included a brief translation in parentheses following; for example, "*Keif halek?* (How is your life?)". The only exceptions are proper names, such as the town of

Thumbrait, or my friend Said bin Ali, which I left non-italicized. These words are commonly used directly in English conversations, and there is no useful translation. Some Arabic items are mentioned frequently in the text, such as *dishdasha* (a light cotton or silk robe worn by Arabs), *gerber* (the goatskin bags in which we carried our water in), and *graf* (a common desert tree). These are translated on their first occurrence and then appear alone in italics thereafter. I assume the reader will remember the meaning, or be able to discern it easily from the context.

The Arabic language has its own script. Representations in Latin characters of the Arabic words are phonetic reconstructions. For example, the name عبد الله can be represented as *Abdullah*. As dialects vary widely with geography, many phonetic forms can often be found for a single word or name. For instance, *Abdulla, Abdallah, Abd'Allah* are all correct. Similarly the city *Jeddah* can be correctly spelled *Jiddah, Djetta, Gedda,* or *Jaddah*. I have striven to use the most common where possible.

Arabic also includes several sounds foreign to Western ears. Notable is the 'Ain, commonly represented by '. I have left the 'Ain out of the phonetic translations completely. The name of one of the major characters is correctly rendered as Mana'a, but I have chosen to refer to him simply as Manaa. This avoids an unnecessary repetition of the ', which would be meaningless to most. The letter 'ghain is also difficult, and I have adopted the common *gh* representation. The *gh* sounds as a soft guttural *r*. It occurs rarely, in such names as *Bin Ghabaisha*.

# Southern Oman

## MAY 1998

*I* was searching for "a man with one finger"; he knew I was coming.

My rented Land Cruiser raced across the featureless southern desert, following a lone strip of asphalt that seemed strangely out of place. Gusts of hot wind buffeted the vehicle as I squinted through a sea of glare and dust. Ahead of me long trails of drifting sand stretched across the tarmac in ever-changing patterns. It was the hot season now, and after two long, sweltering hours I arrived on the outskirts of a remote Bedu settlement, grinding to a halt outside a dilapidated gas station.

After months of fruitless efforts, my other leads were drying up; "the one-fingered man" now seemed our last hope. I had been told if anyone could help my two friends and me to lay the foundations for a camel journey across the legendary Empty Quarter, it would be him.

There was no mistaking Manaa Mohammed when we met. His lone finger gripped my hand in its firm grasp like a claw. His one blind eye, its distended form streaked with broken veins, drew my attention despite my every attempt to ignore it. His remaining eye searched my face endlessly, revealing nothing of his thoughts. Frightening scars marked the few exposed areas of Manaa's robed body, grim reminders of a landmine that exploded in his hand many years ago. I had heard rumours of his turbulent past during Oman's southern rebellion, but one thing was apparent: Manaa was Bedu to the core, rugged, canny, proud, a wolf of the desert.

We met for an hour, discussing the proposed expedition in detail. My knowledge of Arabic was cursory at best, and all our verbal communication was through a harried translator, whom I brought with me from Salala. As we talked, Manaa's roving eye continued to examine me. He had grim news. There had been a drought for ten years; wells were low and grazing was decimated. Camels were no longer as hardy or strong as they had been fifty years ago, when they regularly travelled great distances. There were very few Bedu who would be interested in undertaking the harsh journey we proposed. Most would consider us crazy. Why not see the local desert in an air-conditioned Land Cruiser? It would be faster and more comfortable. Manaa could arrange that.

I held firm to our aspirations of an unsupported journey in the style of this century's early Arabian travellers. I had met disbelief before, and was prepared to continue searching elsewhere. Was I being tested? Manaa rolled the end of his thin moustache between his single finger and his thumb, and stared directly at me. Perhaps there was another way, he finally admitted, but it would not be easy, or cheap. Was he serious? I could not tell. It had been an exhausting meeting. How well had I understood the translation?

Bedu are notoriously cunning businessmen, a trait passed on from their forefathers, branded through generations of tribal conflict and survival. Usually confident in my judgement of character, I did not know if he saw an opportunity to take me, a naive Westerner, for all the financial gain he could, or if he would he adopt my dreams of a camel odyssey as his own.

Suddenly Manaa signalled it was time to leave. I was to come back later. He needed time to consult the village elders. Through the interpreter I hurriedly expressed my thanks.

As I stood to leave, Manaa turned with a wry grin and stated in perfect English, "Don't worry, my friend, I will make you a Bedu."

As I came to learn during my time in the desert, the only thing that I could ever be certain of was that nothing would be as I thought.

# Sand Dance

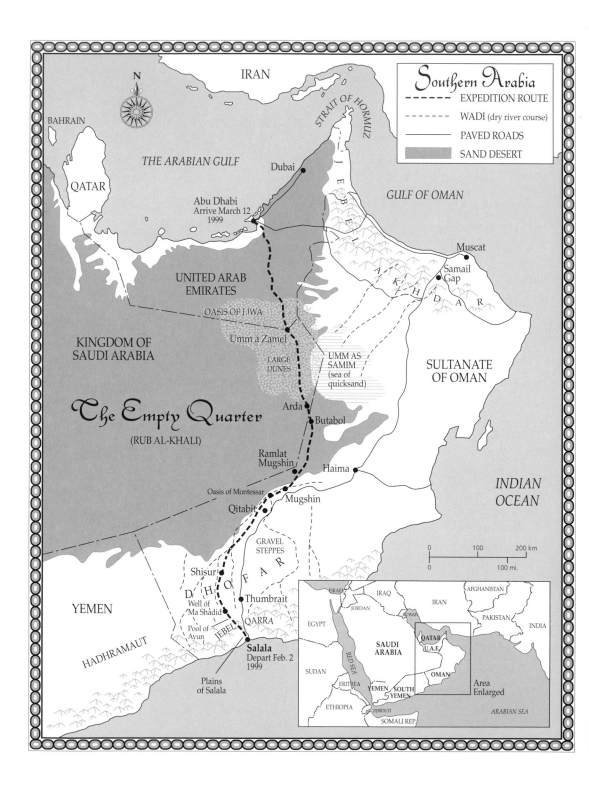

Southern Arabia

EXPEDITION ROUTE
WADI (dry river course)
PAVED ROADS
SAND DESERT

N

IRAN

STRAIT OF HORMUZ

BAHRAIN

THE ARABIAN GULF

GULF OF OMAN

QATAR

Dubai

Abu Dhabi
Arrive March 12
1999

Muscat

Samail
Gap

UNITED ARAB
EMIRATES

J
E
B
E
L

A
K
H
D
A
R

OASIS OF LIWA

KINGDOM OF
SAUDI ARABIA

Umm a Zamel

LARGE
DUNES

UMM AS
SAMIM
(sea of
quicksand)

SULTANATE
OF OMAN

The Empty Quarter

(RUB AL-KHALI)

Arda

Butabol

Ramlat
Mugshin

Haima

INDIAN
OCEAN

Oasis of Montessar

Mugshin

Qitabit

GRAVEL
STEPPES

D
H
O
F
A
R

Shisur

Thumbrait

YEMEN

Well of
Ma Shâdid

QARRA

Pool of
Ayun

JEBEL

Salala
Depart Feb. 2
1999

HADHRAMAUT

Plains
of Salala

0    100    200 km
0         100 mi.

ISRAEL
IRAQ
AFGHANISTAN

JORDAN
IRAN

EGYPT
PAKISTAN

QATAR
U.A.E.

SAUDI
ARABIA
INDIA

RED SEA

SUDAN
OMAN

ERITREA

YEMEN
SOUTH
YEMEN

Area
Enlarged

ETHIOPIA

DJIBOUTI

SOMALI REP.

ARABIAN SEA

# CHAPTER ONE

# The Desert Dream Begins

A cloud gathers, the rains fall, men live; the cloud disperses without rain, and men and animals die. In the deserts of southern Arabia there is no rhythm of the seasons, no rise and fall of sap, but empty wastes where only the changing temperature marks the passage of the years.

— Wilfred Thesiger, *Arabian Sands*

*W*hy the book caught my eye I will never know. Tucked away high on a shelf of a downtown Toronto bookstore, it was a faded paperback in the land of glossy hardcovers. I almost passed it by. Perhaps Wilfred Thesiger's name, emblazoned across its dull orange spine, triggered a distant memory. I had been passing time with my mother and sister, waiting for a Christmas performance of the *Nutcracker* ballet to begin. Now the doors across the street were starting to open. Our browsing time was running short. Yet for some reason I reached for the book, slowly pulled it down from the shelf, and turned it in my hands. Its dusty scent and faded pages invoked visions of a time long past, of romantic journeys, unknown lands, and mystery. The grainy black-and-white photographs spoke the language of hardship and suffering, of freedom and honour, of a forgotten time. It held the promise of adventure. I had only a few minutes to skim through the pages before I regretfully replaced the book high on its shelf. Yet it inspired visions that would burn on in my mind for days. Although I did not realize it on that cold December day in 1997, it would mark my life indelibly, and in ways I never could have foreseen.

The book was *Arabian Sands*, Wilfred Thesiger's classic account of his journeys through Arabia's legendary desert, the Empty Quarter, during the late 1940s. For me, finding it proved a catalyst, a crystallizing moment. In a continuing quest for adventure I had been searching, along with two friends, for a desert to cross. Not just any desert. There was something intangible we sought, something beyond the physical challenge of crossing barren and desolate wastes. I envisaged a remote land, little known and even less travelled, a hidden kingdom with a rich tapestry of history and culture. I did not know exactly what I had been seeking, but I did know that, until that moment, I had not found it. *Arabian Sands* introduced me to the Empty Quarter of Arabia. In that instant, I knew I had discovered the desert we would cross.

ربع الخالي

The Empty Quarter is the world's largest sand desert, a forbidding and foreboding territory. Surrounded by the parched wastelands of southern Arabia, it is a desert within a desert. Covering nearly a million square kilometres (386,270 sq. miles), it occupies an area larger than France. Within its borders lie twenty thousand cubic kilometres (4,800 cu. miles) of sand, more sand than in any other place on the planet – more than even the Sahara, which although six times the size, has large tracts of rock and gravel. Ancient winds, blowing for millennia, have sculpted the Empty Quarter's sand into mountainous dunes, many towering more than three hundred metres (985 ft.) in height. These dunes lie in chains that extend from horizon to horizon, unbroken obstacles spanning hundreds of kilometres. Woven between the colossal sand peaks are vast *sabkha* (salt) flats covering the valley floors. The *sabkha*, a mixture of salt and sand baked to concrete by the desert's heat, mercilessly reflects the sun's glare. During the hot season, which runs from May to October, temperatures in the Empty Quarter regularly soar past fifty degrees Celsius (120°F). The blazing sand surfaces can reach eighty degrees Celsius (175°F), scaring anything that moves. Few living creatures can survive the summer months. No men live there year-round. It is a dead and empty land.

The desert's ancient Arabic name, *al-Rub al-Khali* ("the Empty Quarter"), has its origin in Bedu folklore. The early nomads wandering Arabia believed that the oceans surrounding their land occupied one half of the world. The land they inhabited, the cooler gravel flats and coastal hills lying on the fringes of the peninsula, comprised another quarter. At the furthest extent of their winter grazing ranges lay the great desert, a desolate land perpetually scorched by the sun. There was no food for the nomads' camel herds there. Only a handful of hardy plants could be found, sporadically dotted amongst the dunes and *sabkha* flats. To the forefathers of today's Bedu, this was "the Empty Quarter" of their world.

Despite its strategic location and far-reaching influence, Arabia has long remained shrouded in mystery. Lying at the intersection of three continents, the massive peninsula, while technically part of Asia, is virtually a subcontinent unto itself. It is completely geographically isolated. To the east lies the Arabian Gulf, to the west the Red Sea, to the south the vast Indian Ocean, and to the north, the only land access is blocked by the inhospitable expanse of the Syrian desert.

The region first rose to importance during biblical times when Arabia was a critical link in both trade and travel, controlling the important land routes between the Mediterranean Sea and the Indian Ocean. Yet few reports of the desert kingdoms ever returned to Europe. Early Roman legionnaires were some of the first non-Arabs to travel in the distant and unknown reaches. Although their imperial plans were cut short by the inhospitable lands, they misleadingly named the southern extent of the peninsula *Arabia Felix* or "Happy (Blessed) Arabia," furthering misperceptions. Arabia remained widely known as "a huge white blot on the map of the world," deemed by most to be distant and impenetrable. And soon there was more than just hostile terrain and fierce people with which early explorers had to contend. There was a burgeoning new religion to face as well.

In 610 AD the prophet Mohammed received his first revelation from God in the small, dusty trading town of Mecca, and the religion of Islam was born. The new monotheistic faith suited the Bedu's strict moral code and filled a void within their society. *Islam*, roughly translated, means "surrender," and a *Muslim* is "one who submits." All Muslims are equal before god. The proud and free nomads were permitted to have their own uncomplicated relationship with Allah. In a harsh world, which was ruled by forces over which they had little influence, the Bedu submitted completely. Islam spread across the desert like wildfire, carried forth by word of mouth and by the sword. The influence of Islam penetrated every corner of Arabia, and quickly reached beyond. Within a century, the religion stretched west across Africa to Morocco, northwards into Moorish Spain and France, and east to Persia and Afghanistan.

There are five pillars of the Muslim faith. First, *Shahadah*, to accept and profess that "there is no god but God, and Mohammed is the Prophet of God." The second is *Salat*, to pray five times each day as described and ordained in the Koran. The third pillar is *Zakat*, to donate annual alms of conscience to the needy or poor. The fourth pillar is *Sawm*, the fast observed during the holy month of Ramadan (which in the year of our journey fell in January). No food or water may be consumed between sunrise and sunset during the twenty-eight days of the ninth lunar cycle in the Muslim calendar. The fifth pillar, the *Haj*, had the most enduring influence on the exploration of Arabia, effectively sealing the peninsula to Europe and the rest of the non-Islamic world. The *Haj* is the famous pilgrimage that all Muslims who are financially and physically able are required to undertake once in their lifetime. As Mecca and Medina – where Mohammed spent five years in exile – assumed great new importance, the holy cities were formally closed to all but the followers of Islam, and fanatical anti-Christian sentiments made the entire peninsula inaccessible to Westerners.

As the religion grew, so did the annual influx of believers. Every year the legendary Damascus caravan, with more than forty thousand camels, tethered head to tail, travelled for forty Arabian days and nights to reach Mecca. Each morning a cannon was fired, warning that the march would shortly begin. Anyone not mounted when the caravan surged ahead was left behind in a swirling sea of dust. By the sixteenth century, millions were making the pilgrimage, and the annual human tide was dedicated to preventing non-believers from reaching the holy lands. Despite zealous efforts, which included years of studying Arabic and perfecting disguises, no early explorers were able to smuggle themselves to Mecca or Medina. Their efforts only enshrouded the cities and the surrounding lands of Arabia even deeper in mystery.

It was almost a thousand years after Mohammed, in 1503, that an Italian, Ludovico de Varthema, became the first non-Muslim to visit Mecca and describe the Kaaba, Islam's central shrine. Amazingly Varthema's disguise was so good that he joined the Mameluke guard protecting the pilgrims, and spent three weeks in the holy city. He was able to leave without incident, but his cover was later blown in Yemen, when in a moment of panic he forgot Arabic. Immediately thrown into prison, Varthema was lucky to escape with his life; he was rescued three months later, reportedly by one of the Sultan's concubines.

Not until 1767, when Carsten Neibur returned as the sole survivor of an ill-fated Danish expedition, did the exploration of Arabia begin in earnest. Neibur's records provided a detailed picture of the land and people, sparking renewed interest in the region. He was followed by many famous explorers, including Charles Doughty, Anne Blunt, Gertrude Bell, William Palgrave, Johann Burckhardt, and Richard Burton, each of whom added their own contribution to the world's scant knowledge of Arabia. And from these returning expeditions rumours grew of a great desert to the south. Doughty noted in his masterpiece, *Travels in Arabia Deserta* (1855), that he had "never found any Arabian who had aught to tell, even by hearsay, of that dreadful country." Burton reported that it was "a haggard land infested with wild beasts and wilder men" (*Personal Narrative of a Pilgrimage to Al-Madinah and Meccah* [1898]). None of these early travellers ventured into the *Rub al-Khali*, or even stood on its fringes.

The great desert remained a mystery, and, by the turn of the twentieth century, the Empty Quarter had become the largest unexplored region on earth. Harry St. John Philby was the first to eye this last great prize. As the British adviser to the famous Saudi Arabian king Abdul Aziz, Philby spent fourteen years planning an attempt to cross the Empty Quarter while patiently awaiting the king's permission. Before he could claim it for his own, however, Bertram Thomas, who had earlier been Philby's assistant, stole the prize from under his nose. In 1931, stationed on the opposite side of the great desert, in the court of the Sultan of Oman, Thomas snuck away without the knowledge or consent of his master. He travelled from south to north through the flatter western regions, and completed the first recorded crossing of the Empty Quarter, following a route that Philby quickly noted was the easiest possible. A year later Philby set out, disappointed yet undeterred, and completed a second crossing of the great desert, this time from north to south, again in the west. Between these two, the greatest prize of Arabian exploration had been claimed, yet hundreds of thousands of kilometres remained unexplored.

In 1945, Wilfred Thesiger arrived in Arabia. He had officially come to search for locust breeding-grounds, or "outbreak centres," in the unexplored lands beyond Oman's coastal mountains, but he had other plans. When the Anti-Locust Research Centre in London had offered him the job, Thesiger knew it provided a rare opportunity. He was to be based in Dhofar (southern Oman), which provided a natural approach to the Empty Quarter. At the time Oman was ruled by a xenophobic sultan, and permission to travel in his lands was almost never granted. For Thesiger, a man who dreamed of unmapped places, where the wells and camel routes, dune ranges and desert oases were still unknown, and where the great nomadic tribes remained unadministered, this was the chance he had waited for.

During the next five years Wilfred Thesiger would befriend the hardy desert Bedu, and live as their equal. He travelled over sixteen thousand kilometres (10,000 miles) by camel, through lands never before explored. Twice he crossed the Empty Quarter. He became the first European to reach the fabled oasis of Liwa, and the first to set eyes on the quicksand seas of Umm as Samim ("Mother of Poison"). His travels in Arabia won Thesiger distinction as a traveller – and a life of unparalleled adventure followed. He is widely known today as the last of the great explorers.

When Thesiger left Arabia in 1949 he felt he was "going into exile." Political circumstances were such that he could no longer travel freely through the region's deserts, where visas were now required. Oil companies and governments alike questioned Thesiger's motives, and he realized he would never return to the land as he had once known it. Ten years later, Thesiger chronicled his adventures in the eloquent book *Arabian Sands.* The magical tale recounts his years spent travelling the desiccated wastes with his Bedu companions. While he captures the beautiful strength of the unforgiving land, it was the people that stole Thesiger's heart. In closing he wrote, "I shall always remember how often I was humbled by those illiterate herdsmen, who possessed, in so much greater measure than I, generosity and courage, endurance, patience and light-hearted gallantry. Among no people have I ever felt the same sense of personal inferiority."

Running through the book is a melancholy thread: Thesiger's belief that the ways of the nomads were doomed. The discovery of oil had brought with it staggering wealth, rapid technological advancements, and an inherent materialism, all of which, Thesiger predicted, would drive the Bedu from the desert, and degrade forever the freedom, generosity, and honour of their ancient civilization. Others would travel the land, Thesiger noted, and "they will bring back results far more interesting than mine, but they will never know the spirit of the land nor the greatness of the Arabs."

Thesiger did not return to the desert, nor did anyone else. As of that Christmas as I stood leafing through the faded copy of *Arabian Sands*, no one had returned to the Empty Quarter to travel as Thesiger once had. Certainly oil exploration, international border demarcation, and military activities had on occasion brought men into the desert. But they lived a different life. As they travelled in four-wheel-drive vehicles and lived in air-conditioned barracks, the walls between them and the land could have been miles thick. None lived with the Bedu, travelled by camel across the desert, sought the spirit of the land.

My friends and I were in a unique position. The forbidding desert was still there, largely unknown and untravelled, the same impenetrable barrier to human travel it had always been. And, as Thesiger had foretold, the world around it had changed beyond description.

What had drawn us on this quest? Why, on that winter day in Toronto, was I searching for a desert to cross?

The answer to such a question is never simple. For me it was the next natural step on a long and winding path of adventure that had led ever farther from the city and a "regular" life. In the spring of 1990 I had graduated from university with a degree in Engineering Physics, a course I took more to answer my own innate curiosity about the world around me than to prepare for a future job or career. Afterwards, I happily accepted a well-paid position in Ottawa as a computer consultant, but spent most of the day staring out the window, dreaming of an early escape from my stuffy cubicle to the nearby Gatineau Hills. I began guiding whitewater-rafting trips every weekend, a pastime infinitely more rewarding than my nine-to-five occupation. I had a growing passion and love for the wilderness, which had been instilled by my parents during countless childhood camping trips. I struggled to find meaning in my office job, but each day it grew more suffocating. It may have been right for others, but it wasn't right for me. One day, I simply knew it was time to leave. After only eight months of working, I packed my rusty pickup with what little it could carry, left the rest behind, and headed west, to an uncertain future.

I had no master plan. One thing always seemed to lead to another, and I simply followed my heart. I began with a lucky break, landing a job guiding sea-kayak trips on Canada's West Coast, a position I felt terribly underqualified for, especially with no background in natural history. Knowing it was literally time to either sink or swim, I spent every free moment in the library, trying to improve my non-existent knowledge of West Coast birds, plants, and marine mammals. My eyes were opened to a new facet of the natural world; I had previously sought only adrenaline and challenge in the outdoors, but now I learned to watch and understand the wonders around me. I began photographing with interest what I saw. That first season led to another, and another after that. During the winters I would head south to Belize, leading kayak and snorkelling trips on the barrier reef and raft descents of remote jungle rivers. I enrolled in a hundred-day mountaineering course, and followed that with a winter working in the Swiss Alps. A contact from the mountaineering school helped me secure a position guiding rafting expeditions on the magnificent Tatshenshini River, flowing from Canada's Yukon Territory through the majestic St. Elias mountains out to the Gulf of Alaska. No matter what I did each winter, I was always drawn back to the North the following summer, entranced by the vast wilderness, the midnight sun, the history of the gold rush, and the spirit of the last frontier.

Opportunities for adventure continued to lure me, and with what little money I had, I determined to follow all I could, climbing and skiing throughout the local Rockies, mountain-biking Pakistan's Karikoram Highway, climbing Mt. McKinley in Alaska, trekking in Nepal. Still, in the back of my mind I was never quite sure if it was all just an extended vacation from engineering. Where was it leading me? My friends were quickly moving up the corporate ladder, buying homes and getting married. I still drove the same rusty pickup, and usually slept on their couches when I was in town. I had learned and grown immensely through my journeys, choosing to invest in experience over monetary returns, but my lifestyle was not sustainable. I knew something had to change.

My next big step came on a Northern river trip, when a friend mentioned a possible opening for an upcoming attempt on Mt. Everest. Since the age of twelve, when, with wide eyes and fanciful visions, I read Chris Bonnington's *The Everest Years* time and again, I had dreamt of participating in a Himalayan expedition. A long and intricate dance of faxed résumés and phone interviews finally brought about the unbelievable: I would join the team as their photographer and communications co-ordinator. I immediately moved to Calgary, and the next six months passed in a flash, filled with preparations and training. The team flew to Kathmandu in the spring of 1997 and, two months later, on May 23, Alan Hobson and Jamie Clarke, the expedition organizers, reached the summit, along with four Sherpas. To have contributed in some small way to the success of the expedition provided a feeling of great satisfaction. The experience also marked a turning point for me: my horizons had been expanded beyond anything I had seen through commercial guiding. Initially overwhelmed, I learned to make sense of the complicated world of corporate sponsors, media interviews, photo credits, and contracts. Most satisfying to me was that, upon our return from the mountain, people seemed to like my photographs, and were even interested in buying them.

During the expedition I became good friends with Jamie Clarke. Our friendship had begun when, after meeting me only once, at an interview, Jamie fought hard to secure me a place on the team. Lighthearted and always quick to smile, Jamie had a charismatic and easygoing personality, which overlay a foundation of deep integrity. A very successful motivational speaker, Jamie employed a team of four to manage his busy office back home in Calgary. Sharing an offbeat sense of humour and a love of adventure, we returned from Nepal eager to undertake another expedition together.

At the time, Jamie's older brother Leigh was helping us with the production of a documentary about the Everest climb, and had a keen interest in any upcoming adventure. Leigh had been active throughout his youth, excelling at rugby and travelling through Africa and Southeast Asia with Jamie, but after finishing law school he had succumbed to a grinding, sedentary life. Now tired and worn by his career, Leigh dreamed of an escape from the same office world that had once imprisoned me. Leigh's bond with Jamie was extremely close and, despite a small concern we all had over the effect of a brother dynamic, he seemed a natural to complete our team. The brothers were opposites in many ways, and although I had been associated with Leigh through the movie project for almost a year, I did not know him well. With a quiet and reserved personality, he remained largely an enigma, but I liked what little I did know of him. With building excitement and anticipation, we agreed we would attempt to plan and organize an expedition together, and began to brainstorm ideas.

It was Jamie who initially suggested the idea of a desert. He had made a brief foray into Jordan's Wadi Rum ten years earlier, and wanted to return to that environment. With my rafting background I had been contemplating a major river journey, but slowly I became attracted to the desert concept. A hot, flat desert offered a great environmental and aesthetic contrast to the steep, cold world of mountaineering and to the rough, wet world of rafting. As a photographer, I was drawn by these opposites. We all liked the fact that deserts were not a popular destination in the world of adventuring. A few individuals had made obscure excursions into these unknown regions, but in general deserts remained foreign landscapes – unlike mountains and rivers, which have seen ever-increasing traffic in recent years, and fill current adventure magazines and books with images and stories.

But we sought more than simply a challenging journey in a remote desert region. Aware that uncharted lands existed only in the romantic past, we still hoped to find a desert that remained to some degree unknown. The opportunity to travel and live with local indigenous people was crucial as well. With their rich Buddhist tradition and gentle ways, our Sherpa teammates had opened our eyes beyond the world of climbing we shared during the Himalayan experience. To court the financing we undoubtedly would need, the journey also had to be noteworthy, but we wanted to avoid succumbing to the prevalent game of firsts, tacking unimportant titles on achievements in order to gain credibility. It would matter little to us, for instance, if we were the first Canadians to travel backwards on our heads across the entire length of the Gobi.

Jamie and Leigh were both busy with their careers. The one commodity I had available was time, so I dove into the challenge and began researching the history and geography of the world's deserts. There is only a small number of major desert regions in the world, between fifteen and twenty, depending on how one classifies "major." Many could be quickly ruled out. The Arctic and Antarctic are cold and snowy. Much of the Kalahari is heavily vegetated, and did not provide the aesthetic contrast to Everest that we sought. The Sahara had the most allure; as the world's largest desert it stands as an icon. Within its borders many possible journeys awaited. We considered a trip to Timbuktu, travelling the ancient salt routes with the nomadic Tureg, or retracing the legendary Forty Day Road in the Sudan. Yet nothing seemed quite right. Many areas had seen a proliferation of roads and the associated growth of modern settlements. Other regions experienced constant tourism, and hardly seemed reasonable destinations. Large portions of the Sahara are mountainous or rocky, and do not provide the classic sand-desert environment. After two months I was still searching.

As I stood in the aisle of the bookstore that winter day, everything fell into place. Snow slowly melting from my boots and forming puddles around me, lost in Thesiger's words and images of Arabia's Empty Quarter, I knew I had found the desert in which we would travel. I didn't even think to buy the book at the time, although I would soon, and in the months that followed I read it time and again. That night I called halfway across the country and left a message on Jamie's answering machine. We were going to Arabia, to the Empty Quarter, trust me this much, we could sort out the details later.

CHAPTER TWO

# Planning the Impossible

No doubt there are still corners of Arabia to be explored. The huge
white blot was never just a hole in the map; it was, and is, a hunger
of the soul.

*– Royal Geographical Society History of
World Exploration*, edited by John Keay, 1991

We were staring at a blank page. We knew very little about Arabia.
None of us had ever ridden a camel before or travelled in a major desert.
There was only one Western man alive in the world that had ever
crossed the Empty Quarter by camel, and his journey had been in
another era. Where could we possibly start?

I began by reading everything I could about the great desert, spending endless days in the stacks of the local library. The largest dunes in
the Empty Quarter, a massive series of mountainous sand chains
known as *uruqs* (veins), lie in the northeast corner near the quicksands of Umm as Samim. It was the striking images of these massive
dune fields in *Arabian Sands* that had originally caught our imagination, and it seemed a natural place to aim our attention. After considering many different options, we agreed the most appealing route would
be to retrace Sir Wilfred's first journey of 1946. Not only did this have

the historical tie, but it also crossed extremely difficult and varied terrain.

Thesiger had begun his journey in the city of Salala, on the southern coast of Oman. From there he travelled north, crossing the Jebel Qarra (Qarra Mountains), to emerge on the great gravel plains that lay beyond. Following *Wadi Ghadun*, a dry river course that slowly swung to the east, Thesiger had crossed four hundred kilometres (250 miles) of these flats before entering the sands of the Empty Quarter, just north of the village of Mugshin. Once in the great desert, he had ridden directly towards the oasis of Liwa, skirting the Umm as Samim to the west and crossing an area of massive dunes known as the Uruq al-Shaiba. After reaching Liwa, Thesiger had then swung east and then south, returning to Salala, but we would complete our journey by continuing onwards to the Arabian Gulf, arriving on the coast somewhere near Abu Dhabi.

Our proposed route traversed twelve hundred kilometres (745 miles) of the Arabian peninsula, from the Indian Ocean in the south to the Gulf in the north, and passed through three countries: Oman, Saudi Arabia, and the United Arab Emirates. And we hoped to undertake the expedition in the manner of caravans of the past, riding camels, carrying all our supplies, and moving from well to well, oasis to oasis.

There are many who would suggest this was nothing more than a lark, that we were young fools fancying ourselves in the time of Mohammed. Even Thesiger wrote in *Arabian Sands* "to have done the journey on a camel when I could have done it in a car would have turned the venture into a stunt. To refuse mechanical aid reduces exploration to a sport." We knew that several expeditions had crossed parts of the Empty Quarter by Hummer and Land Cruiser, but that type of journey held no interest for us. The expedition was not about getting from one point to another; we wanted to live close to the land and its people, to experience the hardships and camaraderie of travelling through the desert without a vehicle, or having the annoyance of one trailing us at every turn. We were drawn to facing the desert on its own terms, and we chose to attempt the crossing in that manner and spirit. We would not be ridiculous in the principles of our approach, refusing to drink water from pumped wells or waving off rescue if it were required, but we stood in consensus regarding the proposed expedition's traditional style.

ربع الخالي

Now that we had an initial plan, we needed to assess the feasibility, and I began to seek information and advice.

Searches on the Web revealed little; I posted queries to Internet newsgroups focussing on everything from Middle Eastern heritage to Arabic linguistics. I called everyone I knew with some knowledge of the Middle East. To most, "empty quarter" meant only a frustrating red entry on financial reports, but many suggested others to call, and those contacts led to others still. I opened the phone book and called Arab organizations, Middle Eastern advocacy groups, embassies, and trade commissions.

All these initial inquiries led to the same answer: the expedition we proposed was impossible. The reasons we were given were endless. Arabia and its people had changed irrevocably in the last fifty years. The Bedu no longer had the skills or the interest to accompany us. It would be difficult to find camels that would last more than a few days on such a journey. Permission to travel in the Empty Quarter was never granted. Political tensions and anti-Western sentiment in the Middle East were dangerously high. We would be putting ourselves in unacceptable danger. Although the information later proved incorrect, we were vehemently warned that parts of the region remained littered with landmines from an earlier conflict, and it was rated as one of the world's most dangerous places. A local businessman who dealt extensively in the Middle East assured us that his inside information indicated the region was unstable, and a civil war was threatening. When we occasionally met at the gym, he would urge me to change our plans, and look at me with great concern when I told him we were still planning to proceed. A friend's father even noted that, with my light complexion, I would probably suffer greatly in the desert. Why not try the Arctic? he suggested.

I remember during those formative days a brief conference call Jamie and I had with a local oil executive. He had worked in the Arabian Gulf region for years, and immediately told us to forget the idea of our journey. He suggested that, if we did go, we had better know exactly what we were doing and set off with official support, or else we would never be heard from again. It wasn't a very encouraging response, but over the years we had all been told the same thing about many of our other plans, so it hardly fazed us. Jamie's assistant, overhearing the call from her neighbouring office, emerged with a long face. We assured her that this was actually good news. If it were an easy goal then everyone would be doing it. It would take much more than this to thwart us! She stared at us sceptically, but said nothing.

Leigh and I began taking Arabic lessons. After class we would linger behind to chat with our teacher, Giovanni de Maria, a former diplomat in the Gulf states. He knew the political challenges we were facing, and confirmed how difficult it would be. The process is very slow, he warned, and new ideas are often viewed with concern. Our aims could be misinterpreted. The legendary city of Ubar, fabled in *Arabian Nights* as rich beyond all measure, and then lost in the desert's sands after its destruction by Allah, had recently been linked with ancient ruins buried at Shisur, a small village lying on our proposed route. Government officials might think we were secretly searching for other archeological sites or artifacts. Or they might worry that we were geologists, hoping to study oil production and distribution in the region. Why else would we want to travel in the Empty Quarter?

Even learning Arabic, he admitted, might be a problem. We needed some Arabic to communicate with the Bedu, but if we spoke too well, Giovanni warned, we would risk suspicion of being spies. "*Ghralee balek* (Be careful)," he always said. "Oh, how dangerous it will be!" Giovanni tried valiantly to encourage us with his kind advice, but in his heart I knew he too thought we were facing the impossible.

I slowly began to comprehend and appreciate the immensity of the task facing us, and the picture that emerged was daunting. Arabia had changed almost inconceivably in the years since Thesiger's journeys. With the discovery of oil, and the onset of major production in 1938, monetary wealth rushed into the region in staggering quantities. Modern cities sprang up across the peninsula where a few years earlier only mud huts stood. Saudi Arabia today accounts for more than one-quarter of the world's known oil reserves. The 8.8 million barrels of oil shipped abroad each day account for 90 per cent of their total export revenues, financing a gross national product of $148 billion (U.S.). Sixty years ago Saudi Arabia was still an infant country ruled by their first king and founder Abdul Aziz Ibn Saud, its borders with Oman and the then Trucial Coast States (now U.A.E.) were undefined. Great Bedu tribes still roamed freely. The land, people, and culture had endured unchanged for centuries.

Today the nomadic Bedu have settled, drawn to the cities and towns, many trading their historic freedom for cheap wages and government-subsidized housing. Automobiles and jet aircraft have supplanted the massive caravans that once plied the peninsula. The camels that Thesiger, Thomas, and Philby used on their journeys were tough and resilient, accustomed to travelling long distances with little food or water. Today nearly all camels in Arabia are bred for racing or raised as livestock for meat. The massive herds are watered daily, and fed hay and alfalfa. These camels would simply collapse after a few days' hard march, unaccustomed to the work, refusing to eat the tough and thorny desert shrubs.

As we continued to press forward, the assignment of responsibilities amongst our team slowly clarified. The scope of the project meant that some financial support would be required. The challenge of attracting sponsors, likely one of the most difficult we would face, fell to Jamie, who had twice before raised funds for Everest expeditions. If no sponsorship could be found, we were committed to seeing the journey through, and proposed to pool the little money we each had personally for a bare-bones attempt. I would continue to plan and organize the expedition, pursuing details that ranged from diplomatic permissions to logistics. Leigh, still heavily committed to the law career he dreamed of escaping, offered to assist Jamie and me wherever possible. With Leigh and Jamie's hectic schedules, the three of us found little time to meet. As our plans evolved, we stayed in touch by e-mail and phone messages, sharing every advance and setback, fuelling each other with enthusiasm, and lending support.

While Jamie refined a list of potential sponsors, I helped him prepare for the difficult search by creating a glossy one-page brochure describing the challenges of the Empty Quarter, and highlighting our proposal to cross it. With a busy schedule of presentations, Jamie constantly appeared in front of groups to talk about his experiences on Mt. Everest, and some expressed interest in becoming involved with future adventures. Gaining support for any major expedition is difficult, and the Empty Quarter would not be an easy sell, as deserts did not hold the appeal of other, more mainstream adventures. We focussed on trying to offer tangible benefits for corporations that joined us, and not simply taking the money and disappearing off to the wilderness. Product endorsement rarely offers enough returns to justify a heavy financial involvement, and Jamie was a master at creating synergistic fits with larger corporate agendas. For Everest he had engineered a deal with a firm that had the declared goal of becoming number one in their industry in the upcoming five years, and the summit stood as a metaphor for their target. The firm was rapidly expanding, with new employees all over the world, and our communiqués from the mountain served as a rallying point. Whether or not anyone in the public had heard of their involvement, the sponsorship was a success for both the firm and our team. Now we sought to repeat this winning situation.

My biggest challenge of all, however, remained simply attaining permission to undertake the expedition. Our proposed route passed through three nations, crossing two international borders in remote locations. I learned others before us had tried to gain permission for a similar journey and had failed.

From my search, leads slowly started to emerge. The uncle of a partner at Leigh's law firm was a former Canadian ambassador to the Kingdom of Saudi Arabia. Doug Valentine considered the idea interesting, but his first e-mail warned us it would not be easy. "It is not possible just to get a Saudi Arabian visa," he wrote. "There are no such things as tourist visas. Everyone visiting the country has to be sponsored, and that sponsor is fully responsible for everything the visitor does. Therefore it is imperative to get authority for everything you want to do."

Mr. Valentine provided us with what would be our most important breakthrough, putting us in contact with the current Canadian ambassador to Saudi Arabia, His Excellency Daniel "Ted" Hobson. I sent Mr. Hobson a package outlining the proposed expedition, and in his prompt reply he wrote: "My first response is to say that this sounds very exciting and we will do all we can to help, and in the same breath warn you not to underestimate the sensitivities, obstacles, frustrations, delays, etc. that we might well encounter. But I assume in your business that you are used to all this and will not easily lose heart."

This promise of official help provided our first solid glimmer of hope. Ted Hobson would prove to be one of our greatest allies in the struggle to gain Saudi Arabian approval and sanction; contacting him was an immense stroke of luck.

In conjunction with the diplomatic efforts in the Middle East, I was seeking contact with Bedu from the Dhofar region of Southern Oman where our journey would start. So far, my requests for help on the Internet had elicited little response. I did receive one message from an American professor studying Bedu linguistics, but before revealing any of her contacts she wanted to know more about what we planned. Obviously my answer was not impressive, since I never heard from her again. Two weeks later, however, out of the blue, I received another response to my initial query.

Dear Bruce (from, and on behalf of Chris Beale, Heide Beale
Tours, in Oman.)
– Please send your fax number as soon as possible
– Because of our activities here, we have close liaison with
government organizations
– I have been in Oman for 20 years – first as a soldier, and sub-
sequently as an adventure tour operator.
– It is important that we talk and meet!!
Many thanks, Chris Beale

The above note was actually sent by Chris's neighbour, who had
seen my posting and decided that Chris, who had no Internet access,
should look at the cryptic request for help. A flurry of faxes revealed
that Chris, with his wife, Heide, operated an adventure-travel company
in Oman, catering to German tourists. During his days as an army
officer, Chris had been stationed in Dhofar (southern Oman), where he
drove many patrols along the fringes of the Empty Quarter. Familiar
with the area – and having recently watched a film project that had
attempted a similar journey in the region fail miserably – Chris was
eager to join the challenge.

In late May 1998, I planned a reconnaissance trip to Oman. Meeting
Chris Beale there would be valuable, but most important would be the
sense of reality this would bring to our project. Until now, the Empty
Quarter, camels, and Bedu had all existed for us in another world, a
world of theory. We had spent more than six months immersed in texts
and articles. A visit to the region was long overdue.

ربع الخالي

After a brief stop in London, where I met with the curator of an Islamic
art museum who had offered to help, I flew on to Muscat, the capital of
Oman. Chris Beale met me at the airport. He was an amiable gentleman
in his mid-fifties, smoking an ever-present pipe, and shuffling about in

strangely shapeless shoes. Carrying the faintest hint of eccentricity, he struck me as the epitome of an aging British expatriate, never quite happy at home, but reminiscing endlessly about England. Having lived in Oman for twenty years, Chris was a wealth of knowledge about the land and its recent history. He verified that no one had completed a similar journey since Thesiger in 1946. Together we spent several days discussing plans, while in the evenings I would escape the hotel and explore the crowded markets and bustling streets of Muscat.

Oman was one of the last Gulf states to see the sweeping changes of modernization. In 1970, Sultan Qaboos usurped the throne from his father and introduced radical changes to a country that had remained locked in the past. During a few short years, what is known as Oman's Renaissance vaulted the country into the twentieth century. New foreign and domestic policies brought a booming change to the economy. Export revenues, almost entirely from oil, grew 500 per cent in five years. Imported goods and services supporting the new state grew by 1,000 per cent. Some of the obscure facts are the most staggering. In 1970 there were only ten kilometres (6 miles) of paved road in the country. Five years later some four thousand kilometres (2,500 miles) had been developed, and the number of cars had grown from 840 to more than 30,000. A new international airport handled 170,000 passengers a year in a country which had previously offered no commercial air access. The country's schools multiplied from three to 207, enrolment jumping from 900 boys to 65,000 students of both sexes. Within four years, national media – television, radio, newspapers – had been created, none of which were available before.

Despite these developments, today a strong flavour of the past lingers in the capital city, which is built amid the craggy pinnacles and rocky inlets of the eastern coast. Along Muscat's waterfront, amongst the neon signs of modern kabob shops, market vendors still noisily ply their trade in frankincense and spices. Heavily veiled women and traditionally dressed men stroll through the multicultural crowds.

ربع الخالي

Through a web of Chris's contacts we began searching for Bedu interested in our journey and who might be willing to join us on the expedition. After three days in Muscat, we flew to Salala, the capital of Oman's southern Dhofar province where the journey would begin. Our search eventually led to Thumbrait, a dusty village hidden in the gravel steppes that lie beyond Dhofar's coastal Qarra Mountains, and Manaa Mohammed, an elusive Bedu who we were to recognize by his single finger and protruding blind eye. Manaa brushed aside our proposal, at first suggesting that we would be better off if he showed us the local desert by Land Cruiser. We pressed further, and he eventually conceded that the expedition might be possible. For the right price he could help. He needed time to consult the village elders, he insisted, and we agreed to reconvene later.

Chris and I drove to a nearby archeological site to pass the afternoon. En route, we stopped so I could photograph the bleak expanses. It was midday, and the temperature had already soared above fifty degrees Celsius (120°F). Leaving the comfort of the air-conditioned vehicle, I felt the suffocating weight of the heat surrounding me. The dusty plains stretched interminably, mirages wavering on the horizon in every direction. The light desert gusts raised a fine dust, coating my throat. I felt exposed as I never had before; I could not imagine surviving more than a few hours in this environment. If the car broke down, we could drink our meagre water supplies, and then in desperation finish the windshield-washer reservoir, but our strength would soon fade. On a high mountainside I knew how to dig a snow cave, melt ice to drink, stay warm on the coldest nights. Here I was out of my element. Although it was June, the height of the hot season, and we planned our journey for January to March when the temperatures were substantially lower, it was my first taste of the desert's power. The feeling of intimidation lingered as I jumped back in the truck and we sped off.

We had planned to rejoin Manaa by four in the afternoon at the house of his friend. By seven-thirty he was still not there, which was not unusual, as the Bedu have a relaxed attitude to time and timeliness. We waited in a traditional Arabic meeting room. Large hand-embroidered pillows were arranged in a circle around the walls, and we sat on the carpeted floor. There was no other furniture. We were joined by an elderly gentleman, Nazir, draped in robes and wearing a rich green-and-gold headdress, who sat silently beside us. A young boy appeared and served Arabic coffee in tiny cups. He reappeared with a plate of barbecued camel pieces. Finally Manaa entered, quietly talking on a mobile phone held firmly in his single finger. He sat and smiled. After another round of coffee, we settled down to business.

Maana proposed a team of three Bedu and twelve camels to accompany us. Finding men willing to travel in the desert would be difficult, he said, and would require a lot of money. The negotiating game had begun. Camels would also be a problem. He would have to find special camels, those that could withstand the rigours of a two-month expedition. The sand in the Empty Quarter is soft and deep, Manaa explained; a regular camel from the coast would falter in the dunes, exhausting itself within days. We would need camels raised in the desert, with characteristically large footpads. And the camels would need to be trained for months in advance. Manaa insisted that a special diet of alfalfa, honey, eggs, and dates would be required to strengthen them. The list went on, and it was hard to know where reality ceased. The final cost Manaa proposed was nearly ten times what Chris had earlier estimated would be the maximum we should consider.

Manaa and I revisited every point in succession. Chris joined in to help. We negotiated food rations for the journey, and the cost of building a camel pen at our training camp. As soon as one item was finalized, another we had already agreed upon would suddenly jump into negotiation again. It was like trying to herd chickens with a farm dog. One thing was eminently clear: the costs we had estimated at home in Canada were completely unrealistic. At the end of the exhausting evening I finally shook hands with Manaa. We were both pleased with the outcome. I had been able to accomplish my goal, and leave for home with a logistical plan in place. Manaa would recruit three Bedu with the necessary skills for the journey, and organize a team of twelve camels, which would be trained and fed a special diet for two months prior to the start of the journey. In return, I committed our team to paying more money than we had. I found it a difficult decision, but I had to make it myself, at that instant, trusting Jamie and Leigh to back me, as I knew they would.

Two days later we met at Jamie's office in downtown Calgary. Together we excitedly watched the hours of shaky video footage I had shot. I tried to impart a sense of what I had seen and learned. Jamie and Leigh supported my decision to move ahead and commit with Manaa, but the costs made it clear we needed to continue our hunt for financing. Our own funds were quickly drying up, and although Jamie had several strong leads in his search for sponsorship, no one had yet signed a cheque. There was no doubt, however, that we would continue. The Empty Quarter had taken hold of our hearts. The expedition had become real, and we were bolstered by the recent progress.

From the beginning we had realized that we needed to learn at least the basics about camels and riding before arriving in Arabia. We were grossly underqualified for the expedition as it stood: none of us had even spent much time on a horse, let alone a camel. After an extensive search for riding opportunities in North America, we found seventeen dromedary camels in southern Texas, at a juvenile detention facility, part of a rehabilitation program for serious youth offenders in the state. Doug Baum, who oversaw the program, kindly agreed to spend four days training us. At roughly the same time we discovered that David Alloway, America's leading desert-survival authority, worked at Big Bend Ranch State Park, only a few hours' drive from Doug's camel ranch. When we contacted David and told him our plans, he offered to design a survival course for us – and promised it would be tough. A month after my return from Muscat, we took our first trip together as a team, flying to Texas on July 4, 1998, for ten days of training.

Nothing I had seen or read prepared me for the sight of Doug's camels as we rounded the final bend on the dusty drive to the VisionQuest Ranch. They were massive. The immense beasts sat chewing their cud in the midday heat, their bodies instinctively turned into the sun to reduce exposure. Several lumbered to their feet as our car slowed outside the compound, and the crest of their humps towered over the two-metre (7 ft.) fence. They weighed upwards of nine hundred kilograms (2,000 lb.) Doug explained. By comparison, standard riding horses usually weighed between four hundred and fifty and five hundred and fifty kilograms (1,000-1,200 lb.).

Large heads darted and wove atop powerful necks as they eyed us curiously. I could not help but think they looked like creatures from a *Star Wars* movie. There was even one called Chewbacca! As Doug led us into the pen for the first time, I felt my stomach knot with tension. We had pockets full of carrots to offer as treats and bribes, but the camels smelled the food and crowded around us as we tried to push through the gate. I was particularly aware of their rear feet, one often unweighted and cocked to the side, apparently always ready to kick. Doug calmly walked through the herd, pulling camels aside to gently kiss and cuddle them as he began to teach us about these incredible animals.

The dromedary camel, distinguished by its single hump (the Bactrian camel has two), has played a pivotal role in Middle Eastern history. Able to travel long distances with little food or water, and to carry colossal burdens, it is known as "the ship of the desert." To the Bedu, who relied completely on the hardy beast for transportation, milk, food, clothing, and shelter, it is *Ata allah* ("God's gift"). The dromedary is indigenous to the hot, dry desert belt running from Morocco to India. Today very few are wild. Most of the estimated ten million dromedary camels in the world have been domesticated. The largest feral population exists in the Australian Outback, where a herd of sixty thousand has grown from a small group imported during the last century to help supply the building of a north-south railway.

Although not normally associated with North America, camels have been on the continent for more than a century, and possibly much longer. Some evidence suggests that the ancestors of today's camels actually evolved on the North American continent, later crossing a land bridge to Asia. Jefferson Davis championed the use of camels in the U.S. Army while he was secretary of war. After much debate, a herd of seventy dromedaries was shipped from India in 1857, and began working patrols between forts on the southern frontier with Mexico. The hardy beasts easily outperformed both mules and horses in the hot, dry environment, showing staggeringly more strength and endurance. After Congress repeatedly failed to act on recommendations that a regiment of a thousand camels be purchased, the experiment was eventually scrapped. The initial herd was then assigned to the U.S. Postal Service, where they began travelling mail routes between California and New Mexico. When the officers in charge objected to dealing with the ornery beasts, the camel's use was finally discontinued for good. Over the years, several escaped and, amazingly, reports of wild camels persisted in remote areas of the American Southwest up to the early 1940s.

Camels are supremely adapted to the harsh environment in which they have evolved. An uncanny ability to conserve moisture, combined with the capacity to withstand major dehydration, allows camels to survive lengthy periods without water. In a single day their internal temperature can vary as much as seven degrees Celsius, from thirty-three degrees Celsius (93°F) in the morning to forty degrees Celsius (105°F) during the heat of the afternoon. Thick fur on their backs protects camels from the sun, and prevents the evaporative loss of sweat. Conversely their bellies have only thin coats, allowing for the easy dissipation of heat from surface blood vessels. Their stool is almost completely dry, and their sparse urine sees a final use, splashing on their rear legs for cooling. As they slowly lose water, camels can survive dehydration levels of 25 per cent of their body weight (most mammals will go into shock and die between 12 and 15 per cent).

When water is available, camels can drink more than one hundred litres (26 gal.) in a few minutes. Doug demonstrated this by inserting a garden hose into a camel's mouth. After he turned it on full blast, we chatted for five minutes before he transferred it to the next camel. Not a drop was spilled. Contrary to popular belief, the humps on their backs do not contain water. Rather, they are made up of large stores of fat, which can be slowly metabolized during long periods without food.

Camels are an architectural wonder. Viewed from above they are extremely thin, thus reducing their exposure to the Arabian sun, which shines directly overhead much of the day. Their bodies are raised high off the hot ground on long, thin legs. The slow, majestic gait of a camel, while not comfortable for a rider, is an extremely economical use of energy. They move both legs on the same side forward at once, unlike a horse's more energetic opposing stride. Their huge padded feet act like snowshoes, allowing them to walk over soft, loose sand, where horses and mules would flounder. Large tear glands perpetually wash their eyes, which are protected from sand by a double set of eyelashes. Each eye has a translucent inner eyelid, which camels can close during a sandstorm, allowing them to continue on through blowing sand and dust. Thick guard hairs protect the entrance to their nostrils, and specialized muscles constrict the nostrils, which also close during storms.

Inside the pen Doug showed us how to carefully brush and groom a camel's fur before saddling it, and then got us to practise. I worked on a camel named Chug, whom Doug assured me was one of his best-behaved. Approaching from the front to say hello and let him know who I was, I kept one hand lightly touching Chug as I moved around him, so he wouldn't be surprised or scared. As I carefully pulled twigs and dirt from his knotted hair, Chug slowly and imperceptibly shifted his weight, until all of his nine hundred kilograms were pressing me against the tall, steel fence. I raised my heel against a fencepost and shoved with all my might, but nothing could move him; Chug happily chewed on hay, pretending to be oblivious to my plight. Doug hurried over and explained that camels move away from pressure. The key to controlling them was learning what points to press to get a response. A single finger positioned on his rear flank would easily move Chug in the direction I wanted. Doug demonstrated and left to help Jamie. Chug resumed squishing me against the fence, no matter where I pressed on him.

By the second day we were ready to ride – or, rather, we were ready to sit on the camel and be led around the pen. As Doug tried to coerce Chewbacca into a sitting position, he bellowed, spit, kicked, and pulled at the reins. It was not the type of behaviour that made me want to jump on his back. Luckily, Leigh had drawn the short straw. As Doug held Chewie down, Leigh tried to stretch his leg over the camel's immense back and settle into the strange aluminum contraption Doug used as a saddle. During the morning we all took turns being led around the small corral. It felt embarrassingly like we were riding at a petting zoo, and certainly a long way from being competent desert travellers. After lunch we were ready to work in pairs, and went for longer walks, while leading a camel with a rider or being led ourselves. Perched high on the back of the strong animal, I felt totally at its mercy. The camels were very obstinate, and loath to leave the company of the herd. They fought the entire afternoon to return to the others. With every lurch I would grab the saddle with both hands, preparing for the worst.

As we sat in our hotel room that night, we agreed that riding the camels was the scariest thing we had done in a long time. Climbing big mountains, bungee-jumping from bridges, kayaking racing rivers, none had scared us like what we had done that day. I had been acutely aware of the strength of the camels, and I did not want to be riding one when it was demonstrated.

As fate would have it, I got this chance. By our fourth day we were riding by ourselves, using only the reins and a riding crop to control the camels. I was on Chewbacca, with Chug tied behind, keeping him company. At Doug's urging, I applied a small whip to Chewie's bottom as we rounded a corner, trying to keep the sluggish camel moving. What happened next is open to interpretation, but from the saddle it seemed as if the world had gone out of control. All I could see was Chewie's neck rearing back and a blur of flying hooves. As he charged across the paddock dragging Chug behind, I was flung further and further out of my saddle. Soon I realized that a fall was inevitable, and chose to eject as far as I could to avoid the hooves of Chug, racing behind. The hard landing from two and a half metres up gave me a good shock, knocking the wind out of me and taking the skin off my forearm. I knew I needed to clean myself up, but if I didn't get back on then, my next opportunity would be when we arrived in Arabia. Leigh and Jamie ran to my aid, and helped me remount Chewie for a quick circle of the ring. That evening, back at the hotel, I was a sad sight as I delicately pulled off my dusty clothes to shower. From head to toe I was covered with yellow and purple bruises. It hurt to move or breathe, and X-rays in town later revealed two separated ribs.

Dealing with the camels had been more difficult and intimidating than we bargained for. Doug had taught us a lot, and, despite my example of how not to dismount, we left for home enthusiastic. The memory of that fall, however, stayed with me through the next six months of preparations, a reminder of the challenges that lay ahead.

# CHAPTER THREE

# Final Preparations

> To the desert go prophets and hermits; through deserts go pilgrims
> and exiles. Here the leaders of the great religions have sought the
> therapeutic and spiritual values of retreat, not to escape . . . but to
> find reality.
>
>            – Paul Shepard, *Man in the Landscape*

As the larch and aspen along Calgary's Bow River turned a brilliant yellow and slowly dropped their cover in the cool autumn breezes, the speed and urgency of our preparations increased. Gear began to pile up in our tiny office as Leigh researched and purchased the masses of equipment we would need, from handheld GPS (Global Positioning System) units to canvas overbags. Jamie was in the final stages of arranging sponsorship support from NEC Technologies and Bausch & Lomb Eyecare. National Geographic Television expressed interest in producing a documentary from footage we planned on shooting after we pitched the idea to their director of story development at a local film festival, and contracts flew back and forth.

We were committed to involving children's education in the adventure, both because we enjoyed working with the students and because it felt like an important way to return something of value to the community. Jamie had pioneered a children's program on his '94 Everest expedition with live updates from the mountain. In 1997, again on Everest, we had seen this program expand, and the climb had been covered by a commercial firm that created a children's Web site, and – for a fee – would supply teachers with related manuals and worksheets. Although the program had been well received, all three of us felt that this time it was important to provide something more substantial than an opportunity to follow the journey vicariously. Working with Jamie and Leigh's father, who helped oversee the program, our goal was to provide free curriculum online that would complement updates and digital photos we planned on sending back from the field. We approached the Calgary Board of Education with our idea, and they eagerly joined us, helping to create a comprehensive Web site and forty standardized units of study, for students ranging from kindergarten to Grade 12, all freely available to anyone. For our part, we would visit schools both before and after the expedition, as well as answer students' e-mail questions and send reports from the desert. We struggled endlessly to create a light yet reliable arrangement of solar panels, satellite phone, and laptop that would function in the remote, dusty, hot environment.

The expedition began to take on a momentum of its own; no longer did it require us to breathe life into it. More and more people became interested in what we were doing, and many were relying on us to follow through with our commitments. Most worrying to me was that, as this momentum built like a tidal wave, so did the uncertainties surrounding the permissions for our trip.

With only three months left until our January departure, everything was up in the air. Although we had received agreement in principle from the Saudi Arabian ministry of foreign affairs, neither the ministry of the interior nor the ministry of information, both vital links within the country, had recognized our requests. Beyond these initial permissions there were a myriad of details that needed to be addressed. Passing the borders would be confusing; there was no protocol established in the desert, where the patrols were only there to guard. If we did not have everything prearranged, we would undoubtedly be turned back, delayed, or worse. Once granted, authorization would need to filter down through the convoluted administrations of the police, army, and border patrol, all of whom held jurisdiction in the region. We also sought information on the location and condition of wells and tracks within Saudi Arabia's boundaries. The Canadian embassy in the capital, Riyadh, worked heroically on our behalf, and I remained in awe of their efforts – and very grateful. Still, they had been unable to obtain even a preliminary visa for me to visit on a planning trip. The grinding bureaucracy of the region can stall business ridiculously, and now precious time was ticking away. Chris Beale's efforts in Oman and the United Arab Emirates were on hold: any progress with the two smaller countries would be contingent on positive results in Riyadh. The outcome of our trip hung in a balance beyond our control.

Even as our efforts bogged down, international events took centre stage in the Middle East. In November, when Iraq expelled U.N. weapons inspectors, and shortly afterwards when kidnapped foreigners were killed in Yemen, my fears grew that outside forces might prevent the expedition. I sat glued to the television as the United States threatened to renew bombing. CNN reports indicated that another crisis was looming with Baghdad. I was concerned about the situation beyond our own desire to travel in the Middle East, but I was unsure, even if the bombing was averted, what effect the growing Iraqi unrest would have on our plans.

This fear of the unknown and of unquantifiable dangers nagged at us throughout our preparations. I was not worried about the physical challenges of the desert or the camels. I was confident that we could deal with those as they presented themselves. All our previous experiences had helped prepare us for adverse physical conditions and mental challenges. It was possible anti-Western sentiment and the threat of random violence, a concern raised by many, that kept me awake at night. I found it very difficult to gauge the danger. Everyone has their own comfort level and acceptance of risk. Were those advising us against the expedition being conservative, or were we being foolish and placing ourselves in unnecessary danger?

I had recently read an article about an American university professor lecturing in Saudi Arabia, who was accosted in the desert during a field trip. It was reported that an aging Bedu had learned that Korean tourists were stealing eyeballs from camels. Since he didn't know what Koreans looked like, or what a telephoto lens was, when the old man saw the professor taking a picture of his camels, he confronted him with a drawn gun. It took the combined efforts of all the Arabic students on the field trip to prevent the old Bedu from shooting their teacher. In describing the situation, the professor noted that, in the ensuing ruckus, some students argued loudly with the Bedu, others yelled at each other, while some simply joined their voices to the din, shouting apparently at no one. Finally the Bedu was convinced that the professor was a good Muslim, and should not be killed. Immediately the group was invited around the fire for the standard desert show of hospitality: coffee and dates. The students fidgeted impatiently, indicating that they wanted to leave as quickly as possible. Later they explained that, if they had still been at the camp when the evening call to prayer came, the professor would have exposed their lie, and he surely would have died.

I have no idea as to the truth of this story, but it is both inflammatory and sensational. I can now say after our journey that it seems very far-fetched, and certainly spreads misconceptions. But at the time stories like this hovered in the back of my mind, another uncontrollable variable creating concern.

## ربع الخالي

I knew I had to visit the Middle East again soon. We needed to help bolster the diplomatic efforts in Saudi Arabia, and the ambassador felt my presence could provide the additional support required. I also wanted to visit Manaa one more time. With us living in Canada, half a world away, I worried expedition preparations would be too easy to forget or postpone. Aware of how tight the time was between the end of Ramadan in late January, the earliest we could begin the journey, and the hot season that would follow three months later, we knew we could not afford to arrive in Arabia without everything ready to go.

I also hoped to contact Sir Wilfred Thesiger, who at the age of eighty-eight, was living in a country retirement home outside London. I had always postponed any contact until our plans became more settled, but when an article featuring Thesiger appeared in *Outside* magazine that autumn, I decided it was finally time. I contacted the author of the article, who kindly gave me the phone number of Sir Wilfred's close friend, Alex Maitland. I nervously dialled, and, when the friendly British voice answered, I quickly yet concisely tried to outline our proposed expedition. To my delight, Maitland was interested and enthusiastic about our proposal. He promised to discuss what I had told him with Sir Wilfred, and insisted we visit him and Sir Wilfred when we next passed through London. He suggested I write a letter to Sir Wilfred explaining our background and plans, and I hastily scribbled down Thesiger's address and phone numbers below Alex's on a scrap of paper.

Careful not to disturb Sir Wilfred by phone until he knew of our expedition, I prepared and sent a package outlining our background and plans for the Empty Quarter. A week later I called Alex Maitland to check if the package had arrived, and, glancing down at the scrap of paper, I accidentally focussed on the wrong phone number.

"Hello," a raspy and tired voice answered. It sounded irritated, as if the owner had just been disturbed from a deep afternoon sleep.

"Hello, is Alex Maitland there?" I asked meekly.

"Who?" boomed the voice, now stronger and more alert.

"Alex Maitland?" I asked slowly, trying to enunciate my words, but already realizing my mistake.

There was a short pause, and then the curt, heavily accented voice announced, "This is Wilfred Thesiger."

I had carefully tried to avoid this very situation. I thought of just hanging up, but that would have been silly. I took a deep breath and dove in. Thesiger's fading hearing, combined with the echo and delay of our transatlantic connection, made communication very difficult. Most things I repeated two or three times, finally having to yell, feeling all the time more and more like a boorish intruder. Sir Wilfred was unaware of us or of our plans; Alex had not yet discussed the matter with him. After the little I was able to describe, Sir Wilfred seemed interested but sceptical – and nervous for our safety.

"It will be difficult to find Bedu who want to do it," he yelled over the line. "They will say, why on earth should we do it on a camel when we can get there in a few days in a car? They all drive trucks and automobiles now, you know. Very few Arabs today have ever ridden a camel.

"I don't think you will have much luck," he continued, half to himself. It was not meant to be discouraging, just the old explorer thinking aloud.

After we hung up I sat reeling in my chair. It was hard to believe I had just discussed our desert expedition with Sir Wilfred Thesiger. *Arabian Sands* had inspired our efforts, and I had eagerly read his other works. I had a deep respect for him and his achievements, and I felt privileged to have talked with him.

Sir Wilfred Thesiger's life is that of legend. He remains one of our last ties to a past era, the mythical age of exploration and romantic imperialism. His compatriots, the likes of Burton, Speke, Livingston, and Scott, have long since passed away. As David Attenborough notes, in a comment on the jacket of Sir Wilfred's autobiography, "He is one of the very few people in our time who could be put on the pedestal alongside the great explorers of the eighteenth and nineteenth centuries." Most famous for his journeys in Arabia, Thesiger spent his entire lifetime exploring the far reaches of the planet. He lived for eight years living amongst the Marsh Arabs, a virtually unknown people at the confluence of the Tigris and Euphrates rivers in Iraq. He explored the Hindu Kush mountains of western Pakistan, and trekked with the Hazaras and Nuristanis of Afghanistan. He hiked through the remote mountains of Tibetsi, traversed the Dasht-i-Lut in Iran, and travelled through Kurdistan on horseback. The list is unending, but there is a theme tying his adventures together. He was drawn to unspoiled lands, where the traditional spirit of the people remained untouched by encroaching civilization. Thesiger, ever an idealist, is saddened and disgusted by modern technological society. He believes, as he later told me, that "the internal combustion engine is the worst invention in the history of mankind. It has shrunk the world, and robbed it of its diversity."

Wilfred Thesiger was born in 1910 in Abyssinia (now Ethiopia), the son of the British consul general at the imperial court. He led an unusual childhood. By the age of three he was already accompanying his father on great safaris to hunt lion and oryx. At six he watched spellbound as triumphant Zulu warriors, their clothes streaked with blood, paraded through the streets of Addis Ababa with the rebel king, Negus Mikael, captured during the last battle of the Great Rebellion, in chains. When his father died in 1919, Thesiger's family returned to London, but Wilfred's heart yearned for the wild.

Thesiger returned to Abyssinia in 1930 as the guest of Haile Selassie at his coronation as emperor. During that visit, Thesiger undertook his first great journey. The Awash River in northern Africa had long posed an unanswered question. It flows east from the Ethiopian highlands into the untravelled Danakil country, but never emerges to the sea on the far side. The Danakil was a forbidding land where the local headhunting tribes collected testicles rather than heads. These were strung on a necklace worn by the warriors as a symbol of their standing. Already three expeditions had been massacred while attempting to cross the unknown territory. Thesiger's first attempt to follow the river ended when a letter from the Abyssinian government arrived by runner, ordering him to return. Thesiger went back to England to complete his studies at Oxford, but three years later he returned to Africa. This time, with the permission of the local sultan, Mohammed Yayu, he followed the Awash across the fertile plains of Aussa, deep into Danakil territory. Here Thesiger discovered that the river flowed into a massive salt marsh, where its waters slowly evaporated. At the age of twenty-three, he had solved one of Africa's last great mysteries.

Thesiger spent the next ten years roaming northeastern Africa, employed by the Sudan Political Service as a field officer, the Sudan Defense Force during the 1940 Abyssinian campaign, and the British SAS regiments in Syria and Egypt. During these years, he rode countless miles on camel patrols, and learned to speak fluent Arabic. As he would later write, all this was but a prelude to his five years in Arabia.

It was in Arabia that Thesiger found all he sought. The hardship and freedom with the Bedu marked the rest of his life. His accomplishments were astounding. He travelled more than sixteen thousand kilometres (10,000 miles) by camel, twice crossing the Empty Quarter, in a time when the merest hint of his true identity would have brought certain death at the hands of many fanatical tribes. He survived horrendous conditions, running low on water and becoming lost in unmapped desert.

The biggest reward for Thesiger was the unmatchable spirit of the Bedu with whom he travelled. Their companionship, he wrote, "gave me the five happiest years of my life." Their codes of honour and hospitality had been forged over thousands of years in the unforgiving desert. When Thesiger left Arabia in 1949, he was destined not to return again until 1991. After a string of journeys taking him around the world, he settled in Kenya in 1968, which would remain his home until 1994. Only after the untimely deaths of Lawi and Lhapoto, his two young companions, who had become like adopted sons, did Thesiger leave his hut in Maralal for the last time and return to England.

When the Canadian Embassy in Riyadh called in late November to let me know the preliminary visa they had requested had been approved and needed only final authorization, I booked a flight for the next week. By the time I stood in the long boarding line, I felt tired and resigned. I was exhausted from the other preparations and, despite every promise, the visa for Saudi Arabia was still trapped in bureaucracy. If I did not visit Riyadh on this trip, it would sound a death knell for our hope of entering the Kingdom during the expedition – and likely also end negotiations in the other two countries. The only remaining chance would be to apply for an emergency visa at the Royal Saudi Arabian Embassy in London, where I would be stopping to visit Sir Wilfred. That seemed a long shot at best.

I arrived in London to a typical English fall day. A light but sharply cold rain beat down, and a thick fog hung outside the Heathrow arrivals hall. Due to the urgency of procuring a visa, I set off immediately for the embassy, with all my luggage in tow. After train, tube, and finally a long walk, I arrived wet and tired. The lines at the visa office were slow. When I finally reached the thick bulletproof glass I was told immediately that, to get a visa, I needed to return to Canada! There was absolutely nothing that the embassy could do for me in London, despite faxes I had from the Canadian ambassador in Riyadh and the Saudi Arabian ministry of foreign affairs. I knew I had to persist, but I first needed to contact our embassy in Riyadh, which was now closed for the day. Dejected, I went outside and found a phone book. A distant cousin of mine and her husband lived nearby, along with their newborn boy. They insisted that I stay with them during my three nights in London. While the laughs and cries of the baby proved a welcome distraction, my unease continued. I found myself tossing and turning all night, more from worry over my lack of progress than from jet lag.

An early phone call rocked me from hard-won sleep. It was Ian Shaw, the Canadian second secretary in Riyadh, with details of a visa authorization number. Ted Hobson, the Canadian ambassador, then came on the line. He had arranged several strategic meetings with government officials while I was to be there. I was overjoyed. The tide seemed to be turning and, after feeling that I was fighting alone for so long, it was heartening to see their efforts on our behalf. The ambassador also kindly invited me to stay in his official residence during my visit. A few minutes later Ian Shaw called back with confirmation of my authorization number. This was a tremendous breakthrough.

Later that morning, I arrived at the Saudi embassy to present the authorization number, but a fax confirming my visa could not be found. The attendant agreed to take my passport and wait for clearance to arrive. I hurriedly stuffed some crumpled bills and an official application under the thick glass, since I was already running late for my appointment with Sir Wilfred. Dashing through crowds outside Victoria Station, I arrived at my train just as the conductor's whistle blew. Feeling unprepared for the meeting, I hurriedly leafed through a copy of *Arabian Sands* as London's endless grey suburbs eroded into green countryside outside the train windows. Within an hour I reached my station. I dove into a waiting cab and gave directions for the short drive to Sir Wilfred's retirement home.

Huge willows, swaying gently in the breeze, lined the lane leading to the old country estate. Fallen leaves lay scattered across the gravel surface, swirling aside as the cab sped by. Beside the white mansion, horses lazily grazed in the rolling fields. Tattered wool blankets lay draped over their backs; as they turned their heads to watch the cab pass, each forceful breath condensed into a swirling cloud. I brimmed with eagerness as the car swung around the wide circular drive and pulled up to the white front doors.

Through a large glass pane I could see Sir Wilfred quietly waiting inside. He sat bent forward on a wooden bench by the door, one leg crossed over the other. His hands were folded and resting on a carved Zulu walking stick. Our eyes met, and he smiled. It was a magnificent moment. He emerged slowly but deliberately from the house, towering over six feet tall despite a noticeable stoop.

"Hello," he said, extending a large, shaky hand. "Wilfred Thesiger." His mottled brown skin was marked indelibly by years of exposure. A hawk-like nose and deeply furrowed brow, as distinct as they had been fifty years earlier, added to his imposing figure. His steel-grey hair was brushed straight back. For a man who had walked an estimated one hundred and sixty thousand kilometres (100,000 miles) in his lifetime, he showed little sign of surrendering to his eighty-eight years. There was a welcoming in his deep, sun-bleached eyes that I had not expected.

We entered the sprawling home and navigated an endless maze of corridors. Sir Wilfred grasped my arm firmly for balance, and grumbled impatiently about his ever-reducing pace. We stopped to retrieve his coat before we walked to the nearby golf club for lunch, and while Sir Wilfred rooted in his closet I marvelled at the simplicity of his barren room. Above his small bed hung a single photograph, a stunning black-and-white image of a bustling Arabian market. While I stared at it, he turned and noted, "I took that in Marrakesh in 1965. I was there with my mother. I had taken her to see Morocco. When we went it took us seven days to travel by train and steamer," he said, emphasizing the seven. "Now you can fly there in a single afternoon. It is ludicrous, sad really."

On a crowded bookshelf sat several copies of *Among the Mountains*, his newly released book, containing images and stories from his travels in northern Pakistan and Afghanistan. It is his seventh, and three more are currently in the works. On an old wooden dresser stood a fading photo of his beloved mother, who had a profound influence on Sir Wilfred's life. Beside a small table of books and under a tall reading lamp sat a well-worn armchair. It was positioned to face into the room, looking towards the books and his spartan desk, rather than out over the rolling green pastures beyond the bay windows. It seemed symbolic for a man whose greatest treasures lie in memories of his past.

I carefully helped Sir Wilfred into his bulky felt overcoat. He leaned heavily on my arm as we strolled to the nearby clubhouse where he likes to take all his guests for lunch. Our time seemed so precious. I hardly knew what to say. It felt like I should have a thousand questions, but none came to mind.

We settled into our table, and after ordering, Sir Wilfred began to ask detailed questions.

"From what tribe are the Bedu that will accompany you?" he demanded. I felt embarrassed that I did not know the tribe or even the names of the men Manaa planned to have with us.

"It will be critical you travel with the right men. You will need to find someone to whom a camel still matters. And that will not be easy. They all use cars now. You will want Rashid tribesmen, I suspect," Sir Wilfred continued, demonstrating his lifelong allegiance to the Rashid, whom he considers of a higher moral stock than the other nomads of the southern desert. The Bait Kathir, another predominant tribe of southern Oman, had abandoned him on his first journey. He had never forgiven them, and had later written that he found them to be "degraded with a corroding avarice."

"It was Al-Auf who got us across the sands. We could have never done it without him. He knew when to graze and when to ride. He made all the difficult decisions.

"How will you communicate with the Bedu?" he continued. I explained that Leigh and I had been taking introductory Arabic courses.

Sir Wilfred looked perturbed. "That is all well and fine to say hello, but what are you going to do when you need to communicate about something complicated, such as making a difficult route decision?" Again I had no answer.

"How will you find camels that can survive a trip like this? The camels we rode had been travelling difficult routes for years. I do not believe the camels in Arabia today can do what you will ask of them.

"I wrote in *Arabian Sands* that all my life had been but a prelude for my time in Arabia. I spoke Arabic and had travelled for years on camels in Sudan. If you had previously spent a fortnight riding through the Hadramaut, as I did the year before crossing the Sands, then perhaps crossing the Empty Quarter would be a more reasonable proposition. I am worried for you," he concluded. "It will not be easy. The journey is terribly formidable." Then he added with a smile, "I was just happy to emerge from the Rub al-Khali alive and uncircumcised."

The afternoon passed quickly, and soon it was time to leave. Although I had taken them to heart, I was not discouraged by Sir Wilfred's warnings and obvious doubts. I had not come to learn any facts or details, in particular, but simply to be in Sir Wilfred's presence, to show him my respect, revel in the gift of his company, and to take something intangible away, a sense of place for our journey. I was sad to leave. I promised I would return with Jamie and Leigh before the journey began. As I packed my briefcase, he shook his head. "You will be in Riyadh tomorrow. It is incredible. The world has changed and it is dreadfully sad." A distant look passed over his face. "Indeed, I don't know what I would do with myself if I was a young man today."

We shook hands and I could see him watching politely from inside the pane-glass doors as the cab pulled away.

ربع الخالي

Early the next day I stopped by the Saudi Arabian embassy once again. The morning was designated for the drop-off of visa applications only, but I wanted to ensure that everything was in order. The processing agents, speaking through barely audible microphones from behind a protective tinted layer of glass, were surprisingly cheerful. They assured me that everything was fine. I should drop by in the afternoon to collect my passport and visa. I spent the rest of the day in the dark and musty map room at the Royal Geographical Society, researching early Arabian journeys.

When the Saudi embassy opened for the afternoon, my luggage and I joined a long line of visa hopefuls, eventually arriving at the fateful window. Greeted with a friendly smile, I was asked to produce a copy of my plane tickets, which I quickly did. After a brief delay I was told to take a seat. Someone would come out to talk to me personally. My apprehension began to build. This was my last chance. Check-in for my flight was about to begin miles away at Heathrow.

Forty-five minutes later a well-dressed gentleman appeared beside me and announced that my visa application had been rejected. I had not given them enough time for processing. I couldn't believe it. My heart started to sink when he added with a smile that he could sort out the situation, and quickly disappeared again with both my passport and my plane tickets. The visa office soon closed. Cleaners arrived and the floor was swept and mopped. The last stragglers left, and still there was no sign of the visa. One of the cleaners asked me to take my luggage and wait next door in the embassy's main hall, so I moved down the street one building and continued to wait as the embassy emptied. I was almost convinced that there could not possibly be anyone left on the premises when the original attendant appeared, my passport in hand. I breathed my first sigh of relief in two weeks, and thanked him profusely. With little time to spare, I jumped on the very next train, sped to Heathrow, and displayed the rather innocuous but mandatory visa for my flight to Riyadh.

Twenty hours later, late in the evening of November 27, 1998, I was met inside the King Abdul Aziz International Airport by Ted Hobson, the Canadian ambassador, and the second secretary, Ian Shaw. They whisked me through immigration and customs and out into a large, black sedan parked directly in front of the building. As we sped off into the warm Riyadh night, the Canadian flag flying on the hood, I had no idea about the world I was about to enter.

The Canadian embassy lies in the Diplomatic Quarter, an enclave of embassies, consulates, and official residences lying to the west of Riyadh. Although it was after midnight when we arrived, Ted gave me a quick tour of the impressive facilities. The main embassy building had been constructed from beautiful rose granite, hewn in Quebec. A spacious atrium was highlighted by a wide waterfall flowing amid myriad plants and small trees. Behind a set of locked and push-button-coded doors lay the diplomatic offices. Outside, a series of groomed and terraced gardens surrounded a pool and tennis court, and to one side the ambassador's residence adjoined the embassy. Ted showed me to a guest room, bade me goodnight, and then added in his booming voice, "Welcome to the Kingdom, Bruce."

Saudi Arabia traces its origins to the early morning of January 16, 1902, when young Abdul Aziz, a leader of the al-Saud tribe exiled to Kuwait, travelled through the northern reaches of the Empty Quarter and secretly returned to Riyadh, recapturing the city from long-time rivals, the Rasheed. In the years that followed, Abdul Aziz al-Saud established the Saud dynasty, uniting the fragmented patchwork of feuding tribes and sheikhdoms that covered the peninsula, and founding the Kingdom of Saudi Arabia. During his rule, the legendary king begot, at conservative estimates, forty-three boys and twenty girls, and today more than three thousand descendants claim direct lineage. In discussions with Ambassador Hobson and Ian Shaw, who had been spearheading our efforts in Riyadh, we agreed that the best way to present our expedition was as a recognition of Abdul Aziz's recapture of Riyadh, since he had travelled through the northern reaches of the Empty Quarter to arrive at the city. By coincidence, our journey would take place one hundred years after his trek, as marked by the Islamic *hijra* calendar.

Our first meeting had been arranged with His Highness Prince Turki bin Sultan bin Abdul Aziz, a grandson of the founding king, and the current deputy minister of information. As our black sedan pulled up at the palace gates, the driver lowered the window and yelled, "*El safir el Canadiya, el safir el Canadiya* (The Canadian ambassador, the Canadian ambassador)." Guards scrambled to raise the barrier, and we drove through into an expansive marble courtyard, where a glittering white tower soared above us. The chauffeur stopped in front of the main doors, and we sprang out into the midday heat. Men impeccably dressed in flowing white robes and crisp red-checkered headdresses floated effortlessly up and down the stairs as we rushed by. After several security checks, we were ushered into an opulent office, where Prince Turki bin Sultan was occupying one of the enormous couches that filled the room. After we gave him a brief account of our plans, he immediately agreed that the expedition seemed a good idea, declared the ministry of information had no objections, and wished us luck.

It was a relatively noncommittal response. We had come hoping for more active support, and possibly a recommendation to the powerful ministry of the interior (police, army, and border patrol), where we were making no headway. "We will just keep plugging away," the ambassador promised.

We were scheduled to meet Prince Sultan bin Salman bin Abdul Aziz, another grandson of the late king, later that evening. Commonly known as the "Astronaut Prince," Prince Sultan was a jet fighter pilot, and had been a member of a 1986 space-shuttle flight. As our black sedan neared its destination, our chauffeur played a delicate game, adjusting his speed, and I realized how carefully choreographed a diplomatic meeting was. One would never arrive late, but it appeared that it was equally important never to arrive more than a minute early. Prince Sultan bin Salman's house lay on a darkened and deserted road, and, in perfect form, we arrived at 7:59. Inside, the prince listened attentively to our ideas, and assured us that he wanted to help in every way that he could. He suggested that we contact his uncle, Prince Saud bin Naif, who, as the deputy governor of the Eastern Provinces, held command over police and border patrols in the Saudi Arabian territory through which our proposed route crossed. Prince Sultan bin Salman assured us that he would act on the matter that evening and, *inshalla* (god willing), arrange a meeting. A curt nod to one of his assistants signalled that his decision had been recorded. Suddenly our time was up, and we left as quickly as we had arrived.

When we returned to the embassy, a phone message had already arrived, inviting us to visit Prince Sultan bin Salman's uncle in his palace. Two days later we drove across four hundred and fifty kilometres (280 miles) of desert to Dharan, in the Eastern Provinces. After we phoned the opulent palace from a nearby Burger King where we had stopped for lunch (an irony that was not lost on us), the driver attached the Canadian flag to the hood of the car, and we raced to our meeting.

We waited tensely in an antechamber, fidgeting and reviewing our notes, before the doors swung open and we were led into a huge office. The prince rose from behind his desk, and showed us to a circle of sofas in one corner of the large room. As we took our seats, the prince told us he already understood the purpose of our visit, and he would do whatever possible to help. Surprised and very pleased, we drank coffee served by two silent servants while the prince called in his personal assistant and ordered him to take charge of our file immediately. Any requests, questions, or concerns we could address directly to him, and we should encounter no difficulties. The prince's only wish was that we send him some photos from the journey and that we leave our Web site address, as he wanted to ensure his young daughter followed the Internet education program. "You will be very lucky to see this area of the desert," he concluded. "Few have ever travelled there, it is not an easy land. *Inshalla*, your journey will be a success."

With his approval, the expedition had finally received the sanction we sought, and – theoretically – we could proceed with confidence. With the active support of the deputy governor of the Eastern Provinces, all the small but essential logistical details we had battled for months to solve, such as border-crossing protocols and finding the locations of government wells, should fall quickly into place. We drove home brimming with a sense of accomplishment and all the tensions that had hovered over us during the last week dissipated. In a semi-delirious state brought on by too little sleep and too many hours in a car, we joked, laughed, and slept, as the desert raced by outside.

The approval had come just in time, since I had already pushed back my flights as far as my tickets would allow, and that evening I was to fly on to Muscat. As twilight turned to darkness, we sped smoothly down the brightly lit six-lane highway connecting Riyadh with the modern Abdul Aziz airport. I had fought so hard to arrange the visit, and now the hurried stay seemed too brief. The six days had been an endless chain of meetings and planning. I felt as if I had never been outside an office or car. Even so, it had been a rare privilege to visit Riyadh, and see this face of the Kingdom, and I wondered how long it would be before I could return.

## ربع الخالي

In Muscat my goals were twofold: to finalize the logistical and operational support plans for the expedition with Chris Beale and, more importantly, to visit Manaa. I wanted to ensure the Bedu were continuing to prepare, and to check what had been done so far. For two days Chris and I buried ourselves in his office, poring over maps, discussing the next steps required to solidify permission in Oman and the United Arab Emirates, and analysing route possibilities. On the third day Manaa would arrive in Muscat for a meeting.

After dinner on the appointed day, we waited in the hotel conference room. Shortly after seven o'clock, gruff voices rang close in the hallway outside. The door swung open and Manaa strode in. He took my hand and smiled. His lone finger wrapped tightly around my wrist.

"*Salaam aleykum* (Peace be with you)," I greeted him.

"*Aleykum as salaam* (With you be peace)," he replied.

"*Keif halek* (How is your life)?" I asked.

A smile spread across his thin lips. "So, my friend, you have learned Arabic. It is a good thing, as I do not speak English," he said, with a clear British accent. And, as during our earlier encounter, he uttered not another word of English in the ensuing two hours.

Manaa assured us all the plans were progressing well, and gave me the names of the three Bedu who would accompany us, describing their impressive backgrounds. Camels were already being bought; special feed had been ordered. Although the meeting was mostly for show, now that our Saudi Arabian permission had been settled, we all knew we had to move ahead quickly. After I left for home, Manaa and Chris would travel to Saudi Arabia's Eastern Provinces, meet with our new contact there, and ensure all the border-crossing protocol had been approved. Manaa would also seek local Bedu there to gather information on the condition of grazing and wells in the heart of the desert. Manaa told me not to worry about the camels, everything would be taken care of. He was most concerned about crossing into *El Mamlika* ("The Kingdom" of Saudi Arabia). Manaa warned that everything had to be in order, or there could be major problems, and the Bedu would not go. Smiling disarmingly, he said he knew about the problems, having crossed a few borders that he was not supposed to cross.

صحراء

When I arrived home days later it felt for the first time in months that we might actually pull off the expedition. Things had been busy in my absence, and I met with Jamie and Leigh immediately so we could bring each other up to date on the progress. The most exciting news was that the Saudi Arabian embassy in Ottawa had called earlier in the day to request our passports for expedition visa stamps. The recent efforts in Riyadh had paid off. Leigh had continued to amass more piles of gear in the basement, which we went through, carefully trying to envision what we definitely would need, and what would be extraneous. Long-awaited funds had finally come in from our sponsors, as well as sunglasses and eyedrops from Bausch & Lomb and laptops to send updates for the education program from NEC Technologies. Everything was finally falling into place.

The only problem we faced at the meeting was a dispute over the expedition's publicity program, and it was a very emotional one. Months earlier, when the educational Web site and related curriculum were finally complete and in place, we had begun working with the Calgary Board of Education to spread word of the free program to teachers and students around the world. At the same time, local media began to show an interest in the unusual expedition, and while it was hard to capture or convey the essence of the journey in a single sentence, naturally that is what most reporters sought. We felt uncomfortable with sweeping phrases such as "first time in fifty years" or "world's largest sand desert." Not wanting the expedition to be misportrayed, and to facilitate the dissemination of accurate information, we had contracted a communications firm in Toronto to represent us.

While I was away, this publicity program had taken an unexpected turn. Jamie wanted to enlarge the coverage of the event – and specifically his involvement. He was a public speaker, and this could certainly help his career. Jamie also faced large pressures supporting a business and employees, so I understood his motivations. Still, it just didn't seem right, or fair. During the year of preparations, the three of us had all worked together, seeing ourselves as equal partners. After many heated discussions, Jamie finally decided to continue and contributed additional money himself, ensuring he received the personal coverage he needed. I was frustrated at myself for letting it bother me, because it seemed petty. I wished I could forget about it, but found myself torn. Was I being vain and attention-seeking, or were my concerns legitimate? Several days later when the firm representing us issued the first major press release entitled "Canadian Adventurer Jamie Clarke to Cross Arabia's Empty Quarter" I was shocked, and despite my rationalizations, felt bitterly disappointed.

My strong friendship with Jamie was strained by the anger, on both sides. Although we each understood the other's point of view, the issue had become so emotional that nothing seemed able to resolve the tension, and it only continued to get worse. Previously we had always been able to take opposing views, argue passionately over them, and then move on with our bond strengthened. Now the hurt seemed to linger, and there was nothing we could do but shelve the problem. It was an incredibly busy time as the journey loomed closer: eighteen-hour days seemed the norm, and even five spare minutes to discuss the problem were hard to come by. We rushed to finalize a mass of expedition details, and all grew tired and worn. We each needed the support of the others, and luckily we were able to provide it despite the simmering tensions. The weeks over Christmas flew by, and the day of our departure rolled inexorably towards us.

January 7 arrived bitterly cold in Calgary. Blowing snow rimed our eight duffel bags where they were piled awaiting taxis. By the time we had arrived at the airport and checked in, we were all thoroughly exhausted. The flight was full, and we sat separately, already asleep as the plane took off for England, where we would meet Sir Wilfred before flying on to Muscat.

ربع الخالي

Sir Wilfred looked as impeccable as he had on our previous meeting, waiting in a pressed suit and vest, his slightly long, steel-grey hair brushed back, hands carefully folded over his hand-carved Zulu walking stick. He escorted us to a large sitting room in his home, where Jamie, Leigh, and I took chairs around the old explorer and huddled close, leaning in, paying reverent attention. A National Geographic crew had arrived to film our meeting, and although he had agreed to it, Sir Wilfred was obviously perturbed by their presence. Trying to ignore the lights and cameras around us, we discussed details of his past journeys, and our upcoming one.

"Water is desperately important. You must carry your water in goatskins," Sir Wilfred began. "I accidentally bought some sheepskins, and they leaked rather a lot. I used to watch those bags hanging on the camels," he said, demonstrating the slow dripping with his fingers, "and it felt to me like blood from an unstaunched wound." He looked directly at each of us with his piercing blue eyes.

As we gazed at old black-and-white images from the desert, Sir Wilfred talked of the desolation, and his group's struggle to find grazing. "Think the whole time of saving your camels' strength. You are going to depend on them, and if your camels collapse you will not walk out alive."

Eventually the film crew left, and we continued chatting more easily as we walked to the nearby golf club for lunch. Thesiger talked of his Bedu companions warmly, explaining and in the same breath warning that "their standards of behaviour are very, very high, and their loyalty is absolute. You will have to live up to this. They notice everything, and they remember it, and they pass it on to their friends." He once again inquired as to the Bedu we would be travelling with, and sat back to ponder when we confirmed our companions were from the Bait Kathir tribe.

Three hours seemed to pass in an instant, and before we were ready, it was time for us to leave.

"All I can really tell you is that I wish you every success," Sir Wilfred said as we prepared to bid farewell. Although the meeting had been somewhat rushed, and we had been distracted, already thinking of what lay ahead, all of us would come to remember Sir Wilfred's words many times in the months to come.

CHAPTER FOUR

# In Arabia

Of the gladdest moments in human life, methinks, is the departure
on a distant journey into unknown lands. Shaking off, with one
mighty effort, the fetters of Habit, the leaden weight of Routine, the
cloak of many Cares, and the slavery of Home, one feels once more
happy. The blood flows with the fast circulation of childhood. . . . A
journey, in fact, appeals to Imagination, to Memory, to Hope – the
three sister Graces of our moral being.

– Sir Richard Francis Burton, *Zanzibar*

The Boeing jet banked and eased back its thrust, continuing a comfortable descent towards Seeb International Airport in Muscat. From
the air-conditioned comfort of my seat, I peered down on the craggy,
broken rock of Oman's *Jebel Akhdar* (Green Mountains). The dry, sun-
baked range runs north from Muscat, paralleling the eastern coast
until its crumbling ramparts drop into the waters of the Arabian Gulf,
forming the strategically important Strait of Hormuz. Below the
plane, countless *wadis*, or dry river courses, transected the coastal
flats. Beds of rounded white gravel and stone highlighted their short
but tumultuous trip from the highlands. There are no permanent
rivers or lakes in Arabia. When the rare rains do come, they are hard

and short. *Wadis* take up the precious water the parched ground craves but cannot absorb. Within a few minutes these dry canyons can be transformed into rushing torrents of thick, reddish-brown water, sweeping away everything in their path. Quickly the flood passes; the *wadis* are dry again, and the surrounding land returns to its patient wait for water.

I could make out sporadic dykes intruding into the *wadis* as they fanned into wide deltas before disgorging into the sea. These dykes were not designed to hold back the waters, but rather to capture some of the rich soil which is transported from the mountains during the floods. Small plantations flourished in the fertile sediments behind the barriers, oases of green in the otherwise desolate, brown world.

As we settled in to the final approach, the distinctive white clay architecture of Muscat's suburbs, marked by the rising towers of frequent mosques, rushed past underneath our wings. Six months ago this had been my first view of Arabia, foreign and romantic, inciting visions from my reading. Now it felt comfortably familiar. The plane stopped outside the terminal, and a mass of passengers scrabbled to retrieve their carry-on luggage. Jamie, Leigh, and I caught each other's eyes, and smiled; it was January 10, 1999. We had finally arrived.

A blast of warm air rushed in to meet us as the rear doors of the plane swung open, carrying with it the scent of tropical flowers, sea air, and diesel fumes. As I walked down the stairs to the tarmac below, I could already feel the sun baking my skin. Sweat beaded on my forehead, and my shirt stuck to my back. We were borne along by the bustling crowd of foreign labourers, cheap workers, typically from Pakistan, Bangladesh, and India, who provide essential support and maintenance for Arabia's vast new infrastructure. The long immigration lines moved at a snail's pace, as serious-looking officers entered every visa detail by hand into massive logbooks. We eventually reached the front of the queue and practised the traditional Arabic greeting, "*Salaam aleykum,*" on a rather unimpressed guard. He noted our particulars and then waved us on.

The baggage-claim area was almost empty by the time we arrived. Scattered around the conveyor belts were boxes and dilapidated suitcases of all description. Some seemed to have been there for months. Our brightly coloured duffel bags were notably conspicuous amongst the disarray, but only six of our eight could be found. While we searched through the piles, Chris Beale shuffled in, smoking his trademark pipe. After quickly introducing Jamie and Leigh, I went with Chris to report our missing bags to the luggage manager. He seemed unconcerned, and was decidedly lethargic, since he had had nothing to eat or drink since sunrise. The month-long fast of Ramadan, which moves forward by approximately eleven days each year marked by the Christian calendar (Islamic countries follow the shorter *hijra* calendar, see Notes on Usage, page xi), has a great effect on the efficiency of workers, especially when it falls in a hot month. At home the gear we packed seemed vitally important. I had checked and rechecked every list. Now we had lost a quarter of our equipment before even unpacking it, but somehow it no longer seemed to matter. We left a contact number with the tired luggage manager and departed for our hotel.

Jamie and I had both arrived feeling sick and rundown. The final months of preparation for the expedition had been staggeringly hectic, and the effects of the effort had now caught up to us. Chris recommended a local doctor, and we spent our first morning in Muscat searching for her office amidst a mayhem of traffic in the narrow streets and alleys.

The friendly Pakistani we visited did not seem satisfied until she had prescribed at least one course of medication for every symptom that we mentioned. Afterwards we went from pharmacy to pharmacy, seeking somewhere that could fill our handful of prescriptions. Eventually we were directed to a shop advertising women's perfume in the front window. At the back counter we found all the inhalers, pills, and syrups we required. Anxious for any quick cure, we took a little bit of every medicine as soon as we returned to the sweltering car – including each other's. Despite this effort our afflictions would continue unabated for several more days.

That evening we joined Chris for coffee to review our plans as a team. Although he had sounded very enthusiastic over the phone, it now appeared that Chris had made no progress in pursuing the challenges facing us in Oman. We still did not have official permission for the journey from Oman, and we would be obliged to leave the country in three weeks if nothing changed. This was not nearly enough time to complete our training and the first stage of the journey to the Saudi Arabian border. We would need to begin visiting senior officials Chris knew during the next days to press forward the approval process. Chris also had planned on obtaining accurate maps of the Empty Quarter through his contact with a local military attaché, but the approaching tourist season had kept him too busy. I had seen Chris's role during the expedition as that of a general manager, keeping daily track of our progress and, most importantly, organizing any search-and-rescue efforts if they were required. An emergency-response flow chart that we had neatly drafted in the comfort of our Calgary office showed Chris with the title of "Gulf Region Co-ordinator." On top of the pressures of his business, however, Chris was coping with the illness of his wife, Heide, which I knew must consume his thoughts and energy. I was beginning to realize that we would have to rely on ourselves now that we were here. I worried about what would happen in case of an emergency in the field.

Sheikh Said bin Ali, a Bedu airforce pilot who worked with Manaa, dropped by to visit us. I had met Said during my last visit to Oman, when he had joined Manaa for the final negotiations over the expedition schedule and costs. As a respected and influential member of the Bait Kathir tribe, Said had a strong interest in our proposed journey. After fifteen minutes of greetings and small talk, we got down to the business of the expedition. We were all eager to learn of the status of our Bedu travelling companions and the new camel herd, which we assumed was now well trained. Over a cup of coffee, however, Said bin Ali casually mentioned that Manaa was presently in Abu Dhabi (capital of the United Arab Emirates), searching for camels to use on the journey. My jaw dropped. Months earlier Manaa and Sheikh Said bin Ali had insisted that the success of the expedition would rely on having strong, well-trained camels. After much haggling, I had agreed to pay for a special diet that was to be fed to carefully chosen camels for two months prior to our arrival. One month, they had insisted, would not be enough. I was disappointed that the plans we had agreed to had been ignored, and annoyed by the casual manner in which we were informed. Leigh and Jamie were even more shocked. This was their first introduction to the confusing and contradictory world of the Bedu, where the importance of time holds much less value than in the West, and affirmative replies are often given to all queries, in a kind effort not to disappoint the questioner.

There was a long, uncomfortable silence when Jamie challenged Sheikh Said as to why the camels had not been purchased earlier and trained. The sheikh's eyes burned with anger, and he appeared ready to leave. He did not consider that he or Manaa had broken their promises. Rather, he was offended that we did not appreciate the extra effort Manaa had made in driving to Abu Dhabi to find good camels, instead of choosing second-rate ones locally. His pride and honour, both paramount in Arabian society, were offended by the questioning. The situation soon calmed, but this highlighted the incredible difficulty Westerners encounter in dealing with the Bedu, and our different cultural expectations. It would be a challenge throughout the journey, and is especially frustrating for foreigners accustomed to open and frank dialogues.

We were more anxious than ever to continue on to Thumbrait, the small settlement in Dhofar where I had first met Manaa, to gauge at what stage the Bedu preparations really were. We had a lot to accomplish before we could begin the journey, and our planned start date of January 24 was just two weeks off. Time was also ticking away towards the hot season, which could arrive in earnest as early as the beginning of April. However, there was still more than a week left in Ramadan, a time when Muslims around the world devote extra time to prayer and reading the Koran. During the holy month of fasting foreigners are often advised to stay politely secluded, and I felt uncomfortable intruding in Manaa's tight-knit Bedu village. While waiting in Muscat, we visited a number of senior police officials, and eventually left our passports behind, assured we would shortly get permission for an extended stay in the country and approval of our proposed expedition routing.

Two days later, before the final visas had been issued, Manaa called and urged us to travel to Thumbrait as soon as possible. He assured us that Ramadan was not a problem, and we would be welcome. We didn't need to be asked twice, and Chris promised to visit us soon, bringing with him all the paperwork.

Early the next morning, January 14, we loaded a rented Land Cruiser with our heavy duffels (the lost pair had miraculously arrived after being found on the tarmac in Dubai) and left Muscat for the one-thousand-kilometre (620-mile) drive to Thumbrait. Starting on the coastal flats we wound our way along palm-lined *wadi* gorges which cut deep into the Jebel Akhdar. After passing through the strategic Samail gap, the only overland route joining the capital, Muscat, to the rest of the country, we watched the crumbling mountains fade behind us. The *wadi*'s deep paths widened and spread, opening onto the unending gravel plains of Oman's interior. The lush vegetation dotting the irrigated villages of the mountains also began to fade. Ahead of us the highway was a narrow ribbon of dark asphalt running across an otherwise unbroken landscape. Traffic signs warned of the local hazards, drifting dunes and wandering camels. We saw little other traffic.

Outside the Land Cruiser hundreds of kilometres of nondescript desert rushed past. I stared through the window, trying to imagine living in this environment. The land seemed singularly unappealing. This was not the romantic Arabian desert of common lore. It was mirror-flat, without even a single twig or plant to break the stretching planes. Occasional red-and-white metal towers appeared on the horizon, flaring off waste gas in huge, shimmering orange plumes, the only interruption in the surrounding visual monotony. Mirages wavered in the distance, reminiscent of the illusory puddles that linger just beyond one's reach on hot black highways. Outside it looked hot – hot and dry. I felt intimidated. Inside our air-conditioned vehicle I was comfortable, living in the artificial cocoon of safety and shelter. Vehicles have a tendency to diminish the force of the land one rushes past, shielding the occupants from the reality that can only be grasped by living with the land, walking its contours, knowing its moods. I tried to imagine coping with the inescapable heat. We would cross four hundred kilometres (250 miles) of similar gravel flats at the start of our journey. How could we possibly survive in this environment?

The desert was foreign to me. As I stared at it, trying to grasp its essence, however faintly, I wondered if I would grow to love it in the same way I had the other lands I had lived in. During the months of preparation, a sense of anticipation had built inside me. The desert was a land that seemed to inspire spirituality, reverence, and respect in those who knew it, but I had never understood the allure. I suppose I had never spent enough time in a desert environment to develop any understanding of its seductive powers. I had grown up in Canada, and felt most at home near its Northern mountains, rivers, and forests. I had read somewhere that the desert is a mirror, reflecting back what we see and feel about ourselves. I pondered this. Did the monotony of the land heighten one's sense of observation, and the unremitting passage of hours encourage reflection? Its vastness seemed to reduce travellers to insignificance, and paradoxically magnify everything else; even the smallest blades of grass began to assume a vast importance.

We stopped that night at a highway rest-house in Haima, halfway to Thumbrait. The small building complex surrounded by a stone wall was the only break in the desolation we had encountered. There were no other cars in the large parking lot; we were the only guests at the remote outpost, and probably the first for months.

During the night I was awakened by Jamie rushing around our room. He had been roused by a large bug crawling across his back. When he casually flicked it off, its weight and bulk alarmed him. Despite his fatigue, he got up to investigate. To his amazement a large black scorpion dashed across the stone floor, disappearing into the bathroom. It backed into a corner, facing Jamie with its tail raised menacingly over its head. A quick swat with a sandal dispatched the scorpion, but afterwards I stayed awake, carefully investigating every small itch I felt.

The next morning, when I mentioned the incident to the rest-house manager, he invited me into his office to proudly display a wall covered with large scorpion corpses neatly pinned in a row. They had all been found in the hotel and its surrounding grounds, he told me with a smile. I advised him to keep the display where it was, hidden in his office.

Four more hours of driving across dusty gravel flats brought us to Manaa's village of Thumbrait. The dilapidated gas station marking the turnoff from the highway was deserted, save for two Pakistani truck drivers, lounging in the shade of their vehicle. Manaa had promised to meet us at noon, and when we pulled into the village we were fifteen minutes early, so we bought some bottles of cold Orange Fanta and decided to look around. We would not be hard to spot if anyone wanted to find us.

Thumbrait did not exist in Thesiger's era, but grew as a waypoint with the construction of Oman's "north-south" highway. Today it is home to over two thousand people, as well as the site of a large military air base which lies on the outskirts. As with many other villages in Arabia, to describe Thumbrait as an organized settlement is somewhat of an exaggeration. Rather, it is an unlikely collection of buildings, stores, and houses, arbitrarily erected in a sprawling manner across the dusty flats. Little if no city planning was apparent; it looked as if the buildings had dropped from the sky and landed where they did by chance. The single road leading from the highway ended abruptly in a roundabout with no exits. Rutted tracks led on, weaving through the muddled subdivisions. Warm desert gusts blew trash across the plains. Camels wandered the paths, belligerent at the approach of our truck. Elsewhere they sat lazily outside the cement-block homes, peacefully chewing their cud. Every house was surrounded by shoulder-height brick walls. Inside, the yards were carefully cleaned and raked. Sadly, it seemed most of the household refuse was dumped over the wall. Out of sight, out of mind.

We had stopped to explore the only "restaurant" in town when a grey truck sped up. A young, dark-skinned Sudani man emerged and introduced himself as Manaa's assistant, Mohammed. Asking us to wait where we were for him, he sped off again. Several minutes later he reappeared with a young Bedu in the cab beside him. This was Ali bin Salim bin Amir al-Hazar al-Kathiri, whom we came to know as Ali Salim, one of the three Bedu to accompany us on the expedition. Ali Salim spoke no English, but he shook our hands vigorously, his eyes flashing as he smiled. Long curls of thick black hair hung from under his loose headdress. Ali was short, even for a Bedu, and with his youthful smile he did not look close to his eighteen years. But he seemed confident and friendly. I liked him immediately. Ali Salim signalled for us to follow the Land Cruiser, and jumped back in with Mohammed.

We drove a kilometre out of town and turned west, away from the highway and into the broken land surrounding Thumbrait. Here the stretching gravel plateau of the interior begins to give way to the coastal mountains. Rocky outcrops dot the dusty flats, reminiscent of a lunar landscape. Mohammed raced along faint tracks in the gravel, his truck raising a swirling trail of dust. We strove to keep up, straining to see through the billowing clouds. Fine sand poured through the vents in our Land Cruiser, a thin film coating everything in the cab. Careering around a low rocky outcrop we arrived at a small camp, braking hard to avoid Mohammed's slowing truck. A large Bedu tent, or *haima*, had been set up here. The immense dark canvas shelter was held aloft by two sturdy bamboo centre poles and a multitude of guy-lines, and it could easily accommodate fifty men. Large roll-up panels in each wall allowed the desert winds to cool the sultry interior. I felt a pang of disappointment when I realized the tent was completely barren. None of the food or camel saddlery Manaa had promised to supply appeared to have been organized yet.

Across a small gravel clearing stood a dilapidated camel pen, its bent and twisted wiring held together in a makeshift manner. Rather than the strong proud herd that I had envisaged for months, there were only two tattered camels, which glared at us malevolently, pacing back and forth and roaring intermittently. It seemed that we were now the owners of the two skinniest, most sickly-looking camels in Arabia.

Ali Salim settled in the tent's shade to smoke a tiny pipe not much larger than his thumb. Attached to the bowl by a thin cord was a small plastic canteen, full of a potent blend of crushed tobacco. Carefully shaking a small quantity into his palm, Ali packed the bowl with the end of a wooden match. Not sure what the plan was, or if there even was one, we sat down beside him.

"*Ali, keif halek* (How is your life)?" I asked, wanting to open our communications and establish that we spoke some Arabic.

"*Hamdulilla* ("Praise God" – the normal and polite response throughout Arabia)," Ali smiled. "*Wee enta* (And you)?"

"*Hamdulilla, shukran* (Praise God, thank you)." I paused. What else did I know how to say? "*Enta mabsoot maa el beasa fee el Rub al-Khali?* (Are you excited/pleased about the journey in the Empty Quarter?)?" Ali looked bewildered. My bungled Arabic and strange accent were obviously confusing. Suddenly he appeared to understand.

"*Mabsoot, mabsoot* (Very happy, very happy)," he answered, smiling and nodding his head vigorously. This was the first feedback we had received from the Bedu who would accompany us, and it was encouraging.

Ali lit a match and raised it above the small bowl on his pipe in a single motion. With eyes closed he inhaled deeply, finishing the bowl with one draw, and casually flicked the smouldering ashes in the sand. He lay back to wait. We waited too. Two weeks earlier, Sir Wilfred, with a rare flash of a smile, had told us "Find your own Bin Kabina [Thesiger's trusted young companion during his Arabian travels] and you will be all right." I glanced at Ali with his friendly smile and confident manner, now asleep in the shade. I wondered hopefully, had we found *our* Bin Kabina? Only time would tell.

An hour later Mohammed returned and roused us from our repose, announcing that it was time to visit a tailor in town. Manaa had mentioned during our first meeting that he hoped we would wear Bedu clothes, although I had not known if this would actually happen. In the large cities it is considered silly, even rude, for Westerners to dress in *dishdashas* (traditional Arab gowns). Chris Beale had once scoffed at a tourist wearing a traditional headdress together with a tank top and shorts. I could see his point, but we hoped to embrace the culture as closely as we could, and were honoured when Manaa had originally suggested we dress in Bedu clothing. As we sped back towards town, I was happy and surprised that he had followed through so quickly.

Behind one of Thumbrait's five ornate mosques we found a collection of tailor shops. The open-fronted stores occupied the bottom floor of a building that was still under construction. A crowd of children appeared from nowhere, jostling around the truck to catch a glimpse of the new strangers. Pointing fingers they excitedly yelled, "*Americani, Americani!*" "*Canadi*," Ali Salim shot back with a stern glare, and ushered us into one of the shops. Whether we personally deserved it or not, our nationality brought us favour in the region. Especially as we were most often judged initially to be American, and tensions with the United States remained high.

Inside, the sudden darkness blinded me momentarily. As my eyes fought to adjust, I made out a line of sewing machines against one wall, operated by small, politely smiling Bangladeshi men. Bales of material, mostly muted tones of silk and fine cotton blends, lined the walls. Around us the scene quickly descended into utter confusion. Several of the attendants presented bale after bale of material to Jamie and me, eagerly waiting for us to decide on one from the growing pile. Leigh was dragged into a far corner to be measured by one of the tailors, who loudly announced every number, but wrote nothing down. Ali Salim and Mohammed both haggled with the owner over costs. I seemed to be involved in three conversations at once, understanding none of them.

Suddenly a silhouetted figure appeared in the door, and the commotion stopped – at least momentarily. Sheikh Salem bin Mohammed al-Toof introduced himself as a friend of Manaa's and welcomed us to Thumbrait. Under the direction of the sheikh the mayhem resumed as quickly as it had ceased. Jamie and I were quickly measured, the numbers were again announced with pride, but this time recorded in a thick dog-eared volume on the counter. We were presented with an endless series of choices: the type of material, the colour, the number of *dishdashas* we should order. Everyone seemed to have a different opinion, and they argued amongst themselves while trying to convince us. Some insisted that we needed dark colours for the desert, while others looked at them in shock and astonishment, claiming a light colour would be essential. The importance of each decision took on a greater weight with each moment we pondered, trying to absorb the contradictory information. We chose to follow Sheikh Salem's advice, ordering two *dishdashas* each, both to be made of a light-coloured material that he assured us would be perfect for the journey. The new robes would be ready in two days.

Outside the shop the sheikh stopped. "*Esmak eh?* (What is your name)?" he said, pointing to each of us in turn. He struggled to repeat our English names, but found the pronunciation difficult. "*Ackhhh. Mafi zain, mafi sahal* (Ackhhh. No good, not easy)."

We would need Arabic names now that we were here, he said, good Bedu names from the past. He looked at Leigh intently. "*Khamis*," he announced with a flicker of a smile. The boys who were gathered around us erupted with laughter. The sheikh assured us it was a fine name; Leigh wasn't so sure. *Khamis* means "Thursday." Jamie and I now called him "boy Thursday," which he did not seem to think was as funny as we did. The name would last only a few days, since the consensus in town was that Sheikh Salem had chosen an old and stodgy name. "Khamis" was soon revised to "Abdulla," which stuck for good.

The Sheikh now shifted his attention to Jamie, and after a brief pause declared, "*Sohail*." The name means "easy," and was bestowed because of Jamie's easy smile. But a single name is not enough in Arabia. Rather, there should be a long string, showing one's heritage, background, and family.

"*Sohail bin Canadi al-Musalli al-Kathiri*," the sheikh now added. The onlooking children once again squealed with delight. Sheikh Salem's choice no doubt arose from Thesiger's legacy, when he was known across the land as "Umbarak bin London" (*Umbarak* – the blessed one; *bin London* – son of London). In our names, *bin Canadi* (son of Canada) referred to our homeland, *al Musalli* referred to the predominant family in Thumbrait of which all our Bedu companions were members, and *al-Kathiri* was of course the larger tribe to which they all belonged.

Finally the sheikh pondered me. "*Saleh. Saleh bin Canadi al-Musalli al-Kathiri*." It was a great compliment, I discovered later. *Saleh* means "good man."

With the naming done, Sheikh Salem jumped into the driver's seat of our Land Cruiser, and held out his hand for the keys. Jamie reluctantly handed them over, and the sheikh began to ferry us around town. We visited a parade of small general shops, each carrying everything from fresh produce to frankincense burners to massive displays of cheap perfume. We were searching for headdresses and camel sticks, which the sheikh seemed to think we needed that instant. Finally, hidden among storefronts piled high with bald tires and spare auto parts, we found a shop with a suitable assortment of headdresses. We each spent several minutes sifting through the vast selection of colours and patterns, trying to decide between wool or cotton, fringe or no fringe. Once we had chosen, Sheikh Salem carefully showed us his technique for wrapping the headdress and, after a few aborted tries, we found we could quickly tie our own. We sat together, laughing and trying new arrangements, as the setting sun turned our faces orange and cool desert gusts fluttered the large squares of cotton. Sheikh Salem had shown us a traditional, tightly wound, wrap. Ali Salim preferred a loose, sporting wrap, with a long tail left hanging at the back. It appeared so loose I could not understand why it did not fall off his head. I assumed Ali's style was the equivalent of rebellious North American youths wearing their baseball caps backwards.

The sheikh spoke a little English, and, with our pidgin Arabic, we were having a splendid time, although we did not know exactly who he was, or how he was related to Manaa and the expedition. Being new in town we remained a little cautious of his intentions. When he invited us to dine with him, and stay at his home that evening, I was concerned that Manaa may have other plans, but since Manaa had still not appeared, and no one knew where he was, we accepted. There was really no other choice.

Sheikh Salem's two-storey brick home lay on the northern outskirts of Thumbrait. In the courtyard inside the brick wall surrounding the house was an open firepit surrounded by blankets and covered by a roof of corrugated aluminum. A crowd had gathered and continued to grow as townspeople filed in all evening, eager to view the newcomers. The broken conversation quickly turned to money, a favourite topic of the Bedu. A blind man called Ali began questioning us aggressively as to where we got the money for the trip. How much did it cost? How much did we pay for the camels? How much we were paying Manaa? After each pointed inquiry, the group would fall silent and intently await our response. Dark eyes shot us serious glances, and the chiselled faces in the flickering firelight showed little emotion. I avoided the questions as best as I could without being rude. It was a difficult situation. Everyone was sure we would become rich and famous like Umbarak (Thesiger). How were we going to share the money with the Bedu, blind Ali asked?

Sheikh Salem finally intervened, leading the conversation to more casual subjects. Did we listen to Michael Jackson? Why did he not sing about camels? Were there camels in Canada? Why not? Had we eaten camel meat? Did we like it? Our answer of "Yes" brought much applause and laughter. Were we married? How many wives did we have? Jamie was married, which met with obvious approval. As advised by our Arabic teacher, I answered, "*Lissa, ana schaab* (Not yet, I am young)," to get around this potentially sensitive issue. The Bedu looked at me sus-piciously. How old was I? Thirty-one! I must be crazy not to be married, they laughed. Soon the questioning became intense again. Were we Christian? How many times a day do Christians pray? Did we burn our dead or bury them?

As the night wore on, the crowd showed no sign of abating. We were tired and would have preferred to leave and sleep out at our desert camp, away from town, hoping to find our first moments of solitude since arriving. But it would have been rude to suggest, and the Bedu cer-tainly would have had none of it. Instead we settled in to sleep on carpets by the fire, surrounded by townspeople. Wrapped in blankets, I listened to broken fragments of animated Arabic conversation breaking the otherwise silent night. The word "*Canadi*" stood out often, and I wondered what they were saying.

The following day we began settling into the desert camp. After we unloaded our gear and tentatively approached the two camels, who bel-lowed with displeasure and caused us to retreat, there was not much to do. In the late afternoon, Jamie and I left on foot to explore the land around our camp. It had been baked hard by the sun, and with each step the gravel crunched underfoot. A few sparse plants had broken through the parched surface. Behind a shallow rise we discovered the weathered corpse of a camel. Only tattered fragments of its hide remained, cover-ing a tangle of sun-bleached bones. A short loop of baling twine, hope-lessly tangled around the two rear ankles, told the sad story of its demise. The camel was a victim of discarded garbage, which blows end-lessly across the desert here. I stared out across the cooling wastes as Jamie filmed the scene. In the dying heat, a tranquillity was descending on the land. For the first time since leaving Canada, I felt relaxed.

Honks and clouds of dust interrupted my reverie. A heavy diesel lorry loaded with camels appeared in the distance, roaring across the flats towards our camp. Behind it I noticed a pickup, swerving sharply back and forth. The lorry rushed by, honking, with waving men hanging from the windows, their *dishdashas* billowing in the wind. The pickup drew near, and we could see four camels galloping in front. To my delight, Manaa was driving. He stopped and waved, yelling something unintelligible over the noise. The camels began to veer away, and Manaa sped off to continue herding them towards camp. Jamie and I packed our gear excitedly.

By the time we arrived back at the camp the large lorry was already being unloaded. It had been backed into a low mound of soft gravel, and three men were fighting to lead roaring camels from the back, down the makeshift ramp of dirt. Ali Salim had arrived with the truck and explained to us that these six camels had been bought in the U.A.E. They appeared very impressive, large, strong, and healthy, but the thousand-kilometre journey in the cramped truck bed had taken its toll. Their thick, golden-brown coats were matted with hay and dried feces. The camels appeared stiff and tired as they lumbered to their feet, but in no time they bucked and roared frighteningly as the handlers attempted to lead them into the camp's makeshift pen. Eventually they were all tethered to fence-posts and fed a few armfuls of hay.

Meanwhile, Manaa was having troubles of his own herding his four camels towards the pen. Speaking only Arabic, he barked commands at us: "*Raboot!* (Tie [the gate])" "*Habel* (Rope)!" In the confusion I had no time to introduce Jamie and Leigh. We struggled to help, but we were intimidated by the big animals, and acutely aware of our incompetence in a situation that demanded fast reactions. Finally, the last beast rushed in, and the small pen was full of thrashing bodies. After welcoming us warmly, Manaa explained with pride how the four wild and unbroken camels he had brought were descendants of a herd his grandfather once owned. Their heritage could be traced back within Manaa's family for generations. Along with the two sickly camels already here when we arrived, they were to be broken and would act as pack camels on the journey. Many of Manaa's friends had told him that he was crazy to use his own camels on this expedition. They would surely die in the great desert. No one in the local area would sell him their camels for the trip. Manaa smiled as he explained this. "Do not worry," he said, "I know my family's camels are strong."

For now Manaa's wild camels still ran free in the pen, milling around the tethered camels from the U.A.E. Our final challenge was to catch, halter, and tether them. As we walked through the herd, I remained mindful of their big feet, knowing they could kick at any moment. Twilight in Arabia is very short, and darkness was already descending quickly. The first three camels were captured easily. Manaa approached each one stealthily and slipped a loop of rope over its head. By adding a twist under its chin and sliding the second loop over the camel's nose, he formed a makeshift halter. The fourth camel, however, presented a considerable problem. She would run wildly when approached, and soon Manaa resorted to swinging a western-style lasso overhead in an attempt to catch her. Jamie, Leigh, and I all took turns in the fading light, but the technique seemed to hold little promise of success. Manaa decided to try another technique: leaving a lasso on the ground in a far corner of the pen. After several attempts at herding the camel towards it, she inadvertently stepped in the waiting loop, and Manaa quickly pulled it tight.

As the loop closed on her rear leg, the wild camel went completely berserk, and Manaa yelled for help. While he attempted to halter her, Jamie, Leigh, and I struggled to hold the nylon lasso rope but, with only a short length of rope and the powerful back legs flailing dangerously close, it was nearly impossible. We were dragged helplessly around the stall in a losing tug-of-war. Finally Leigh was able to brace himself, while Jamie and I managed to wrap the rope around a fencepost and tie it off. Manaa, who apparently could see well in the darkness, inched forward to delicately place a halter on the angry beast. Then he moved tentatively towards the rear leg, clicking and cooing to calm the camel. The lasso on the rear ankle had jammed under the terrific tension of the camel's tantrums. Manaa gave a few ineffective tugs on the knot, carefully trying to stay out of the range of a kick. Suddenly, in a moment of inattention, a quick swipe of the large padded hoof hit Manaa square against the chest and right forearm. The thud of the impact resonated in my ears, and Manaa flew backwards, almost lifted off his feet. This was enough for one night. Manaa gave up and cut the rope near the camel's foot, leaving the lasso tightly attached. As we walked away exhausted, he favoured his arm, but smiled. "*Hunna, yimkin ghralas* (Here, maybe finished)," he said, pointing towards his head. If the kick had struck him there, he might have been killed.

We drove the short distance to Thumbrait, and ate at Manaa's house, sharing a large platter of rice. His two young boys ate with us, but his wife, or wives, stayed out of sight, handing the food into the room while remaining hidden behind the door. We returned to camp and slept outside the tent, in the stillness of the dark desert. For the first time the magnificent Arabian sky revealed itself overhead. Stars dotted every corner of the heavens. The familiar North Star marked the sky over Thumbrait, while the Southern Cross floated low over the opposite horizon. A thin sliver of the waning moon indicated that Ramadan was almost finished. Apart from the camels shifting quietly nearby, the only sound was an almost imperceptible scurrying of beetles, crawling over tiny ridges of sand and gravel, searching for food in the night.

# CHAPTER FIVE

# Amongst the Bedu

Bedouin ways were hard, even for those brought up in them, and for strangers terrible, a death in life.

> – T. E. Lawrence, *Seven Pillars of Wisdom*

The sun rose at six o'clock the next morning, just as it did every day so close to the equator. Within fifteen minutes the blessed coolness of the night had passed, and the heat soon drove us from our sleeping rolls and camel blankets, despite our fatigue. It was January 17, 1999. Leigh boiled a pot of tea over a small fire of dry, thorny shrubs. We ate the remainder of a piece of *khobz* (unleavened bread) that Manaa had given us. A staple of the traditional Bedu diet, *khobz* is prepared using only flour and water. After the dough is well mixed, it is flattened into a large pancake shape and set directly onto the embers of the fire to sear. It is flipped quickly to sear the opposite side, and then buried in the hot sand beneath the fire. It cooks in ten to fifteen minutes, and after a good shake to remove the sand and traces of embers, is ready to eat.

As we sat in the hot sun quietly eating, Jamie noticed that the wild camel we had lassoed the previous evening now had a swollen foot. The slip knot had remained tight, and was cutting off circulation. The camel appeared tired, probably from standing all night, and it had no intention of letting us anywhere near. I was worried that damage to the foot might become serious, and felt badly about the camel's suffering. We wanted to do something, but were again aware of how inept we were around the camels. All we could do was sit in the hot sun and wait for help to arrive.

My attention was continually drawn to one of the new camels that had been brought in by truck the previous day. He paced incessantly along the twisted fence, from one extent of his tether to the other, never standing still. He was a young male, and the new surroundings and unfamiliar camels had left him distraught and nervous. I felt sympathetic watching him, and took over a handful of hay in a cautious attempt to say hello. He paused, guardedly sniffing at the dry grass, then ate it in one quick mouthful and immediately returned to his nervous pacing. It was a funny type of repetitive motion. He shifted his weight rhythmically between opposite front and back feet, while his head and rump swayed from side to side in unison, a kind of horizontal twist. I continued to linger beside him, talking in a soothing voice. Unfriendly, he stared back at me. As the days passed he would slowly grow accustomed to camp and calm down, but whenever he was agitated he would return to the strange shifting. This strong, stocky camel would become my constant companion and great friend over the course of our journey. When I referred to him offhandedly the next day as a Crazy Dancer, the name stuck.

Several hours later, Manaa arrived with a Bedu we had not previously met. The new man was short, his beard heavily tinged with silver. Obviously skilled with camels, he went immediately to the lassoed camel, and quietly urged her to sit. After soft words, and a few light raps from his stick, the camel protested, but settled to the ground. With great patience and slow movements the Bedu proceeded to tie her front legs in a way that prevented her from rising. Then he carefully prodded her hind quarter so that she readjusted her weight, exposing the lassoed leg. From their rapid conversation I understood that both Manaa and this new man were afraid to use a knife to cut the knot. It was very near crucial tendons. But the knot would not budge, despite all their efforts.

Finally the older man reached under his *dishdasha* and pulled out a long knife. Carefully distracting the camel, he slit the restraining rope in one smooth cut. Leigh whispered quietly beside me, "Tell me this is one of the Bedu who will be coming with us."

Manaa introduced the new man as Musallim bin Abdulla bin Musallim al-Rabat al-Kathiri. He would indeed be the second of our three companions on the journey. His age (forty-one, considered venerable in Bedu terms) and serene countenance seemed a perfect complement to young Ali Salim. Musallim was a poet, knowing by heart thousands of lines. Poetry is an art loved by Arabs, and especially the Bedu of the desert. During our late-night feasts, silence would fall around the noisy fire and the Bedu would listen intently to anyone reciting a poem. Musallim was also a camel doctor, widely sought after in Dhofar. Our confidence in the team that would accompany us was growing daily.

While Musallim went to his truck to retrieve a gun, Manaa told us he had still not found Bin Ashara, our final companion. Bin Ashara often journeyed alone into the desert for days. Manaa had seen the eldest of his ten sons at a gas station near Qitabit, two hours' drive away, and had sent word to Bin Ashara that we were waiting. *Inshalla*, Manaa assured us, he would arrive soon.

Musallim returned with his rifle and we spent the next two hours shooting at rocks and sticks from the shade of the tent. I was not accustomed to the constant presence of guns, but by the end of the journey I would be. A Bedu's gun is a source of great pride, a symbol of both his virility and his freedom. I never saw any of the Bedu as happy as when they were handling or firing a gun. They would sit for hours oiling and cleaning their ancient rifles. The fact that their guns still operated in this sandy environment was a testament to their fastidious efforts. Each Bedu would carefully inspect any new gun that arrived on the scene, feeling its weight, sighting the barrel. They told tales of guns they had seen in the past. In Thesiger's day a man's wealth could be judged by the rounds of ammunition on his belt, which would stay there for years, and often misfire when called upon. Today, boxes of cheap ammunition are available, and hardly a day passed when an excited game of target practice did not occur. As we were newcomers, our manliness seemed largely contingent on our marksmanship, and the group's opinion of us often swung from admiration to shameful disdain with a single poor shot.

We began to settle into desert life and Bedu ways. Ali Salim urged us to discard our boots and walk barefoot around the camp, to toughen our feet. "Bedu sandal," he said, smiling, pointing to the thick pads on the soles of his feet. It went against all common wisdom regarding desert safety, but we tried to walk, or tentatively shuffle, barefoot around camp. At first we could not go more than five or ten steps without having to sit down and pull out a large thorn or splinter. Slowly, our feet toughened.

Learning to sit comfortably and politely proved another major challenge. The Bedu sat with both legs tucked underneath, knees together pointing forwards, and their bottoms resting on their feet, toes pointing backwards. I found this position almost impossible. Certainly it was far too uncomfortable to stay in for any length of time. The pressure on my knees was immense, and they felt as if they might catastrophically fail at any instant. Leigh succeeded the best of all, but still could manage only a few minutes, the whole time grimacing with pain. A cross-legged position would have been unacceptable, as the soles of our feet would have shown, which is extremely rude in Bedu society. We were forced to develop a half-and-half style: one leg tucked underneath and the other knee raised in front, foot flat on the ground. With an arm wrapped around the raised knee, we seemed to be able to maintain the position comfortably for several minutes before switching legs.

Our presence was a cause of both curiosity and celebration by the local Bait Kathir Bedu. Every evening a gathering would swell around the fire at our camp. Often more than fifty men and children would arrive out of the blackness of the night. Many came day after day, and we grew to know them, but others came only once, having travelled great distances to see the Canadians. There was always someone new. Whether they thought we were crazy or brave I never knew; likely a little of both. Huge cauldrons of rice would be boiled, and goats arrived in the backs of pickups, destined to be slaughtered. After eating, the Bedu would dance and sing late into the night. As large groups chanted ceremonial greetings and good wishes, others would take turns prancing around the fire, spinning and throwing their guns high overhead. Their enthusiasm for these gatherings never waned. I wondered if at home such spirited camaraderie would take place without the influence of alcohol, which is *haram* (forbidden) under Islamic law, and is never seen amongst the Bedu. No Bedu would be comfortable attending any social function without a gun, or at the very least a camel stick. Many of the Bedu, despite having arrived by truck and not having ridden a camel in years, appeared with a riding stick. This they kept close by their side all night. In fact, occasionally men who had forgotten their camel sticks would ask quietly on the side if they could borrow mine for the evening. I suppose it was much worse for a Bedu than a Canadian to be seen without a camel stick.

Most nights Manaa would stay long after the gathering had dispersed, and took special pride in sharing with us Bedu ways and traditions. He showed us how his grandfather had taught him to sleep in the sand, carefully scooping out a shallow body-sized depression, running his fingers through to remove any rocks or camel droppings, explaining intently that only uncivilized people did not first prepare the sand this way before laying out their blankets. By the smouldering remains of the fire, Manaa recounted old tales and legends passed down to him by his father. Once, as we sat listening raptly, I absent-mindedly tossed a date pit into the embers. Manaa leaped up, and quickly retrieved the seed with his camel stick. After settling back down he explained that the date tree is a very special tree for Muslims, because it is mentioned in the Koran. "We believe God told Mary to shake a date palm while pregnant," he said with a gentle smile, "and after she ate the freshly fallen fruit, Jesus was immediately born underneath the tree. So as a sign of respect we cherish this tree and never throw its seeds in a fire."

I mused at how lucky we were to have found Manaa. At times he had been frustratingly unpredictable, but he cared deeply for us and had invested his heart in the expedition. I would miss him once we were travelling. I asked him why he did not make the journey with us, and he laughed, saying only that he was an old man now. "One day," he added, with his two young boys asleep, wrapped deep in the thick coat thrown over his shoulders, "one day I hope Tanuf and Mohanee will make a journey like this, *Inshalla*."

Our biggest challenge in the coming weeks would be learning to ride and handle the camels confidently. Manaa was eager for each of us to have our own camel for which we would be responsible. After a few days of observing both us and the herd, he decided that Leigh should ride Labian (Arabic slang for "white"), an aging white beast of Sudanese descent, and the largest camel. Jamie was assigned Mr. T., so named by us for two prominent T-shaped brands on his right front shoulder. I was paired with the nervous camel we now called Crazy Dancer. The Bedu were initially delighted with our English camel names, and adopted them immediately, although they struggled with the pronunciation. Musallim took exception, though, when I translated "crazy" (*majnoon*). He insisted the camel was fine, and I could not explain that the two words, "Crazy" and "Dancer," were linked. He would angrily object whenever he heard me whisper the name to my camel while riding.

"*La, la, mafi majnoon. Gamel waged zain.* (No, no, not crazy. Camel is very good.)" I found myself nervously glancing around before talking to my camel to ensure Musallim was out of earshot.

As we sat in the shade of the large tent, sorting the saddles, Manaa explained that camels are very intelligent. If we treated them with love and compassion, they would become our faithful friends, a bond that would last forever. However, if we wronged them, even once, they would never forget it. For years they would patiently wait for a chance to exact their revenge with a kick or a bite. A man in Thumbrait had once beaten a young camel badly. A few weeks later, the camel's mother had jumped onto his passing car, crashing through the front window and killing him. "*Ghralee balek min gamelek* (Be careful with your camel)! It will become your best friend," he said, looking straight into our eyes. The bond could become so strong on the journey Manaa warned, that if we jokingly play-fought or tussled with each other, a camel might come to its owner's defence.

The Bedu love to sing at any opportunity, and while riding they often chant hauntingly beautiful and melancholy verses. Manaa suggested we each choose a song we knew well, and sing it to our own camel over and over while riding. The camel would grow accustomed to the tune, he explained, and it would calm the beast if it was nervous or excited. Leigh, the best singer amongst us, chose ever-varying songs from a wide repertoire of Bruce Springsteen and Neil Young, which I was always pleased to hear when riding nearby. Jamie settled on "Frère Jacques," a French song from his childhood. I picked the "Huron Carol," a Jesuit missionary hymn written for the Huron first-nations people in 1649, and "Land of the Silver Birch," a Canadian campfire song. Not only did both songs remind me of the wild northlands of Canada, but they also are two of the very few that I can manage to sing in tune.

I began spending as much time as possible with Crazy Dancer; I would often sneak over to the compound after the frenzy of evening feeding had passed, simply standing nearby and quietly whispering. At first my presence seemed to bother him, and he would eye me suspiciously. Soon he became accustomed to me, and I could gently stroke his mane as he nibbled at the remains of hay and alfalfa. I always saved a few dates from my dinner, and I was amazed at how delicately he took each one from my hand. After a final sniff, to ensure he had found them all, Crazy Dancer would once again turn away to keep me at his back. As the days passed, he began to linger longer by my side, occasionally nuzzling his soft nose against my chest.

Each afternoon, after their prayers at the mosque, Manaa, Ali Salim, and Musallim would arrive at the camp to train both us and the camels. The massive animals would be led from the pen to the front of the tent, where they were couched and saddled. A camel sits, or couches, by low-ering itself to rest on its callused chest pad with its legs tucked under-neath its body. To instruct a camel to couch, the Bedu give a sharp tug downwards on the halter, accompanied by a guttural "*khhhhh*" sound. If the camel is obstinate or unco-operative, it can be encouraged by gently tapping the sand near its front feet with a riding cane while con-tinuing to pull down and "*khhhhh*." Often even this is not enough. As a last resort, a sharp rap to one of the forward feet will cause the camel to pull that foot back, and immediately drop to its front knees, the first action of the couch. Once the front knees are on the ground, the camel lowers its back end, and rests on its hind quarters. Finally it slowly moves both front knees forward in a shuffling action, easing its weight onto the large thorny pad on its chest.

Camels can sit comfortably couched for hours while resting or chewing their cud. Yet, as soon as saddles or loads appear, they will jump up violently – given the opportunity. To prevent this, it is necessary to tie the camel's halter firmly and tightly around one of the folded forelegs. In theory, this should keep the camel from rising, because, as it tries to rise, it pulls its own head down with its foreleg. At first I found that, no matter how tightly I tied the halter to my camel's leg, as soon as I turned away, he would jump up. The knot always slipped forward off the knee in the violent process. Luckily there were always Bedu nearby to recapture the roaming beast, but I knew it would be a more serious problem in the desert if I did not solve it. Soon I began wrapping the leg twice before tying the rope, and this worked much better. Still, many of the camels were strong enough to jump up on one front leg, with the tethered one hanging ineffectively at shoulder height. They would hobble around on three legs, roaring and spitting, until someone dashed in and grabbed the halter. After receiving a sharp tug down and a loud "*KHHHH*," they would then settle back to the ground, but would continue waiting for another opportunity to attempt an escape.

The Bedu of southern Arabia traditionally use a light saddle built of blankets, different from the larger double-poled cedar saddles found farther north. Manaa had searched widely to find us authentic saddlery. It was important that we had things just as they had in the old days, he said. Now he proudly presented each of us with the multitude of ropes and blankets we would require. Every piece had been lovingly hand-crafted by elders. While sitting on mats outside our tent, Manaa patiently went through the large pile, and taught us each name in Arabic.

The basis of the Omani saddle is the *hadut*, a wedge-shaped piece of cedar padded with a mat of woven palm fibres. Nothing other than palm fronds or wool should rub against the camel's fur. Modern synthetic materials can wear the hair away after only a day's riding. The *hadut* is positioned forward of the hump and firmly hitched in place, using a wide strap run under the camel's belly. A crescent-shaped fibre pad is then fitted behind the hump, the thickest point of the curved pad lying just above the camel's rump. A section of rope joins the two forward ends of the crescent, and this loop is passed over the front of the *hadut*, preventing the crescent from slipping backwards. A second long, black strap of woven wool is hitched around the camel, just in front of its rear legs, holding the crescent down. Now the rest of the seat pad is built over this base. Every Bedu seems to have a different method for arranging the blankets and padding, and eventually we each found what worked best for us. I often had to stop well-intentioned visitors to our camp from rearranging my seat once I had built it. Early on I made the mistake of allowing others to change my set-up, and then suffered for the entire day on an uncomfortable rig.

The arrangement that I liked best was quite simple. I would carefully fold and roll a camel blanket, forming a pad which was thicker at the rear than at the front. This I would lay between the hump and the padded crescent, forming a natural dip in the camel's back where my weight would rest. On top of the blanket I laid my saddle bags, two large pockets of woven wool which draped across the camel's back. Finally, I would add a large black sheepskin, or *souf*. The tail end of the wool strap already holding the crescent in place was now run over the pile of padding, around the *hadut*, and back to be tied off on the original loop. This held the entire platform of blankets and sheepskin firmly in place.

Learning to saddle the camels was a surprisingly difficult and challenging process. It forced us to work closely around the intimidating animals. I recall tentatively trying to pass a strap below Crazy Dancer's belly, which was pressed firmly into the sand. As I carefully excavated a small tunnel in the sand beneath him he turned his head and snapped at me with his large jaws, roaring belligerently. I beat a hasty retreat, wondering how long it would take me to master this seemingly simple task. No matter how hard we tried to learn ourselves, as soon as we faltered even slightly, the good-hearted Bedu would rush in to do it for us. Although they were trying to be kind, this prevented us from learning skills during training that would be critical in the desert.

While learning to saddle helped ease our trepidation marginally, learning to ride the camels presented a new set of challenges. Just mounting was a scary process. Once saddled, the camels would continue to sit comfortably for hours, only to jump up as soon as they sensed a rider preparing to get on. The Bedu, much quicker and lighter than we were, used a sudden jump to mount their camels. The camel would begin to rise immediately, but the Bedu would be firmly settled in the saddle before it was up. Being heavier and less sure of ourselves around the big animals, we tried to straddle the camels while they were still on the ground, as if they were giant motorbikes. Initially the Bedu helped us, firmly gripping the halter and holding it down, but despite this, the camels would still struggle to stand. Often we had only just started to swing a leg over the hump before the camel began its quick rise. Invariably we ended up being thrown for a painful landing on our backsides beside the snorting camel's feet.

Crazy Dancer was particularly impatient. During the first days at camp, Manaa always helped me mount. He would bend Crazy Dancer's long neck around in a curving arch until his head was pinned back against his own flank. Although it sounds awful, it did not appear to cause the camel any pain. In this position the camel was unable to – or would not – stand up, and it was a trick many of the Bedu used. While Crazy Dancer rumbled ominously and shifted in the sand, Manaa would stand on his folded front leg, further preventing him from rising, while motioning for me to quickly get on.

Soon I learned to perfect the trick myself. I always knelt and talked to Crazy Dancer before riding him, scratching behind his neck and ears. Then I would reach under his chin and grab both reins where they joined the halter. As I slowly worked my way back towards the saddle, Crazy Dancer's head came with me. Finally, I stood beside him, with his halter firmly held in my outside hand, his head pressed against my outside leg. He would look at me, and a gurgling rumble from deep inside him would indicate his displeasure. Still, he never moved as I put one hand on his hump and swung my leg over the saddle. When I slowly let the reins out, and his head swung forward, Crazy Dancer would immediately spring up, and it required all my strength to keep him from galloping off.

Camels instinctively walk in a train or line, nose to tail. Before we left camp Manaa always carefully tied our reins to the back of Musallim's or Ali Salim's saddle. Behind the others we were free to concentrate on staying aboard. We would have our own "control" soon enough, Manaa promised. For now, when the camels did jump or buck, as they were occasionally wont to do, they could not go far.

Our very first excursion was a two-kilometre (1.2-mile) ride across the flats surrounding the camp. I gripped the tufts of mane on Crazy Dancer's hump so firmly that my sweaty hands started to cramp after a few minutes, since I was precariously balanced on the pile of blankets that is the Omani saddle. Memories of the painful fall in Texas no doubt added to my trepidation. The wide back of my camel seemed to spread my legs to the splitting point. Without stirrups, no matter how I adjusted my position, all my weight remained centred squarely on my quickly bruising coccyx. After only ten minutes, every step shot a flash of pain through my tender backside. When we returned to camp, our legs were so cramped that we almost fell to the ground upon dismounting, and none of us could walk properly for quite some time. We had all developed saddle sores, which would likely get worse in the days to come. This was worrisome, as we were facing more than a thousand kilometres (620 miles), in unsanitary conditions.

Each afternoon, while we grew accustomed to saddling and riding our own camels, many of the local youth would arrive at camp to help in the frightening process of breaking Manaa's wild camels. Kept outside the main pen, tethered to makeshift anchors built from huge feedbags filled with sand, these menacing animals would snarl, kick, and spew forth regurgitated cud (a bright green repulsive-smelling mixture), whenever anyone approached. It required a whole team of boys just to saddle one. To begin, a crowd would surround a camel and dart in, trying to grab hold of its halter, all the time avoiding kicks and bites. Once someone had a firm grasp of the halter, he would pull down on it with all his might, while the others whipped the camel from every side. The roars were frightening as the indomitable beast violently resisted couching. When the camel eventually settled to the ground, the team of boys would work feverishly to tie both folded forelegs securely. Even so, camels occasionally struggled to stand using only their back legs, pivoting violently on their front knees and scattering the crowd. The young boys' patience was exceptional. They would fight for hours to get a saddle in place. As soon as it was ready, one of the barefoot youths would jump on without fear and ride the charging animal around the nearby flats.

One hot afternoon, a group of young Bedu spent almost an hour attempting to teach Tynoona, the wildest of these unbroken camels, to couch and stand on command. As soon as she gave in and settled down, responding to "*khhhhh*" and tugs on her halter, the boys would get her up again and repeat the process. Tynoona became progressively enraged, and then, suddenly, with a burst of strength, she broke free and sprinted off. Immediately the group ran to nearby Land Cruisers and sped across the plains after her. Tynoona had run more than a kilometre before being cut off and turned around towards camp. She careered back at a full gallop, long strings of white saliva streaming from her mouth, huge roars of outrage echoing across the desert. Suddenly Salim Ali, a tall, thin boy who was standing beside me, began jogging barefoot towards the returning camel. The camel saw him and changed course, veering away from camp once again. Salim Ali started to run, and then sprint, across the rocky, thorn-covered ground. He ran with graceful fluidity, and to my amazement he caught the fleeing camel. I watched open-mouthed as he reached up with his long, thin arms and grabbed hold of a tuft of fur on the camel's hump. He lifted himself a few inches off the ground and lightly swung his legs forward. When they dropped to touch the ground rushing past underneath he was vaulted high in the air, and landed squarely on Tynoona's back. Almost instantly she slowed, and then stopped. Salim Ali calmly rode her back to camp, an awe-inspiring example of how some of the traditional skills are still retained by today's Bedu, despite their demise predicted by Thesiger and others. I doubted there were many other youth in the world who could do what we had just witnessed.

Living amongst the Bedu was both a joy and a continual challenge that required immense patience. We were learning a lot, but I felt we could be much more efficient. Nothing was ever planned or organized, and any attempts to bring order seemed doomed to failure. Some days the Bedu would arrive and sit for hours in the shade. When we asked if we were going to ride, the answer was always "*Inshalla*" (God willing). Sometimes we did, sometimes we didn't. Days passed when no one showed up at camp. The constant uncertainty was frustrating. The hot season was fast approaching, and we knew there was much to be done before we would be ready to begin the journey.

Then, when we were lounging around aimlessly, one of the Bedu would suddenly declare it was time to ride. Many helping hands would rush to arrange our saddles, urging us to hurry up and mount. If we protested that we first needed to fill our water bottles, find sunscreen, or get film for the cameras, the delays were met with looks of frustration and loud grumbling. Often we set out on the long, hot rides unprepared, burning ourselves in the sun, carrying no food or water. It was our own fault, since we should have realized that we always needed to be ready. Heat and exhaustion made these frustrations even more difficult to deal with. It was at this time we most poignantly realized that the word "please" did not appear to be a part of the standard Bedu vocabulary. Instead single commands were yelled loudly at us as we scrambled to prepare. "*Sekin . . . Hut el sekin! . . . La . . . Habl, HABL!* (Knife . . . Get the knife! . . . No. . . . Rope, ROPE!)" Usually several people yelled at once, adding to the confusion.

Slowly we were all worn down. Despite our efforts to go with the flow, it was difficult to abandon our ingrained Western concepts of planning and efficiency. Leigh faced the biggest challenge, coming from years in a busy law practice, where every minute is accounted for. He had not been on a major expedition like this. Jamie and I had the advantage of years of expedition experience, where things never went as planned. As logistics were my primary responsibility, Leigh was understandably frustrated with me and my inability to effect any change. Despite the internal friction, however, we all worked together to continue moving the training forward.

ربع الخالي

After a week at camp, Manaa decided we were ready for an overnight trip. We would ride to Wadi Douka, a wide, shallow drainage that ran through the flats west of Thumbrait. Our camp was busy with excited preparations as word spread through town about the trip. As we saddled and mounted, a column of pickups set out ahead of us on the dusty trail, soon disappearing over a distant rise. Getting to camp would be our longest ride to date, and as the twelve kilometres (seven miles) wore on, the pain of the saddle grew insufferable. I tried to shift my weight, but could find no relief. The discomfort of the saddle monopolized my thoughts and not a minute passed that I was not conscious of the pain. When we finally entered the *wadi*, I temporarily distracted myself by marvelling at the new terrain. Scant traces of moisture from previous floods must have remained below the bed of rounded gravel, for green flourished everywhere, a welcome respite from the parched environs of camp. Glorious miniature palms were interspersed with groves of tall acacia. An hour after entering the *wadi* we spotted a gathering of trucks through the intermittent foliage. Two blazing fires had been lit in a small hollow, and large pots of rice sat boiling in the flames. More than fifty members of the al-Musalli family were already on hand to welcome us. In the fading light I tethered Crazy Dancer to a nearby acacia, careful he had enough room to avoid the thorny branches.

As we packed our saddles away for the night, two goats were slaughtered, their bodies hung to bleed from the back of a pickup. A short time later the boiled meat was served atop platters of steaming rice. The gathering silently divided into circles around four large platters of food. I found myself in a group with nine others, including Jamie and Sheikh Salem. Jamie and I tentatively picked at the rice. When we arrived in Thumbrait it had required little prompting for us to eat with our hands, as is Bedu custom. We quickly learned not to be greedy. The searing burn from one snowball-sized fistful of the hot rice ensured we never did that again. We watched the Bedu, who would skilfully scrape away only the top layer, using their right hand. With a tossing motion they systematically packed the loose rice into a small ball, and then shot it into their mouth with a flick of the thumb.

While we ate, Bedu in the circle dug through the pile of meat atop the rice, and generously placed particularly succulent morsels on the rice in front of Jamie and me. Unfortunately, these morsels often consisted of the heart, liver, and other unidentified organs and glands that we preferred to do without. It was very impolite not to eat the food placed in front of you, and we always finished a meal full beyond our capacity. Occasionally in the dark I would try to move one of these portions in front of somebody else, but they invariably noticed, and immediately passed it back. They never considered that we might not want to eat it, they simply assumed we were being generous and polite, as they were being by returning it.

Now, with the Bedu completely immersed in eating, I began poking in the remains of the meat. I was happy to find a long, white string of intestine, the thickness of a dew worm. This I stealthily placed in front of Jamie. He of course knew exactly what had happened, and, in turn, found something resembling a short length of a radiator hose, with roughly the same consistency, which he left for me. We both diligently searched for remains of the goat's head. The cheeks and the brain are considered delicacies, but it was the eyeball that we hoped to pass to each other. Fortunately, the head was nowhere to be found, or at least was indistinguishable in the dark, and we both returned to feasting on the massive piles of meat in front of us.

After eating, singing, and dancing, we settled in to sleep around the fire. Manaa told us that, when we awoke, everyone would be gone. Our challenge would be to saddle and ride our own three camels back to camp alone. He suggested Labian ride in front, being the oldest and a natural leader, with Mr. T. and Crazy Dancer tethered behind. I lay in my bag contemplating this problem. It would be very difficult for us. Neither Jamie nor I could get on our camels without someone restraining them, and both of our camels would need to be tied to the back of Leigh's before he mounted. We chatted about plans in the darkness.

During the night Manaa seemed to have a change of heart. Perhaps it was the cold air that kept him in his blankets. Whatever the case, when we rose the Bedu had not left, and we were helped onto our camels and tied behind Leigh. Still, we would ride home alone, for the first time untethered to a Bedu.

As soon as Labian was released, I sensed something was wrong. She surged ahead and our camels were dragged along behind. Leigh magnificently managed to rein her in, but she continued to buck and pull. She surged again, and Leigh once again stopped her. Jamie and I were hanging on for dear life with both hands. Our reins had been used to tie our camels to Labian, so all we could do was watch and offer unwanted advice. Leigh was forced to bend Labian's neck backwards to stop her, and when he released the pressure a touch she would prance and jump forward. Each time it took a little longer to stop her, and finally I realized we were losing control. Labian came to the edge of a small ditch crossing the track. She accelerated down the small drop and just kept going. We raced along the curving path, ducking overhanging trees, and brushing overgrown bushes. I was using every ounce of strength and concentration to stay on. I could feel myself bounce higher and higher out of the saddle, only to pull myself back down with both hands locked to Crazy Dancer's mane. We went faster and faster. I occasionally stole glances beside me at Jamie, just a short distance away, caught in his own battle to stay aboard. Leigh had dropped his reins to hold on with both hands, and the camels charged on unchecked.

"I can't take much more, I gotta bail!" Leigh yelled, the sound floating back, almost drowned by the pounding hooves.

"Come on, buddy, hold on. Hold on!" Jamie screamed in encouragement. "Can you get one hand free to grab a rein?"

"No way. I can barely hang on with two."

It went on and on. There was no resolution in sight. Somewhere behind us one of the Bedu must have seen what was happening, and soon a speeding Land Cruiser passed far to our right, turning ahead to cut us off. The camels galloped even faster as it drew near. At the last moment the camels darted to the right. My weight was high off the saddle and, when I came down, Crazy Dancer was no longer underneath me.

Incredibly, I landed on the hard rocky ground on my butt, and bounced back up to my feet. I joined the others, who had stopped just ahead.

"*Mafi mushkilla* (No problem)?" Ali Salim asked. "*Hamdulilla*," he uttered when I nodded. I was fine. We were all okay. Only my pride was bruised. I had fallen in Texas, and now here. Why was I the only one falling from the camels?

It was lucky that the Bedu had not left us alone. Manaa told us we were strong to stay on for so long. But the camels are very strong too, he added. "It would not be a problem for them to ride at that speed all day. Then what would you do?"

Five minutes was certainly all we could take. This incident was a wake-up for us, and tempered our growing confidence. And all of us now had fresh saddle sores.

By the planned departure date of January 24 we were nowhere near ready to leave, and no end seemed in sight. In fact, the Bedu appeared to have no plans ever to leave. If we had been training diligently every day, it would not have seemed so bad. But, as days went by when the Bedu would not even come by camp, our frustrations mounted. Chris Beale flew to Salala, the coastal city an hour and a half drive from our camp, where we planned to begin our journey. We met him there with Manaa to address the faltering progress, in what we came to call the Salala Summit. Manaa's biggest concern appeared to be arranging more press coverage for the Bait Kathir tribe and their involvement in the expedition before we left. This was understandable, since our journey offered the opportunity for the Bait Kathir to restore their pride after Thesiger's scathing judgement of them in *Arabian Sands*, but we were still shocked. It seemed at this point publicity should be the last concern on anyone's mind. Manaa had brought a Sudanese interpreter, Mohammed Sami, who was also Manaa's business partner. Chris and Manaa were at odds, and Sami only served to inflame the differences by becoming involved

The Empty Quarter of Arabia, the world's largest sand desert, covers nearly a million square kilometres (380,000 sq. miles), occupying an area larger than the country of France. During the winter of 1999, our team travelled 1,200 kilometres (750 miles) by camel, crossing this vast expanse.

In preparation for the expedition we trained with camels in Uvalde, Texas. Above, left to right: Me, Jamie, and Leigh during the training week in Texas. The injury to my forearm occurred when I was thrown from a camel on our third day of riding. Left: Jamie becomes accustomed to the high perch aboard Chewbacca, while Doug Baum, our instructor, slowly leads him around the pen.

Opposite, left to right: Ali Salim, Bin Ashara, and Musallim, proud Bedu of southern Oman, and our companions during the journey across the Empty Quarter.

*A camel couches, or sits, by first dropping to its front knees (top left), then settling on its haunches (top right), and finally shuffling its knees forward, lowering its immense weight to rest on a large callused chest pad (bottom left). But getting the camel couched is only half the battle: you still have to get on, which can be very difficult (bottom right). As Touarish prepares to mount Swad, the massive bull pulls his head back and gurgles in defiance.*

*While preparing to brand one of our wild pack camels, Musallim narrowly avoids being bitten. Note the hobbled front legs, essential at night during the journey to prevent the camels from wandering off.*

*Top: An infuriated Tynoona, snarling at the camera, ready to spray a mouthful of regurgitated cud.*

*Below: Our training camp on the dusty gravel flats surrounding Thumbrait, in southern Oman. We spent over two weeks here preparing for the journey.*

*Above: February 2, 1999. Moments before setting out we paused for this photo. Front row (left to right), Manaa (with his single finger clearly visible), Leigh Clarke, Bin Ashara, Musallim, Bruce Kirkby, Ali Salim, Mr. T., and Jamie Clarke. Back row: Not wanting to miss the opportunity to have their photo taken, several bystanders we had never seen before jumped in, joining Touarish (third from left) and Salim Ali (far right).*

*Left: Manaa Mohammed al-Musalli al-Kathiri, "the man with one finger" I had been sent to find in Thumbrait, who played an essential role in organizing the expedition.*

On the beach at Salala. Toward ish holding (left to right) Labian, Lucy, and Mr. T.

Overleaf: Following a gravel road towards the crest of the Jebel Qarra, Oman's coastal mountains. The day before, we had travelled through the forested valley in the background, struggling up steep slopes along winding trails.

in the disagreement, adding his own personal distaste for the British. I struggled to keep the meeting focussed as personal agendas sprang up. Negotiating a firm start date was our key issue. Leigh insisted we could learn what we needed as we travelled, and pushed for departure in two days. Manaa would not listen to this, arguing that ten days was the absolute minimum. Finally we agreed on four, but in reality it would not be until the beginning of February, eight days later, that we saw the camels trucked from Thumbrait to the coast.

In the meantime, more uncertainty struck the expedition. Bin Ashara, our third guide, had still not arrived. During one of the evening gatherings at camp, a local confided to Leigh that Bin Ashara thought Manaa was running the expedition poorly, and would not come. I will never know if this was true, but it caused another major group disagreement. Leigh, who had had enough of the delays and poor planning, voted that we abandon Manaa as a co-ordinator, and empower Musallim to run the expedition. Jamie and I both balked at the idea, not ready to interfere in the complicated Bedu hierarchy.

Luckily for us the problem was solved the next morning when Salim bin Musallim al-Musalli al-Kathiri arrived in camp. Widely known as Bin Ashara ("son of ten"), forty-five-year-old Salim earned his nickname strangely enough by fathering ten children. Ten children actually meant ten boys; shockingly, girls were not included in the total when a man described his offspring. Soft-spoken, and graced with an air of confidence and dignity, Bin Ashara was obviously deeply respected by all the men at camp. His dark face, always smiling, was framed by a short, trimmed beard, heavily flecked with grey. Bin Ashara stayed at camp and trained with us for the next two days. Like Musallim and Ali Salim, he was obviously both an expert rider and a skilled camel handler.

Finally Manaa agreed we could delay our departure no longer. Later that afternoon a truck arrived to transport six riding camels to the coast. The remaining six pack camels would meet us after we had crossed the coastal Qarra Mountains that separate Salala from the interior of the country. This would save them from a difficult journey over rocky paths – and save us the added complication of caring and tending for them on our first days. For now, the loads normally carried by the pack camels would travel in Manaa's pickup, since he planned to visit us every evening during the first week.

Many of our Bedu friends from Thumbrait gathered to help in the loading. We laid out a thick bed of carpet and hay to protect the camels' knees during the drive. As we led them one by one towards the truck, the camels kicked and fought, refusing to be forced into the confined space. It was hot work, and the Bedu soon stripped down to only their *wasir* (skirt-like undergarment). Young Ali Salim whipped each camel from behind while Bin Ashara and Musallim heaved forward on the reins. Finally, each camel was dragged, skidding and halting, into the truck, thudding heavily down as they couched. Bin Ashara passed ropes under their hind legs and cinched them tight over their humps, preventing them from rising. Once settled, each camel, which had previously fought viciously, lazily ate hay from the truck bed, apparently oblivious to the tantrums of the next. Amazingly the Bedu managed to fit all six camels in a space that looked no larger than a double bed.

After carefully driving the one-hundred-kilometre (sixty-mile) paved road transecting the coastal mountains, we unloaded the camels on the white sand beaches of Salala. They looked odd against the backdrop of the tropical blue waters and majestic coconut palms. Although the camels had never seen so much water before, the herd remained calm and simply looked around. The only difficulty was trying to wash them. None would enter the water, and each had to be gently coaxed towards the edge of the breaking waves. We splashed them down, the last rinse they would receive in two months, and then tethered them behind a grove of nearby trees. There was a tranquillity on the beautiful beach as we packed our gear in preparation for departure. After a year of effort, the journey was about to begin.

# CHAPTER SIX

# The Journey Begins

I knew instinctively that it was the very hardness of life in the desert
which drew me back there – it was the same pull which takes men
back to the polar ice, to high mountains, and to the sea.

— Wilfred Thesiger, *Arabian Sands*

*I* awoke with a start the morning of February 2, 1999. My face was
pressed against a dank carpet in a small hotel room. I had wanted to
stay at the beach and sleep beside Crazy Dancer as he shifted restlessly
in the sand, but the Bedu, never willing to believe that we liked to sleep
outdoors when a proper bed was available, had urged us to accept the
manager's invitation at the Holiday Inn. We argued that we would be
happier on the beach, beside the camels, suggesting they stay at the
hotel alone, but the Bedu were insistent. It would have been an insult
to their strong sense of hospitality if we had slept out in the sand, so we
eventually relented. However, when important guests arrived late in
the night we found ourselves suddenly roused and shuffled into a tiny
back room with only one bed. I slept on the floor, questioning my previous judgement.

We dressed and packed quickly. A commotion was already building
at the beach. The camels, still tethered to the palms, stared expectantly

as we approached. Bin Ashara and Musallim, smartly dressed for the day in freshly cleaned and pressed *dishdashas*, had arrived just before us. Each carried a gun slung over his shoulder with carefully polished ammunition adorning the strap. Ceremonial *kunja* knives, their polished sheaths decorated in fine silver weave and coming to a characteristic sweeping curve at the tip, were strapped around their thin waists. They looked as if they had stepped off a page of a history book.

All around, pandemonium was breaking out. Many of the Bedu's friends and relatives had come to watch the departure, and everyone wanted to lend a helping hand. Manaa strode through the gathering crowd of onlookers, yelling commands in every direction. I caught his eye and smiled, then running to where our gear was piled, I rescued Crazy Dancer from a young man who seemed to be walking him in endless circles. I gathered my saddle and led Crazy Dancer away from the milling crowd to prepare for our first day in peace. He patiently waited while I carefully tightened his saddle and arranged the pile of blankets and wool I would sit on. I drifted over to chat with Jamie and Leigh, who were fighting to retain some control over the construction of their seat pads. Everyone seemed to have an opinion as to the best arrangement. As soon as one knot was tied, another hand reached in to undo it.

I had waited more than a year for this day. Only the day before, when I called my mother to say goodbye, did I first sense the overwhelming personal significance of our impending departure, all the work and effort that this day symbolized. Paradoxically, there was a great sense of completion in having arrived at this beginning; getting here had been a journey in itself. Now, at last, the unknown was upon us. As the final preparations were made, I felt numb and slightly overwhelmed, watching the events unfold as if I were an outside observer. After all the remaining food and blankets were thrown into a pickup truck that would follow us for the first week, we gathered together by the shore for a photograph. Then we walked slowly up the beach with our camels, towards the Holiday Inn, where the media awaited.

Inside a tall chain-link fence separating the hotel grounds from the beach, we found a small gathering of local reporters and cameramen waiting on a lawn shaded by towering palms. The camels, agitated by the enclosed surroundings, interrupted their prancing antics only long enough to stare hungrily at colourful flowers growing in the gardens nearby. Hotel guests peered inquisitively over shrubs surrounding the swimming pool. Predictably, nothing was organized for the event, and we patiently waited. Soon local dignitaries, visiting Bedu, and some of the reporters lined up around the periphery of the lawn, singing traditional desert songs to wish us luck. A few speeches were made in Arabic. The dignitaries, who glanced at the camels nervously, lined up to shake our hands. Although Crazy Dancer did not like the close proximity of so many unfamiliar bodies, he remained calm, but still I was relieved when Manaa finally signalled it was time to leave.

Leading our camels away, we entered a maze of paths through the sprawling hotel grounds. Our animals bellowed in protest, distressed at being hemmed in by the waist-high hedges, and pulled back frantically on their halters. As I struggled to lead Crazy Dancer on, a loud thud from behind, followed by a frustrated expletive, indicated that Jamie had just been kicked in the thigh.

We soon emerged onto the asphalt road running along the front of the hotel, where the Bedu stopped to confer. More and more people clustered around us in the traffic as Musallim argued with onlookers about the best route leading from the city. When Bin Ashara and Ali Salim spiritedly joined the good-natured dispute, it became clear the Bedu had no plan. More and more fingers seemed to be pointing towards the centre of the city, and the group appeared poised to depart. Downtown Salala, a noisy concrete jungle, would be a nightmare with the camels. Jamie and I quickly agreed we could leave the decision to fate no longer. We had scouted a plausible route the night before, just in case of this eventuality. Yelling for the others to follow, we started walking our camels east along the road, towards the beach and away from the crowd. Our Bedu companions and the shocked onlookers beseeched us to stop. We continued, and soon their protests waned.

Bin Ashara and Musallim hurried to join the departing line. After the onlookers dropped from earshot, a few last cars honked their good wishes. We were finally under way.

The bone-white beach reflected the morning sun. It was still early, but we sweated as we shuffled through the deep sand. To minimize the toil, we mounted our camels. Although it is always better to warm the camels up before riding, Musallim did not like to walk. Jamie, Leigh, and I were each tethered behind a Bedu's camel. I struggled to grasp small tufts of mane as Crazy Dancer skittishly surged from side to side. Musallim's big bull ignored my upstart camel, and walked calmly on. I absorbed the first few moments of our trip alone, since Jamie and Leigh were too far away to talk with and Musallim was gently singing, apparently happy in his own world.

I finally worked up the courage to take one of my hands away from the mane, and rummaged through my saddlebags, looking for a small point-and-shoot camera. After brushing sand from the lens, I framed the camels ahead against Musallim in the foreground and slowly squeezed the shutter release. A sudden whir from the advancing film scared Crazy Dancer, who bucked wildly. I held on briefly, but with each bump slid further off the side, almost hanging sideways before I gave up. I landed softly, with my camera held high out of the sand. Crazy Dancer's hooves sang by perilously close to my head. With only my pride injured, I quickly couched Crazy Dancer and remounted, but several days would pass before I found the courage to try another photograph from his back.

We followed the beach to a quiet road that turned north and skirted Salala's developed core. Excited by the events of the day, the camels fought hard to trot and pressed forward on their reins. I tried asking Musallim, who was riding in front, to slow down a little, but I bungled the attempt in Arabic. He looked inquisitively down at the crushed-stone road, thinking I had asked about that.

"*Mafi zain* (No good)," he frowned, shaking his head.

"No good for the camel's feet?" I asked. He nodded in agreement, looking worried. Should we walk instead? I wondered. I had no idea of how difficult the hard surface was for camels, whose soft feet are used to the desert sand. There are not many notches on the Bedu scale of disapproval. Anything that was not like the desert was simply "*Mafi zain.*" The camels seemed to step tenderly, but we rode on. An hour later we crossed the major highway running north from Salala to Muscat. On the other side was a small plantation, and the coastal plains which Thesiger had so clearly described. Finally we were leaving the city behind.

The plains of Salala are a small semicircular intrusion on the dry, rocky hills that run the entire length of the southern Arabian coast. Enclosed to the north by the Jebel Qarra (Qarra Mountains) which rise in a giant arc, and cut off to the south by the blue waters of the Indian Ocean, the plains witness a miracle known as the *Harif* each summer. By some fluke of nature, the hills and flats capture a portion of the Indian monsoon. For three months fog, mist, and rain envelope the lowlands and their neighbouring southern slopes. Along two thousand kilometres (1,200 miles) of coast, only these thirty (20 miles) see regular rainfall. By the end of the rainy season in September, the hills are verdant. In the deep valleys draining the Jebel Qarra, thick forests thrive. A canopy of sycamore, acacia, and jasmine covers quiet pools and burbling streams. Along the coast, coconut palms and mango trees abound and supply the hordes of street vendors who eagerly ply their trade in Salala. Pink flamingoes can be seen wading beside giant white egrets in flooded fields. Even the stony plains bloom into life with tall windblown grasses that ripple in the monsoon breezes.

The last *Harif* had passed five months ago, and now the locals patiently awaited its rebirth. Around us the hills and valleys retained only a fraction of their lush growth. Well-worn paths spread out across the plains like veins over a giant leaf, reconverging again in settlements butted against the distant hills. Heat waves shimmered ahead, dancing over the rocky surface. The broken, black rock appeared burned, as if it had been singed by a terrible fire. Far off, a lone row of telephone poles, ubiquitous throughout Arabia, where the ground is too hard to bury cables, provided the only reminder of the recent changes in this ancient land.

As we rode out onto the plains, a hot sun scorched us unremittingly from above. I wondered how we could possibly survive its onslaught for another two months. We were well covered beneath our *dishdashas* and *masars*, but already the exposed skin on the back of my hands had turned bright pink – despite repeated applications of sunscreen. As I rode along, lost in thought, I suddenly wondered if I had been rubbing the sunscreen off each time I rummaged through my tight saddlebags, and immediately reapplied more. My knees began to feel as if they were suffering internal structural damage from the constant jarring of Crazy Dancer's strong gait. Still spooked by my earlier fall, I tentatively tried to readjust my position, but no amount of stirring seemed to bring relief. Resigned to suffer through it, I peppered Musallim with questions to distract my thoughts. Was he happy to be under way? "*Hamdulilla.*" This common response can mean anything from only slightly pleased to ecstatic. I tried another tack. How long will the ride to the mountains take? "*Inshalla*, two hours, maybe more, maybe less."

Often when we rode, Musallim would teach me Arabic words for things we saw, and I would teach him the English in return. Now he pointed to the sky. "*Sima,*" he said.

I repeated it aloud and then slowly enunciated, "sky."

"Sigh? Sly?" He struggled before capturing the foreign sound. I wondered how the Bedu could possibly understand anything I said in Arabic with all the deep guttural clicks and coughs I tried to emulate. Musallim began to recite a poem. I once again tried to readjust my position in the saddle.

A plume of dust could be seen rising behind us in the distance, and soon a pursuing Land Cruiser caught up. Sergeant Farah bin Said, a friend of Manaa's we had met while training, jumped out. He ran over carrying a transparent plastic bag bulging with cans of cold pop. I feigned indifference, largely because I feared he would spook my camel. My ongoing dispute with the Bedu concerning the ethics of support on our trip hardly mattered at this moment.

"Please, Saleh, take a cold drink. Your journey will be a very long one. You will be thirsty soon enough. Things are different these days. Now people have cellphones and TVs. You have a satellite phone with you. It is no longer the same as when Umbarak [Thesiger] travelled here. How can your trip be the same? You are being foolish. Anyway, no one will know that I brought you this." Being quite thirsty, I finally reached down and grabbed a cold can from his outstretched hand, but, remembering Crazy Dancer's sensitivity to noises, I slipped the can in my saddlebag, where it remained unopened until lunch.

Our trail passed through a small group of old clay homes hidden on our approach by a subtle roll in the flats. At the centre stood a beautiful white mosque, its domed roof painted a deep indigo. From inside, the lyrical voice of a *muazzin* could be heard delivering the midday call to prayer. The religion of Islam has evolved around the practicalities of desert life. Our Bedu, as is universally accepted for all travelling parties to help ease the rigours, had reduced their midday and afternoon devotions, and we rode past without stopping.

As the mountains slowly drew closer, the flat ground of the plains became more undulating. We crossed the outstretched fingers of buttresses extending onto the flats. Small stream beds cut the plains in intervals, dry in the late-season heat. Finally, we entered the mouth of a giant *wadi* and urged the camels down a steep trail with unsure footing to its wide floor. This would be the beginning of our route through the Jebel Qarra. It was here, at the entrance to this great valley, that Thesiger's party spent their first night, taking a final inventory on their stores before moving on. Thesiger travelled with twenty-five men on his first journey, although many more joined them every night. These visitors would often appear from the hills and desert in search of food, which Bedu hospitality demanded Thesiger supply them. For the three-month expedition the caravan had carried nine hundred kilograms

(2,000 lb.) of flour, two hundred twenty-five kilograms (500 lb.) of rice, along with a supply of butter, coffee, tea, sugar, and dates. Although our stores were identical in nature, only six of us would be travelling beyond the mountains, and we carried much smaller quantities.

We dismounted near a small stream and hobbled about, tired and sore. Slowly the blood returned to our aching legs. In almost a month of training, this had been our longest ride. Manaa arrived soon with Sergeant Farah in the pickup, bringing with them a bale of fresh alfalfa that was distributed amongst the camels. Together, we retired under a massive tree, whose sprawling branches were wreathed in a web of flowering lianas. A fire was lit, while meat and rice were set in the flames to boil. I wandered about to explore, washing my hot, dusty feet in a nearby stream and rinsing the dirt from my face. Lying back on a smooth boulder, I watched butterflies float overhead in the breeze, flitting between small yellow flowers in the vines above. Beyond them, small white clouds drifted slowly past, casting intermittent shadows on our hidden grove. For all the lush growth and abundant life, we could have be in an English garden. How soon it would all be behind us, I mused.

The food was laid out on a large communal platter, and I huddled around with the others. The rice was scalding hot, and I carefully fought to scrape tiny handfuls from the surface. As we ate, I began to sense the Bedu were planning to travel further that day. I chose to ignore my suspicions, instead occupying myself by washing down the food with cup after cup of warm tea. Leigh dug out the maps, and spread them under the tree. Using his GPS, he had taken several waypoints during the morning, and, as the Bedu gathered around, Leigh carefully plotted them. Following some friendly debate, the group reached the consensus that we had travelled twenty-two kilometres (14 miles) from the beach. Dutifully recording waypoints from this day forward, Leigh would become the official statistician for our entire journey. During some of the longer days to come, in an attempt to break the monotony, I would ride up beside Leigh, asking him how far we had travelled. Minutes would pass as he busily entered points and made calculations, only to report a distance which always seemed pitifully small.

While Leigh and Musallim continued to inspect the maps, I stretched out on the ground. Its subtle warmth soothed my back and eased me towards sleep. Before I could drift off, however, Bin Ashara jumped up and curtly announced that it was time to go. How much farther did they want to travel today, I asked? What lay in the valley beyond? I could get no answer. Ali Salim was busy untying the camels, and Musallim had already started up the path with his bull. Sergeant Farah came to my side as I hastily prepared Crazy Dancer, and announced that he knew the route. He would walk with us this afternoon as we led the camels through these isolated valleys. By the evening, *Inshalla*, we would have breached the mountains and arrived on the rolling plateaus that mark their crest. Jamie, Leigh, and I wanted to consult our maps, but there was no time. We had to get going. Not knowing the feasibility of the route, and suspicious of the short time remaining in the day, we fell to the mercy of the Bedu's plans. It was our fault. Once again we were not prepared.

## ربع الخالي

A paved road, which soon gave way to gravel, lay against the western slopes of the valley. After less than a kilometre the gravel road itself petered out, and we entered a sprawling network of paths dissecting the thick forest. As our caravan passed makeshift homes fashioned from corrugated aluminum, shy *Jebali* (mountain dweller) families peered out, surrounded in the doorways by milling crowds of goats and sheep. Large cows with long twisting horns reminiscent of water buffalo watched us menacingly from behind thickets of undergrowth. Further down the trail a tortured bellowing caused me to slow momentarily, its mournful lament sounding almost human. It was a baby camel lost in the thick forest, and it approached as we drew near. Suddenly realizing our large bulls were strangers, and not its missing family, it turned and quickly retreated down a dry stream bed.

As the undergrowth closed in tightly on the rarely used trail, travel became increasingly difficult for the camels. Bands of rock traversed the path at intervals. Using subtle tugs on his halter, I found I could successfully steer Crazy Dancer through the maze by guiding his head around the encroaching obstacles. The rest of his body would follow in a twisting pattern. The camels required constant encouragement to continue. At the top of sharp drops in the trail, Crazy Dancer would paw the open air in front of him with one leg before nervously lowering himself with the other. I stroked his muzzle, whispering into his ear as we travelled. The hours passed quickly, as our concentration on the tiring work was complete. In the humid air we were drenched with sweat.

Leigh had started out at the end of the group after lunch, and slowly dropped farther behind throughout the afternoon. Although he could easily rejoin the group now, he seemed to prefer lingering at a distance. I glanced back often, wondering whether he was all right. During our short stops, Jamie and I would chat with him. Despite his assurances that he was fine, something in his averted eyes told me otherwise.

By late afternoon we reached a major junction in the path. Sheer rock faces, emblazoned by the golden light of the setting sun, soared above the misty canopy of the forest. From here the valley split into two arms, both of which climbed sharply towards the rolling plateaus above. Sergeant Farah was not sure which way to go. The light would soon fade, and moving through this undergrowth in the dark would be difficult and dangerous. We were ill prepared for a night out, having foolishly left everything in the truck, which was to meet us at the top. If we did decide to stop, we would need to do it here. The terrain ahead appeared steep and continuous, offering no breaks.

Bin Ashara left his camel behind, and rushed on with Sergeant Farah to determine the correct path. No sooner had Jamie started to look for our maps, than the men were back. They had decided the right-hand valley held our route. Unsure, we glanced hesitantly at each other. In my broken Arabic I tried to discuss the situation with Bin Ashara, but the aging Bedu did not want any part of this. He headed off quickly.

Leigh was livid. He did not like our lack of control, he did not like my leadership, and he was worried about Labian's feet. All three concerns were eminently justifiable. "I need the Bedu to understand," he fumed, "that we plan on taking these camels the entire journey. They are not interchangeable like car parts if they become tired or injured." We had all worried in the last weeks over the Bedu's apparent lack of concern for the camels. Sir Wilfred's final words to us as we had left him in London had been, "Spare your camels all you can; they will mean your life." Now we were driving them on, hurting their feet and obviously exhausting them in the process. We could reach no consensus. The others were already out of sight, and we continued after them with the disagreement still simmering.

The path up the narrow valley arm became less and less discernible. Farah declared that it had not been travelled in at least twenty years, maybe fifty. Soon machetes were needed to clear the way, and our progress slowed to a snail's pace. The crux came at a large rock layer where an exposed strata that circled the valley like a contour line created a vertical barrier. As we approached, a winding path appeared which rose through a previously hidden break in the limestone. At the top we traversed to the right, above the first face of rock and beneath another, following a wide ledge. Crazy Dancer hesitated at the sight of the ground dropping sharply away to the forest below, and instinctively I transferred the halter to my left hand and took the outside position. We did not break pace. I was beginning to understand his moods and thoughts, and there was a great satisfaction in our growing teamwork. Winding through a thicket of thorny acacia trees, Musallim's camel caught its wooden saddle on a branch. In the thrashing confusion that followed, its entire load was strewn across the path. Together we tried to reload his camel, but it was impossible. The path was too narrow and steep. Everyone picked up an armload as they passed, and we carried on.

The backbone of these rugged mountains was exposed here. A loose jumble of rocks lay between the trees, making footing difficult. It was now almost completely dark, and we stumbled on, with the camels tripping helplessly behind us. Jamie yelled forward that he had noticed small dark blotches of blood smeared intermittently on the rocks. Was it from Crazy Dancer's feet, I worried? I peered at the path, and after a short period saw the telltale dark patches also. It must be from Musallim's camel ahead. I yelled to Musallim, but he did not appear to hear me. Crazy Dancer lowered his muzzle onto my shoulder. I could feel his immense weight balancing unsteadily as we struggled forward. I grieved for him with every step we took. Dehydration and exhaustion were making me emotional, but I knew we could not stop now. Finally emerging from the forest to a barren rocky field stretching upwards out of sight, the Bedu stopped for their evening prayers. Abruptly a shot rang out nearby, its frightening report echoing through the forest below. Was it a hunter? Were we trespassing? Where we being shot at? The Bedu kept on praying. I considered joining them.

Five minutes later, as they rose from their prayers, a lone *Jebali* emerged from the darkness below with a well-worn gun of black metal slung threateningly over one shoulder. Word had spread though the valley that we were in the area, and he had been looking for us. Some-where ahead, he assured the Bedu, there was a road and flatter pastures. How far away was lost to me in the rushed Arabic conversation. We obviously could not stop here, as there was nowhere amongst the rocks for the camels to lie down. He signalled for us to follow, and slipped quietly into the night. In the darkness, I stepped blindly forward, feeling for obstructions with my feet, trying to lead Crazy Dancer to easier terrain. Sometime later we arrived on a small path that led upwards to a gravel road. We stopped shortly after in a clearing by an enormous fig tree.

Exhausted we unsaddled the camels and carefully tied them to a nearby fence, worried about the effects of the long day. Many of them had cut their soft feet on the rocks, and now stood delicately favouring their hurt pads. Leigh was in no mood to chat, choosing instead to retire. He retreated far from the group with his bedroll and a copy of *War and Peace*. A truck's headlights were spotted bounding along the nearby road, and it was flagged down. Jamie left, along with Bin Ashara, to find some food for the camels, and they returned with a small bale of hay – and several visitors in tow. The local sheikh had appeared and was now intent on slaughtering one of his camels in our honour. Quietly, Musallim warned that we would have to stay and spend the entire next day eating if this happened. After much negotiation we were able to protect the sheikh's honour by accepting a large bowl of fresh camel's milk and one of his best goats.

Jamie and I watched intently as the plump animal was slaughtered and butchered at the foot of the tree. I was exhausted from the day. How I longed to roll out my bag and fall asleep, but I knew this would not be possible as more and more apparently nocturnal Bedu appeared out of the darkness. The feast carried on late into the night, and afterwards the Bedu sang and danced around the fire. When I finally collapsed, I knew the welcome rest would not last for long.

صحراء

We rose early the next morning, awakened before dawn by Musallim singing the poetic verses of the traditional call to prayer,

*God is most great.*
*I testify that there is no god but God.*
*I testify that Mohammed is the Prophet of God.*
*Come to Prayer!*
*Come to Salvation!*
*Prayer is better than sleep.*
*God is most Great.*
*There is no god but God.*

The chant-like words hung in the cool, damp mountain air, a distant echo returning from the valley walls below. Musallim returned to the smouldering fire. Bin Ashara had already placed a coffee pot in the embers, and now himself disappeared to pray. Buried in a camel blanket beside the fire, young Ali Salim showed no signs of stirring.

"*Ali, salat! Salat!* (Ali, pray! Pray!)" Musallim snapped, as he did every morning to rouse the youngster. I glanced at the slowly stirring form huddled nearby. On this cool morning I wondered blasphemously if prayer really was better than sleep.

Soon we were hastily swallowing tiny cupfuls of milk tea while preparing to leave. The dirt road beside which we had camped now rose gently to the rolling plateaus that crown the Jebel Qarra. As we followed its winding course through the grassy downs, steep valleys fell away in the distance on both sides. In the fields that surrounded us, giant fig trees stood amidst the brown late-season grasses, solitary and wind-swept. At tiny hamlets, old men could be seen hunched in the doors of their dwellings, curiously watching our caravan. Whenever he was asked, Musallim, who was riding in front, would announce that we were on our way to cross the Empty Quarter. Often the men would rush out, not believing their ears, and ask Musallim to repeat his claim. Many had lived here during the time of Thesiger's travels, and a few had met him as he passed. As we were borne by on our unhalting camels, I would look back and return their smiles.

The vegetation progressively thinned and withered along our slowly rising course. Later that day, we crested the final subtle rise of the plateaus atop the Jebel Qarra. Ahead of us stretched an unending sea of brown, the barren moon-like landscape broken only by a few rocky out-crops. In the distance I could see the winding course of a deep *wadi* leading out into the flats. From this divide the Arabian desert stretched ahead of us unchallenged for thousands of miles. To the north it reached as far as Jordan and the lands T. E. Lawrence had once roamed. To the west it extended to encompass the holy cities of Mecca and Medina. And to the northeast more than a thousand kilometres lay between us and the coast of the Arabian Gulf. Not a single living thing could be seen. I paused briefly to look out across the great land we would travel through, and then continued, exhilarated. Already the warm desert air kissed our cheeks, enticing us on.

The heat of the day continued to rise steadily. We descended along a stony path to the wastelands lying below. By evening, we had arrived above the cliffs of Wadi Ghadun, the massive canyon draining this part of the coastal range that we had seen from the crest of the Jebel Qarra. A sheer cut sixty metres (200 ft.) deep in the limestone plateau, this dry canyon attests to the ferocity of the floods which accompany the infrequent rains of the interior. Over the next weeks our route would follow its rocky bed until finally joining Wadi Mugshin far to the north. The combined course of these two dry drainages would take us over four hundred kilometres (250 miles), to the edge of the great Sands.

After unsaddling and hobbling our camels, Jamie, Leigh, and I gathered to chat. We were tired from two hot days of riding, and we lay on the rocky ground away from the campfire. Leigh, who had remained reticent since last evening, was still furious. He felt we were pushing the camels too hard. I understood his concern, but felt helpless. We were handicapped, because we could not judge the capabilities and condition of the animals ourselves. I suggested that, for now, we had to place our trust in the Bedu, and promised to make clear to them our concerns. I worried about delivering too many contradictory messages to the Bedu. In our desire to retrace Thesiger's footsteps we had persuaded them to begin the journey from the coast, a route that for two days had created this challenge for the camels. The Bedu had wanted to leave directly from Thumbrait. We had also expressed a lot of concern about the delays surrounding our departure because of the approaching hot season. I suspected the Bedu were now trying to make up for lost time.

Jamie too was angry, though not at anything specific. Anger just seemed pervasive in the mood of our group. Rather than solving things, the discussion was getting us nowhere. I was very aware of how often we were separating ourselves from our Bedu teammates, talking quietly amongst ourselves about our frustrations. I was tired of it, and concerned that our companions might misinterpret our actions. Privacy is a foreign concept in their society, and I caught their curious glances from the fire. We rejoined the group.

The night before we had discovered Leigh's sleeping bag had disappeared in the confusion of our departure from the beach. Now Jamie and Leigh borrowed the pickup and left for Salala, hoping to buy a new one. I stayed behind, setting up the satellite phone to send a progress report and some digital photos to our education program back in Canada. I was concerned about the distance forming between Jamie, Leigh, and me. I knew we would each need the support of the others in the coming months. My bond of friendship with Jamie ran deep, and we had suffered disagreements before. But I worried about Leigh. I hoped his sullen mood would soon pass. Strangely, I felt more in common with our Bedu friends, and was happy to linger in their company, losing myself in the endless fireside banter. When they returned much later that night, Jamie and Leigh looked tired and worn from their eventually successful efforts to find a sleeping roll in Salala. We chatted briefly. I felt happy to be reunited with them, and the earlier frustrations seemed to have passed.

ربع الخالي

The next morning we saddled quickly, and within an hour had reached the threshold of our entrance into Wadi Ghadun. Below us, hidden by steep limestone cliffs, lay the pools of Ayun. In Thesiger's time a serpent was rumoured to inhabit their dark waters, occasionally seizing a goat from the flocks which congregated here during the long, hot months of summer. The pools are one of the few permanent water sources in this vast land, and their waters remain fresh even during the longest droughts. They are fed, through faults in the sedimentary plateau, by an enormous subterranean water course that flows deep beneath southern Arabia.

From the canyon rim we descended along a wide ledge cutting the broken ramparts of the eastern wall, and soon we came to a winding path that led down through a scree slope covered with jumbled boulders. Below, I could see the waters of the pools, silent and still. They were surrounded by tall reeds. A smattering of palm trees extended from their fringes down the winding valley. The camels rushed forward as they neared, smelling the water, and drank greedily while jostling for position around the edge of a shallow pool. Occasionally a head would rise above the melee, slowly scanning the surroundings with watchful eyes. Then, with a quick shake it would send long strands of frothy white saliva in all directions before diving back into the boisterous turmoil below. Slowly the fervour passed. The camels drifted away from the water one by one.

Bin Ashara lingered by the pool long after the rest of us had mounted and begun to ride down the canyon. He patiently coaxed his shy camel to drink more by singing. Soon we could hear him galloping to catch up. His voice echoed from the walls, moaning and sorrowful in a melancholy riding chant. I turned to watch the aging Bedu, who knelt precariously atop the camel, absorbing every jolt with his bent legs. High over his head he brandished a riding stick, extended in the characteristic signal of a charge. Under his arm he clenched his beloved rifle, a constant companion since youth.

Bin Ashara has seen the tumultuous changes Arabia's nomads have endured. He continues to live a traditional life, spending each winter roaming Wadi Qitabit with his wife and children. They follow the grazing that appears after sporadic rains. Previously I had asked Bin Ashara how large his herd was, but he would not tell me for fear he would appear to be bragging. Others later told me he had well over one hundred camels. Historically, Bedu have been renowned for their ability to recognize the individual hoof prints of their camels, and Bin Ashara's skills as a tracker are legendary. It is claimed that, by the age of twenty, he could identify the track of every camel in Dhofar, which at that time numbered more than six thousand. From the depth of a print in soft sand he can discern whether it was ridden, or alone. The state of the prints and nearby droppings will tell him when the camel passed that way, and on what it has grazed. The strength of the pellets rolled between his fingers even tell Bin Ashara how long it has been since the camel has watered.

Bin Ashara is often recruited to search for missing camels, and on our journey I would hear him questioned around the campfire.

"Have you see my red female with the broken tooth?"

"Was she the one who had the grey calf last spring?"

"Yes."

"Well then, I saw her following Ali Said's herd in Wadi Dauka two months ago."

As we continued riding, Musallim explained to me that Bin Ashara first became famous in his youth for breaking a huge bull camel. Despite the attempts of many locals, this particular camel had remained wild and unridden for some four years. Together with a friend, young Bin Ashara had stalked the camel and approached closely from behind. He then sprang up and charged the surprised bull. Running beside it, he had reached up and grabbed its mane where it grew long and ragged over the hump. After vaulting up onto its back, he had hung on while the camel bucked wildly. Musallim recounted the tale with wonder in his eye, and as I glanced at Bin Ashara quietly riding ahead, his short grey beard standing out starkly against his sun-blackened skin, I marvelled at the life he must have led. I wondered if any of today's youth, herding their camels from pickups while listening to blaring East Indian pop music, would ever share his knowledge and experience, or would it be lost forever?

We stopped that evening at a remote Bedu encampment, tucked to one side of the broadening canyon floor. Here a local sheikh, Musallim bin Ahmed, had spent the winter with his aging father, two brothers, and their children. As we arrived, his herd was returning to camp, a slow stream of brown that steadily flowed around the sparse acacia trees dotting the stony flats. The camels bellowed a welcome to our caravan. Several bulls approached with their heads held high, and tongue pouches thrown menacingly out of their mouths. These inflatable sacs, approximately the size of a beach ball, are used as both a mating display and a sign of aggression. Glistening and quivering in the late afternoon sun, the bright pink pouches were mottled by the streaks of purple veins. The sheikh's four-year-old son bravely charged towards them. He waved only a small stick and was unable to reach even their knees, but the bulls reluctantly deflated their sacs, sucked them back in, and grudgingly retreated to wait behind a clump of nearby shrubs.

We dismounted and joined the family around a small fire, exchanging news. A young camel was ominously tethered apart from the others, bleating loudly. Soon Sheikh Musallim and several of his sons rose. They stripped off their *dishdashas* and approached the hobbled baby wearing only undershirts and their *wasir*. I knew what was coming, and I had to fight my urge to leave or ignore the slaughter. It was hypocritical, I felt, to be willing to eat meat and yet unwilling to participate in the animal's death. I resolved to watch.

The boys untied the camel, running after it and pushing until it fell screaming on its side. As one youngster pulled the head back towards its rear haunches, Sheikh Musallim resharpened his long knife with a few quick strokes on a rounded stone. Without hesitation he reached below the camel's neck, and cut deeply at a point abutting the body with a single stroke. Bright red blood issued forth in terrific spurts, but with each heart beat their vitality waned. The head was now brought forward and Sheikh Musallim cut deeply again into the top of the neck, severing the spinal cord. The last twitches faded from the camel's rear legs as the head fell limply to the ground. The entire process had taken less than ten seconds; still I found myself shaky and light-headed as I exchanged stunned glances with Jamie and Leigh. The animal was butchered into a large pile of bite-sized pieces within an hour.

I watched with grim interest as the sheikh's young son walked obliviously through the blood-soaked rocks, staring with only brief interest at the camel's glistening eyes. Its head was now completely severed and lying separately. The differences between us were staggering. I had been raised in a sheltered society, where meat appeared in cellophane wrappers at the supermarket. This can often engender a casual attitude towards its origin, and a lack of respect for our food. The Bedu were compassionate for their animals, but never loved them as we do pets. They knew from a harsh past that often their slaughter would be necessary for the group's survival. They taught their children respect rather than indifference, and often mouthed a quiet prayer prior to killing an animal.

That night the silence of the deep *wadi* was broken by a massive feast. It was the largest gathering we had yet experienced on the journey. Throughout the late afternoon, pickups arrived, winding their way down a treacherous path on the far side of the valley. The camel was cooked in various dishes, and served all evening. First, small cubes of the tender meat were fried in their own fat, and then heavily salted. Next, the organs were boiled and presented atop platters of rice. The largest joints were placed on rocks to roast near the fire. After scraping them clean, the Bedu would crack them, drinking the translucent white marrow that poured from inside.

As each new group joined our campfire, they would be received by a traditional welcome that has been practised across all of Arabia and beyond for centuries. Generations of survival in a hostile land have led to the evolution of a strict code of honour and conduct for the Bedu, still seen today in the greeting of visitors. Although the routine may vary slightly from tribe to tribe, the essence is the same. The new arrivals will gather beyond the range of the fire or tent, and then approach in a group, without stragglers. Until they announce themselves, the hosts feign ignorance of their presence. When within a stone's throw, they stop and exclaim loudly, "*Salaam aleykum!*" Immediately those present stand, while replying, "*Aleykum as salaam!*" This reply brings the assurance of hospitality and protection for the guests, not only during the evening, but for three days after as well, since it was thought to take that long for the last remnants of food, provided in hospitality, to have passed from the guest's stomach. The newcomers now enter the circle, shaking hands and touching noses with all present. "*Salaam aleykum*" may be repeated as individuals greet each other, but nothing more. The new guests are prevailed upon to sit at a prestigious place in the circle, and after some reluctance and negotiation they will generally accept the honour. After sitting, each new arrival will briefly acknowledge every one of those present with a small greeting, "*Halekum* (May life be good)" or "*Halekum grheir* (May your life be of abundance)."

Now this part of the ritual is finished and the host group will confer among themselves who should ask for the news. The task usually falls to the eldest or most senior man present, although he will put up a valiant struggle. It is considered the height of politeness if he can persuade another to accept this honour. Finally, someone will acquiesce, and the question will be posed to the newcomers, "*Aaluwm* (What is the news)?"

The newcomers will dispute amongst themselves as to who will accept the honour of replying. The response is always "*Ma shay aaluwm* (There is no news)," even if the man has an arrow stuck in his chest. Any bad news is saved for after the official greetings are finished. The minute "*Ma shay aluwm*" is uttered, the reserved silence is broken by a rush of questions. Every newcomer is questioned, and in return questions each host, with a variety of queries. These include "*Keif halek* (How is your life)?" "*Keif el aiella* (How is your family)?" "*Keif el asdegah* (How are your friends)?" "*Keif el jahal* (How are your children)?" "*Keif el bosch* (How is your herd)?" The proper response is always "*El hamdulilla*." Again, bad news is always saved till after the official greeting. This final process is astounding to watch and complicated to be involved in. All members of the group may be both asking questions of some and responding to others at the same time, apparently never losing their place. Finally, as the questioning slows down, the guests are offered sweet tea or coffee and have become a part of the group. In our three months of travel across Arabia, I never once saw this tradition shortened or omitted at a campfire or other formal gathering. This despite the fact that, with as large a group as we had in Wadi Ghadun that night, it can become quite time-consuming. Often new guests will arrive through the night, and most of a feast can be taken up with greetings.

As I finished eating, Pakeet and Mohammed Salim, two of our friends from training in Thumbrait, arrived. I wanted to dash over and say hello, but instead I had to wait patiently through another round of greetings. Before we were finished, more visitors had arrived. I decided to save my hello for later. At the height of the evening, more than sixty men surrounded the blazing fires. The rushed conversation grew too difficult for me to follow, so I sat quietly observing. Orange light danced across the men's chiselled faces. I noted that every single one clutched either a gun or a camel stick. Some carried turn-of-the-century rifles, while others had modern semi-automatic weapons from their army service.

I found myself beside Sheikh Mabhoot bin Said bin Salim, a tribal elder who had travelled with Sir Wilfred down this very *wadi* fifty years before. Sheikh Mabhoot had been thirteen then, and joined the party as a companion of his father. When they reached Mugshin, located at the very edge of the great sands, he was told he could travel farther only if he carried pots and pans on his camel. This he steadfastly refused to do. It would have been an insult to his honour not to carry something more important. Instead he chose to turn around and ride twenty days back to his home.

As the evening wore on, I slipped away from the light of the fire with a handful of dates. Despite their complicated greeting ceremonies, Bedu never say goodbye, they simply drift off from the fire, as I did now. In the darkness I whispered Crazy Dancer's name, and he moaned softly from where he was sitting tethered to a nearby acacia. His lips brushed gently against my hands as he happily ate the dates. I sat by him in the sand, absentmindedly pulling ticks from his coat. The cool night air seemed a perfect temperature. Overhead a brilliant canopy of stars lit the sky above the canyon walls. I found my bedroll, and after creating a slight depression for my body in the soft sand, spread it out. The comforting sounds of the Bedu singing broke the silence of the Arabian night. I drifted slowly to sleep.

# CHAPTER SEVEN

## Tentative Steps

The great Bedu tribes . . . could at any time have dispossessed the
weaker cultivators along the desert's edge and settled on their land.
They continued instead to dwell as nomads in the desert because
that was the life they cherished. Only in the desert, they declared,
could a man find freedom.

— Wilfred Thesiger, *Arabian Sands*

*I* awoke the next morning to a silent campsite. The visiting Bedu had
quietly disappeared into the darkness. A few empty cups lying around
the heap of smouldering ashes were the only signs of last night's large
gathering. Buried under thick piles of camel blankets, the featureless
forms of Ali Salim and Musallim were slowly stirring. Bin Ashara sat
crouched by the fire, carefully tending the morning coffee.

As we prepared to leave, Manaa quietly pulled me aside. Sheikh
Musallim, the host of the feast, had asked to join the journey. He also
wanted to bring along two of his sons, and had offered to supply all the
camels they would require, but a salary would be expected. Refusing
him the privilege after he had slaughtered a young camel in our honour
would be an unacceptable insult, Manaa warned. We both agreed that,
although we liked the sheikh, the extra hands would provide little

benefit and only create more confusion, but I was confounded as to how best to handle the situation. I had been faced with a similar incident on the beach in Salala. A friend of Bin Ashara's had suddenly announced that he was joining us. I disliked his pushy manner, and did not want our small group to acquire an ever-growing number of mouths to feed. After a long and heated discussion under a nearby palm I had been able to convince him that I appreciated his offer but did not have an extra riding camel for him to use. Now I was relieved when Manaa agreed to help defuse this second situation. He took Sheikh Musallim aside, explaining that we had only limited supplies for our small party. If for any reason one of our party fell sick or decided to leave, Manaa promised we would send for him and his sons immediately. The sheikh seemed pleased with this answer, and I was relieved to see him return to the fire smiling. Everyone's pride had remained intact, and we rode off down the rocky *wadi* bed as a party of six.

Later that afternoon we stopped to camp by a well that was hidden up a small side canyon. A concrete water tower had been erected near the well in the mid-seventies to store water that was pumped to the surface. A small oasis of shrub palms and reeds flourished at its base, where in the past years local Bedu had congregated during the dry season with their herds. Sadly, a scattering of garbage indicated man's presence. Sheikh Salem, our friend who named us in Thumbrait, had arrived the day before, bringing the remaining six pack camels, which would now join our caravan. With the entire herd together, we were now a self-sufficient team. After the town of Shisur, one hundred kilometres (62 miles) to the north, Manaa assured me we would at last travel completely on our own.

Shortly before our arrival at the well, a large camel had been slaughtered and butchered. Thin strips of meat hung everywhere, adorning a row of drooping acacias. The bushes looked like strangely decorated Christmas trees. Left to dry in the desert air, unseasoned and unsalted, the one hundred and thirty kilograms (300 lb.) of meat would last for the length of our journey. Carried in two burlap sacks, it would be the final addition to our expedition supplies. Manaa took a raw strip, moist and red, from the acacia. Tearing off an end and eating it, he gestured that I do the same. The meat was tender and tasted slightly salty. I was pleasantly surprised.

Jamie, Leigh, and I rinsed off under a tap by the water tower, and then fell asleep in the warm afternoon sun. As I tossed and turned in an exhausted state of semi-sleep, the sun's last rays lit the distant canyon walls a flaming orange. Several hours later a call from the fire roused me from my slumber, and I stumbled across the clearing in the dark. Leigh, who was reading *War and Peace* beside me, chose to miss dinner. At the fire I found Manaa and Jamie covering the glowing embers with giant joints of meat and bone, remnants of the slaughtered camel, mostly legs and hips, that still had flesh and sinew remaining after the butchery. As the meat slowly roasted, we shaved off pieces with Manaa's sharp dagger and then replaced the immense bones on the pile. I laughed to myself as I realized how prehistoric we must look, three bearded men around a fire eating from bones the size of a dinosaur's. Manaa picked up a particularly strange, whitish piece and shaved us each a thin slice. As I chewed the odd-tasting item he explained that it was part of the giant chest callus that the camel rested on when couched. It no longer tasted quite so good.

We lay back under a thick blanket of stars.

"Saleh," Manaa said to me after a pause, "this is the way life has always been in the desert." We were silent again.

I thought about how I was Saleh now. The names Sheikh Salem had given us only three weeks earlier now seemed intrinsically tied to each of us, representing our existence here – a life so different from that we knew at home to be almost irreconcilable. Jamie really was Sohail, and Leigh was Abdulla. Even when talking alone, amongst ourselves, we referred to each other by our Arabic names. The Bedu knew us by no other. After only a week in Thumbrait, a Bedu named Saleh had visited our camp, and I was amazed how sharply the utterance of his name in another conversation across the campfire caught my attention, as if I was being called. I had always thought I would know myself by nothing other than Bruce, but now I was surprised at how quickly I had assumed another name. The changes went deeper than that, in fact, although I would not realize this until later.

When we finally retired for the evening I found myself lying awake under my camel blankets, sheltered from the desert wind by a thorny acacia. Jamie and Leigh had long since drifted off. I thought of my father. That night marked fours years to the day since he had died in an accident at our farm. It was he, along with my mother, who had instilled in me a love of the outdoors, and since his passing I had deeply missed sharing with him the adventures in my life. Dad had read *Arabian Sands* himself, and been impressed and inspired by Wilfred Thesiger's travels. I knew he once had travelled this very route himself in his mind, learning of Sir Wilfred taking shelter behind small shrubs as we now did. I thought of my mother, and decided, despite my fatigue, that this was the one day of any that I should use our satellite phone to call home. I crept from my blankets and set up the equipment in darkness, guided only by starlight. It was the only voice call I would make during our entire journey, and ironically I connected with my mother's answering machine. I told her that I loved her every day, and was thinking of her especially on this day. I hung up, packed the phone away, and scurried back to the warmth of my blankets. I watched a shooting star leave a blazing green trail across the night sky before exploding in a tiny shower of orange near the horizon. I wondered if my dad somehow knew where I was.

## ربع الخالي

Two of the new pack camels Sheikh Salem had brought were massive bulls. They had not been among the original camels at our training camp, but obviously Manaa had been doing some trading while we travelled. The ungelded males towered above the other camels. Everything about them was bigger, stronger, and more intimidating. Their heads were immense, their jaws and teeth appeared monstrous, like those of dragons, and their thick bodies rippled with muscle. When approached, they would throw back their heads and moan, gurgling loudly as tongue pouches flopped from their mouth. Longs strands of foamy saliva would dribble from their trembling lips. They cowed the other camels into submission and had to be tethered separately. One bit Crazy Dancer directly on top of his head, opening a gash in his thick hide, through which his skull could be seen. Ali Salim helped me pack the wound with salt, and within a few days it had healed.

With the presence of the new camels, the entire herd was excited as we saddled and prepared to move on the next day. The long-term plan was for each of us to ride one camel and care for another pack camel that we would have in tow, but Manaa still felt that we were not ready to ride "in control," untethered to a camel ahead. For now, Ali Salim and Bin Ashara would each tie three pack camels behind them. Jamie, Leigh, and I would all ride in a line tethered behind Musallim. Crazy Dancer seemed anxious about the new arrangement, and wove from side to side of his tether even before we set off. On the trail he kept pushing to pass Mr. T., and I was forced to haul back on his reins. I began to practise using my camel stick, although it really had no effect. The tether leading from Mr. T.'s saddle left Crazy Dancer only a few feet of freedom.

We followed the winding course of the *wadi* for several hours before arriving at the well of Ma Shadid. Here a natural cave in the underlying limestone drops down more than thirty metres (100 ft.) to a trickle of fresh water below, part of an extensive underground aquifer. Thesiger stopped nearby in 1946, but did not enter the well himself, preferring to let his Bedu descend for water. Consequently we did not know what lay below. After tethering our camels, we scrambled up a short rise to view the well. Atop a craggy outcrop the narrow hole dropped quickly into darkness below. A messy collection of aging ropes lay draped over the lip. The oldest appeared to be formed from interwoven palm fronds, which were now dusty and cracked.

A crowd of local Bedu had awaited our arrival, proud to show us the well that had been overseen by their family for generations. A tiny and energetic man named Sheikh Musallim bin Ahmed bin Said offered to descend with us and help fill our goatskins, and Ali Salim declared he would come too, along with several of the young boys waiting around the hole. One after another we lowered ourselves hand-over-hand down the ancient ropes. Dust was thick in the air. Without our head-lamps we would have been blind. The humidity in the hot well was unbearable, and soon we were soaked with sweat. The route continued to drop steeply, winding through occasional keyhole constrictions. Deep grooves worn in the lips of these limestone ledges attested to generations of Bedu who had hauled heavy goatskins of precious water from the depths.

"*Ghralee balek, haya* (Be careful, snakes)!" Sheikh Musallim shouted from the darkness below. The well was full of snakes, he warned, urging us to check every crevice and travertine outcropping before placing our hands and feet. Inspecting the rock ledges in front of me I could see a multitude of winding snake tracks in the dust, leading back into the darker recesses beyond my fingers. Suddenly I found myself claustro-phobic, hot, and not sure I wanted to stay any longer. Still, we descended in concentrated silence. A few minutes later a young Bedu announced we had reached the spot where his grandfather had died. I looked down the well at him with surprise. Before lowering himself over the lip of the next drop he looked up and smiled. "*Haya,*" he explained.

A final narrow opening forced us to breathe in and hold our hands overhead. We slithered down into the small cavern below. A tiny stream of crystal-clear water, only centimetres deep, emerged from a crack near the sandy floor, and disappeared under the opposite wall two metres away. There was room for only two of us on the bottom. The others waited perched on ledges above, descending in turn to drink from the cool stream. As Jamie and Sheikh Musallim bin Ahmed filled a goatskin, we all sang a camel-watering song at the top of our lungs.

*My camel has a big hump, Ya hye bye, Ya hye bye*
*Drink much water my friend, Ya hye bye, Ya hye bye*
*Because you have travelled far, Ya hye bye, Ya hye bye*
*Now we have unloaded you, Ya hye bye, Ya hye bye*
*Under the shady bushes, Ya hye bye, Ya hye bye . . .*

Relieved to be done, and anxious to return to the surface, we scrambled, squirmed, and crawled quickly out of the cave, momentarily blinded when we emerged into the midday sun. Manaa laughed when he saw us, soaked, filthy from the dust that now covered us, and ecstatic to have returned with our prize of water.

On the journey we carried our water in *gerbers*, the traditional goatskins that Arabia's nomads have used for centuries. A gerber is essentially a goat, skinned and turned inside out, suspended by the legs, with the neck pointing forward to be used as a faucet. Any seams opened during butchering are sealed with fat. The skin itself leaks terribly when dry, but once the *gerber* is filled, the hide quickly absorbs water and seals. The *gerbers* we had all varied in size, but each contained roughly 15 litres (4.0 gal.) when full. As we gradually used our water we were careful to always leave a tiny amount in each *gerber* to prevent it from drying out. To pour the contents out, the rope lashed around the neck is undone and the skin tilted forward. Unfortunately all the fur inside a skin had never been completely removed, and thus after sitting in the hot sun, sloshing around with the camels' jolting gait, and absorbing a strong taste of rancid fat from the seams, the water that came out was almost nauseating. When poured into our clear water bottles, it looked like chocolate milk, with a few decomposing hairs and a film of fat suspended on the surface. No amount of juice crystals could disguise the foul taste. However, soon we no longer noticed, and drank the liquid without hesitation during the hot days to come.

We rode on down the *wadi*, leaving the crowd at Ma Shadid behind. By the time we stopped in the fading evening light, another group had appeared from nowhere, racing past us in their trucks, waving and honking their horns. Leigh was annoyed at the constant presence of others and, after eating dinner, he left the fire early to sleep alone, hidden in the sands. I understood his frustration. The trucks we found following us at every turn diminished the sense of adventure that we had come seeking. Still, I felt he was reacting very strongly. This was the Bedu's land, and their ancient tradition of hospitality dictated that they honour us with their generosity. What could we do? Ask them to leave us alone? We had arrived with a vision of crossing a desolate, lonely desert in Arabia. So far it had been anything but desolate, and we still felt untested, but there were more than a thousand kilometres between us and the coast at Abu Dhabi in the United Arab Emirates. Manaa had assured me that he would follow us only as far as Shisur with the support trucks. After that he doubted we would meet anyone in the remote desert. As the main liaison with the Bedu, and our de facto leader, I felt responsible for making the trip a success for Leigh. I desperately wanted him to enjoy the experience. Together, the three of us had invested eighteen months and our hearts and souls into planning it. Now I was at a loss as to how to deal with his frustrations. He was constantly angry, and nothing I did seemed to work. Luckily, I found great pleasure in the company of the Bedu, and tried to forget these worries in the rambling conversation around the flickering fire.

Day after day we continued to follow the *wadi* north. At first it cut a sharp path through the land, and yellow walls rose up steeply around us. Massive blocks had fallen to the canyon floor in places, the smashed limestone diverting us in a circuitous path along the bed. As the *wadi* progressed, however, its course widened, and the walls slowly dropped.

Below us on the trail, a fragile mosaic of life revealed itself in the stark land. Small tail-less lizards began to appear, lazily sunning themselves on the hot ground. As we approached, they would scurry for cover, and then turn to watch as the camels' hooves passed overhead, crunching noisily on the gravel. Long-legged beetles cruised the paths. Like the larger dung beetle, they quickly pounced on the droppings our camels left behind. Occasionally our group would flush hares from nearby shrubs. The Bedu spotted the motion immediately, pointing to the fleeing animals and pretending to fire imaginary guns at them. Gazelle tracks were common in the soft sand, and occasionally we would see their white backsides bounding through the canyon far ahead. A recent agreement amongst the local sheikhs had curtailed all hunting of gazelle, and brought a dramatic resurgence of their fading numbers. One day a gerbil darted from a shrub directly under Crazy Dancer's feet. Leigh and I watched its long tail, three times the length of its body and standing straight up, disappear far in the distance. This amazing small mammal can live its entire life without drinking water, subsisting only on the moisture of the plants it eats. Apart from three snakes we passed over while riding (likely pit vipers), and a healthy bird population near the pool of Ayun, we saw no other wildlife.

A few days later we rose out of the *wadi*, and headed across the open plains towards Shisur, only sixty kilometres (40 miles) away. We had now been travelling for eight days tied behind the Bedu's camels. I fantasized about riding free, but was not sure how much control I really had of Crazy Dancer. Labian's frightening gallop during training had left us all tentative. I knew the Bedu would find excuses to put off our graduation to solo riding indefinitely. As we rode, I stared at the slipknot tying Crazy Dancer to Jamie's saddle. Jamie was tied to Leigh, and Leigh to Musallim. I decided it was time.

"Hey, Jamie, can you reach behind you to untie Crazy Dancer?" I whispered.

"Are you sure?" He looked at me with a half-cocked smile, and raised one eyebrow. I knew he wished he was at the back of the line, but he would have his chance soon enough.

"Go for it," I nodded. "Just let go of the rein slowly, and I'll reach forward to grab it with the crook of my camel stick."

Jamie slowly pulled Crazy Dancer forward as close to Mr. T. as he could, and then in a single motion he undid the thick rope. As the loose end dropped towards the ground, it fell into the crook of my camel stick, and I quickly raised it to my hand. I was free. Crazy Dancer slowed slightly, unsure of what was different, and then fell back into the line. I was lost in my own world, practising steering right and left with taps of my stick. As Crazy Dancer began dropping behind the others I wanted to speed him up with a firm rap to the hump. I had seen the Bedu do it, but was unsure how hard I should rap him. My first efforts produced nothing, not even a faint sound of contact. I tried a little harder, and the cane made an awful sound, as if I had hit a bone directly. However, Crazy Dancer showed no sign of acknowledging my request, so I tried still harder. As we slowly caught up to the group, I looked up just in time to see Leigh untie Jamie behind him. Soon Leigh was unhitched by Musallim, and we rode along together, blissfully experimenting with our new-found freedom. The Bedu shouted and applauded excitedly, encouraging us to try a gallop. With a bit of effort the camels surged into a slow trot. We bounced uncomfortably high in the saddle, and Bin Ashara roared in delight.

At the fire that evening I decided to confirm with Manaa his previous assurance that the support trucks would leave us after Shisur. I knew we were now only a day away, and I did not want to get blindsided by a change of plans. To my surprise, a huge chorus of protest went up amongst the Bedu. Did they not know this was the plan, or after a week on the road were they too comfortable with the current routine? Why did they not protest earlier if they thought it impossible? Were they hoping they could convince us to "take the soft side" as Manaa called it? How long did we have to hit our heads against this wall? I wished we could share a common vision. Manaa agreed with me about our goal, and then entered into long and heated discussions with Bin Ashara and Musallim. I could catch scattered words, but the sentiment was clear. The Bedu did not want to continue without a support truck. Jamie,

Leigh, and I chatted in the darkness. We agreed that we would not capitulate on this demand.

# ربع الخالي

We awoke in the morning to find that several of our camels had drifted away during the night, despite being hobbled. What would we do now without a truck? the Bedu asked rhetorically. Bin Ashara and Ali Salim jumped in the Land Cruiser and sped off to look for the escapees, which they found three kilometres (2 miles) away. Drawn by the scent of water, they had hopped in their hobbles to a nearby well during the night.

When the Bedu returned, they continued to act annoyed and angry. I was frustrated. I felt they were not giving the expedition a chance. Manaa had agreed to this plan since the start, but he had apparently done nothing to convince the others of it.

As always, riding eased all worldly concerns. The familiarity and soft sway of the saddle soothed us early in the day, before the onset of the terrible pain. We rode untethered, joking with the Bedu, whose mood also improved as soon as we were under way. Our maps showed the oasis of Shisur lying due north across forty kilometres (25 miles) of featureless plains. Long before we arrived we could see palm trees floating on the distant horizon, an indescribably welcome sight. An hour passed and Shisur appeared to come no closer. Jamie asked how far we thought it was to the oasis. It looked as though it couldn't be more than a kilometre: I felt I could jump down and dash over to the trees faster than we were getting there riding. Leigh estimated two kilometres, and I thought he was way over, but it was another four and a half kilometres (3 miles) before we finally arrived. Distances on the flats were deceiving.

Behind the last grove of fluttering palms lay a small fenced pen. Dismounting, we unsaddled and hobbled the camels before retiring to the shade to rest. Above us on a small rise lay the crumbling ruins of an ancient settlement. An intensive archeological search during the mid-eighties, employing everything from space-shuttle imagery to helicopters, to fleets of Range Rovers, had finally declared this well-known site to be the legendary Ubar, a flourishing city rumoured to have been destroyed by God for the sins of its inhabitants and lost in the desert sands. The evidence recovered is not conclusive, and many locals we met remained unconvinced.

Running directly into the crumbling ruins at Shisur, a massive cleft in the limestone led down to a tiny trickle of water far below the desert sands. The only water source in these gravel flats that stretched beyond the coastal mountains and deep *wadis*, the well and oasis here have long been of strategic importance to the Bedu tribes passing across these lands in a search for grazing. Thesiger stopped here twice to water during his travels. Then, only a handful of palms had dotted the sands below the entrance to the rocky cleft. Now an electrical pump supplied irrigation water to a small plantation.

Atop the rise and beyond the ruins, a small settlement had recently been established. In 1980 two rows of concrete semi-detached homes had been constructed, and nomads from the nearby steppes first settled here permanently then. In 1990 the Omani government strengthened its influence and support, building an administrative centre. A large brick wall and an iron gate enclosed the small subdivision. Inside, a single paved street led past the office of the *wali* (mayor), a new mosque, and other official residences.

The *wali* of Shisur had organized a feast in our honour. Earlier, as we rode into town, a decrepit old camel was being led past the plantation by a group of youths. Now its butchered meat had been boiled and spiced, prepared in enormous steaming cauldrons. We arrived together at the administrative centre, the Bedu proudly shouldering their polished rifles, Jamie, Leigh, and I brandishing only our camel sticks. A large circle of carpets and pillows had been laid outside the entrance to the town hall. Once again the tightly knit Bedu community had gathered from all around. In the pleasant evening air we ate from lavish piles of fruit, while young boys circled the gathering, offering tiny cups of strong cardamom-flavoured coffee. After a song of welcome and official wishes of good luck, the massive piles of rice and meat appeared. As I ate, I noticed spiders the size of a man's hand darting from the shadows towards the piles of food, only to be absentmindedly flicked away by a camel stick or rifle butt. These were the massive camel spiders of which Sir Wilfred had complained. In England he had told us, "I find spiders ghastly things. Give me a good snake any day." Although camel spiders are not true spiders, as they have only six legs, they are disturbing creatures. They have an incredibly large mandible-to-body-size ratio, and the Bedu told of how, after injecting their powerful anesthetic sting, these spiders could eat away a sizeable chunk of flesh while one slept. It was a terrifying story, but I could never confirm any report of this actually happening, and we lay in the sand undisturbed that night.

The next day we set about trimming down our gear yet again. Until now we had not been forced to pack everything with us on the camels, since the pickups arrived in camp every evening. Now we meticulously went through the supplies, leaving behind anything that we had discovered was not essential. In addition to the clothes I wore while riding, I decided to take a T-shirt and a pair of longjohns for evenings. Gone were my boots, extra shirts, fleece jackets, spare underwear, and socks. Gone also were the bug screens, sextants, canvas buckets, and spare rope that had sounded useful while I was at my desk in Canada. I took a single paperback, a headlamp, and a toothbrush. Everything I had fit into a small stuff sack no larger than a lunch bag. It felt wonderfully liberating to travel with so little. For group gear we had a small repair set and a comprehensive first-aid kit. Our cameras, video, and communication equipment in their protective, sandproof cases accounted for most of the weight. When we finished, the meagre pile weighed only 45 kilograms (100 lb.), a far cry from the 300 kilograms (660 lb.) we had brought with us from Canada.

# CHAPTER EIGHT

# On Our Own

Ships in harbour are safe, but that is not what ships are built for.
— John Shedd

*A* tense mood hung over the camp as we awoke on February 12. Manaa had risen uncharacteristically early, and sat staring into the fire. From now on we would be on our own. Despite his worries he had to let us go.

Manaa had become like a father to us, and I trusted him implicitly. Although I had fought hard to ensure that the trucks and support crew left us behind after Shisur, I was sympathetic to the other pressures Manaa was facing. Musallim and Bin Ashara seemed to have no interest in travelling alone. The presence of the pickups meant that they could take turns riding with the drivers when they were tired, and that the supplies did not all have to be loaded on the camels. They would find any excuse to stow things in the truck instead. Touarish and Salim Ali, two young drivers accompanying Manaa, also wished to stay, not wanting to leave the excitement of the expedition. Jamie, Leigh, and I suspected Manaa must also have been facing an unspoken pressure from the Bait Kathir tribe, pressure for the expedition to succeed, and for us to encounter no harm along the way.

When Thesiger had reached the town of Mugshin during his first journey across the Empty Quarter, his Bait Kathir companions who had been assigned by the sultan to accompany him refused to travel into the heart of the desert. Whatever the reason may have been, after this Thesiger did not hide his disdain for the Kathiri tribe – as we had seen. In a land where a man's reputation means everything, the pain of this insult had not faded. Now our expedition offered an opportunity, after fifty years, for them to regain some of this lost pride, to restore their tarnished reputation. I had little doubt that this had been subtly, but firmly, impressed on Manaa by the sheikhs who had travelled from afar to see us. If our journey was "on the soft side," perhaps our reporting of it would be even more favourable. I tried to explain to Manaa that the opposite was true.

"I think the soft side is better for you. Why do you need the hard life?" he would ask. I told him that "the safe side" was okay, but not "the soft side." I certainly did not want to ask our Bedu companions to face irresponsible or unnecessary dangers in our Western quest for adventure. I suggested it might reflect poorly on the Bait Kathir if we did not attempt the journey alone. We had struggled with this conflict every day since the journey began, but today, finally, we would travel alone, unsupported. I don't think Manaa felt defeated, but he did feel concerned. He just sat and stared emptily at the long tendrils of thick smoke enveloping the kettle.

Leigh, Jamie, and I were ecstatic, but maintained a sombre countenance around the morning fire. Ali Salim seemed excited by the prospect of the new challenges facing us, giving a hidden thumbs-up as we prepared to leave. Musallim and Bin Ashara had grumbled perpetually for the last two days, and now sulked. It had initially baffled me that these men had no interest in attempting the journey in a traditional manner. Both were skilled desert travellers, experts with camels, and extremely proud of their heritage.

Standing by the fire I realized that I always instinctively assumed the more difficult something was, the better it was; the bigger the challenge, the more rewarding the experience of facing it. Others may not always agree, and naturally there are limits to this line of reasoning. Setting the goal for oneself of swimming the English Channel may be arguably reasonable; to do it with five-kilogram (11 lb.) weights on each ankle simply to make it harder would be viewed, universally I suspect, as ludicrous. The line between the two can be vague at times, and a matter of personal judgement.

I felt the journey had meaning, and was not just a stunt or an invented hardship. Undeniably we could complete it more easily with a car behind us the whole way, but that itself seemed silly. Alone in the desert we would be forced to rely on ourselves, and each other, leaving behind for a short time the crutches of our modern life. To me there was an unquantifiable, but undeniable, value in accepting and facing that struggle.

In the West we lead a comfortable existence, and now paradoxically have to seek out the challenge and hardship that technology has removed from our daily existence, hardships that other cultures often suffer daily as a matter of course. Our Bedu, particularly Bin Ashara and Musallim, had led tough lives. Perhaps we were unfairly asking too much of them? Even so I remained surprised that they showed not the slightest sign of interest in rising to the challenge.

The camels sensed the mood in camp, and became edgy themselves. Despite their hobbles, they hopped away vigorously as we approached. After a day's rest their energy had returned, and so had their obstinate behaviour. They were indignant at the thought of working. Crazy Dancer turned in circles, keeping me to his back as I drew near. He reminded me of a big ostrich trying to pretend I was not there. As I went one way, he would turn the other, looking up at the sky as if he did not see me. Finally, with a quick dart, I reached forward and was able to wrap one arm around his long neck. He was caught, and acquiesced immediately, nuzzling my chest as I attached his halter.

The previous day Manaa had worked with us to prepare and pack all the gear we needed to carry. Now six pairs of balanced loads sat together by the fire, carefully lined up on camel blankets. Eight *gerbers* would carry all our water, and were to be loaded in opposing pairs on four camels. Two hard plastic cases containing our camera, video, and communications gear would be carried in a pair of burlap feed sacks slung over the back of a fifth camel. Finally, two large duffel bags carrying all our personal and camp gear, along with anything else that needed to be packed at the last minute, would be loaded on the remaining pack camel. Touarish and Salim Ali kept checking and rechecking the weight of each load by hand, shaking their heads in disgust. "*Mafi zain*," they would mutter and shake their heads, more to cause me consternation, I suspected, than as a comment on the weight.

Loading the camels was not easy. It required two people to approach from opposite sides, each with one half of the balanced load. Two ropes were hastily tied between the heavy loads, one fore and one aft of the hump, and the weight was lowered to rest on the saddlery. Most camels did not like the new encumbrance, and bellowed loudly, turning to spray regurgitated cud. Others would try to jump up before the loads were properly attached, which sent the gear crashing to the ground. This excitement would incite other camels hobbled nearby to rise also. At one point three loose camels were hopping about, partly attached loads falling to the side. The noise was deafening as the camels roared with rage and indignation. Jamie, Leigh, and I tried to help in every way we could, but were not offered much instruction. When we did manage to involve ourselves, our knots and load arrangements never met with Bedu approval. Any orderly knot or rope system was impatiently undone and reworked into a complicated bird's nest. Bowlines and trucker's hitches were viewed with disdain; granny knots seemed the only approved method of tying. Touarish asked how we could ever travel alone when we could not even load the camels ourselves. It was too much work for six men, he said. I started to explain that we just needed to learn, but decided to let it go for now. Several of the local Bedu who had stopped by to watch our departure offered their own advice. Most deemed our chances of success without a truck to be slim, and commented freely on this as we fought to control the bucking camels.

With the ordeal of loading finished, Manaa and Bin Ashara began pairing each pack camel with a rider. From now on we would each be responsible for a pack camel, which we would saddle and load in the morning and unsaddle and hobble every night. Manaa tied a scrawny female camel named Tynoona II (there were three camels on the journey called Tynoona by the Bedu; we differentiated them by number) behind Crazy Dancer. As we stood waiting to leave, Tynoona II began dashing to and fro, yanking on her rope. This annoyed Crazy Dancer, who started circling the tether I held, dragging Tynoona II behind him. I noticed the others were facing similar challenges. Any change in our daily routine seemed to upset the camels greatly.

Eventually we were all ready, and we struggled to lead the excited herd through a gap in the barbed-wire fence surrounding the pen. They jostled and fought, frightened by the small opening. A stampede almost erupted. As the last stragglers darted nervously through, and we led them out onto the great gravel flats surrounding Shisur, the herd began to calm. The lush green of the oasis faded behind us.

Touarish and Salim Ali sped ahead in the truck for a final goodbye. Musallim wanted to ride immediately. I could sense Crazy Dancer was still agitated, and I wanted to give him more time to calm down, but Musallim was already mounting. I knew I had to get on as well or risk being left behind. I had experimented with a little extra padding in my saddle arrangement that morning, searching for a more comfortable ride, but as soon as Crazy Dancer rose, I knew I was in trouble, perched precariously high and unable to grip his torso with my legs. Musallim and Bin Ashara trotted ahead and our camels rushed to join them. From far behind I heard a half-exhilarated, half-fearful cry. I turned to look, and Leigh galloped by on Labian, appearing on the verge of losing control. Mr. T. and Crazy Dancer both jumped to keep up. Jamie and I fought to restrain them. Their excitement came in waves, and we would only just have calmed the camels when they would press forward again.

Suddenly something scared Tynoona II, and she kicked wildly, in turn scaring Crazy Dancer. In an instant we were galloping, and with every bounce I felt myself inch dangerously farther forward on the loose saddle. Seconds later I was thrown forward in cartwheel, landing between the two camels as they ran by. Jamie charged past with a look of amused disbelief as he fought Mr. T. for control. Stupidly, I had tied my reins to my saddle, and was unable to hold onto the camels after I had fallen off. I promised myself I would never make the same mistake again. I watched helplessly as Touarish and Salim Ali raced after my camels in the truck, quickly catching them and returning them to me.

Touarish held out the reins proudly, looking like he had won a point. "*Lesh mafi siyara? Mafi siyara el yom, yimkin mushkilla kabir!* (Why no truck? No truck today, maybe big problem!)" I was humbled and embarrassed, but initially remained defiant. While Touarish held Crazy Dancer, I jumped back on. He was immediately up, and I held on tightly as he ran to catch the others, who were now well ahead of us on the horizon. Slowly the camels settled into their steady walking pace. The excitement of moving again gave way to the ceaseless stride they had inherited through generations of caravan travel. The truck that had hovered in the distance for some time turned and headed back towards Shisur, disappearing behind a low gravel rise. Finally we were alone.

I began to wonder if the Bedu were right. Was I being unrealistic and reckless by continuing to campaign for an unsupported expedition? How could I have the nerve to suggest such a thing when I couldn't even stay on my camel? Although the Bedu should have been the unquestioned experts on the feasibility of a desert expedition, I doubted their willingness to accept a reasonable challenge, and suspected them of being lackadaisical. I had weathered their complaints and arguments without ever questioning my resolve or the validity of our team's goals. But now my internal strength seemed to have evaporated. Were we in over our heads? I was discouraged and found myself starting to believe the Bedu's previous admonishments. Although my despondency did not last long, faint doubts still lingered as we travelled farther out into the gravel flats.

In the featureless terrain the Bedu navigated by the sun and their knowledge of the subtle variations in the flats, while Leigh passed the time charting our progress using his GPS. By noon the GPS showed we had travelled nineteen-point-seven kilometres (12.2 miles), and it was nineteen-point-five (12.1 miles) in a straight line back to Shisur. Musallim had held an almost perfect bearing for three hours. I was amazed, well aware of how difficult this was from my experience travelling on glaciers during a whiteout. The Bedu knew these flats well.

There were very few breaks in the monotony, and every small variation was noted. Occasionally *graf* trees, large thick-trunked trees with a dome of leafy foliage, appeared in the far distance, standing solitary against the horizon. Here, with so few other landmarks, each one was recognized by the Bedu. Even small rocky outcrops had individual names, which Bin Ashara or Musallim would announce as we passed.

We took a short break in the early afternoon, barely long enough to stretch our legs and eat a few scraps of dried meat. Jamie and Leigh handed me their camels' reins and left to relieve themselves. There was no hiding in the featureless terrain, and as a matter of politeness they walked a short distance away and simply turned their backs. I noticed Musallim glance over in horror, and I wondered what the problem could be. Later Ali Salim explained to us, with the most serious countenance, that it was wrong to pee standing up, and none of us should do it again. The Bedu simply raise their *dishdasha* slightly and squat down on their heels, avoiding any need to use their hands. We all tried this, but it was harder than it appeared to master the balance. For the rest of the journey we resorted to dropping to one or both knees to appease the Bedu, but often found ourselves rapidly crawling backwards mid-process, as unfortunately our knees created small yet significant trenches.

We continued on, and as the afternoon passed, the winds grew. At first they blew in warm gusts, occasionally bringing with them a dark cloud of dust that could be seen approaching across the plains. Soon there was a constant breeze. Most of the sand drifted by at ground level, blowing below our camels in a swirling sheet that was reminiscent of drifting snow. The camels' prints disappeared almost as quickly as we passed.

After several more hours, Musallim veered right and stopped by a flat-topped limestone outcrop rising from the centre of a crater-like depression. Conditions continued to deteriorate as we set up camp, the blowing sand making it difficult at times to talk or even to see. Between gusts we unloaded the camels. I felt the weight of responsibility as I tied my camel's hobbles. If the rope was too loose or the knot came undone, there would be no truck to retrieve the lost animal. The consequences could be serious. Conversely a hobble tied too tightly could hurt the camel's ankle so badly as to leave it lame for days. It was a delicate balance. As Ali Salim passed by, I asked him to check the rope. Was it too tight or too loose? He gave it a yank and quickly inspected the knot. Amidst the blowing sand he give me the thumbs-up, before leaving to gather some dry shrubs for firewood.

The *gerbers* were carefully laid on one camel blanket, and then covered with another; any sand on them would leach precious moisture. Once the camels were all hobbled and had settled, we climbed on top of the flat rock, above the blowing sand. Shortly Ali Salim returned with an armful of twigs and started a fire in the lee of the outcrop. Exhausted, we sat in a small circle, drinking tea and chewing on dried meat. There was no meal of rice or *khobz*; no one had the energy or inclination to cook. The simplicity of our new routine was wonderful; finally it felt like the journey that we had sought. The Bedu also seemed very content. Without a large crowd at the fire, they tried harder than ever before to interact with Jamie, Leigh, and I, despite our rudimentary Arabic. Bin Ashara told stories and old Bedu legends while we huddled close atop the rock. Here, alone with only us and the camels, the Bedu were joyful and full of vigour, apparently brought to life by the desert. Yet at the very hint of having a truck come to meet us they would have nodded eagerly, their resilience deadened, the magic of these isolated moments apparently not holding the same value for them. I was never sure if they noticed this themselves.

As the sun set, Bin Ashara climbed to his feet and pointed north. There on the horizon, painted red by the evening light, lay the dunes of the Empty Quarter. It was our first sight of them, and it stirred something inside. We would continue to skirt the sands until we reached Mugshin, where we would turn directly north into them. As the twilight passed to darkness, silence enveloped the land. We settled down to sleep, nestled closely together, hidden from the wind behind small piles of gear and food.

The next day we rose early. The wind had blown all night, and sand covered much of us and our gear. One camel had wandered off, but luckily it was easy to spot on the flat expanse, less than a kilometre away, and, after praying, Musallim left to fetch him. The rest of us packed up camp while tea was brewing. It took an hour to saddle and load all the camels. We were riding by eight, our earliest start yet – and it was without the help of others. There was solace in the simple nature of this existence. Travelling through the empty land we were so alone, united by purpose. Life fell to a natural rhythm.

The day passed as every day did, a blur of separate moments: tranquillity, pain, heat, hunger, thirst, excitement. Afternoon ground on, and I could find fewer and fewer comfortable positions in my saddle. Discomfort had displaced all other thoughts. As we caught sight of the distant well where we planned to stop, I tried to convince myself I could last ten more minutes in the saddle. I had already been in it for over eight hours, but now getting off and walking the last kilometre seemed tantalizingly appealing. To the west a quickly setting sun turned the sky a subtle yellow, illuminating clouds of dust suspended above the plains; sporadic trees and lone scrubs stood as silhouettes on the horizon.

A foreign sound interrupted my concentration. Turning, I saw in the distance a pickup roaring towards us across the flats we had crossed. It was Touarish and Salim Ali. What were they doing here? My heart sank.

They beat us into camp, greeting us with waves, shouts, and even a few rounds from their rifles fired in welcome. As our twelve camels ground to a halt and milled around waiting to be unloaded, Touarish and Salim Ali jumped in and began to work. It was as if it were perfectly normal to meet them here in the middle of the desert. I tried to intervene and asked why they had come, but their only response was to comment on how we could not handle the unloading ourselves. Musallim shot me a dirty look. In the Bedu's world of desert hospitality, it must have seemed terribly rude for me to question the presence of our new guests. Really, I should be making them coffee and offering them dates.

They had appeared so suddenly I was at a loss as to what to do next. I did not want to ignore it, as I knew they would stay on forever. Should I ask them to leave? Tell them to leave? I felt they could never understand. They were proud to be doing us a favour, but their presence changed everything good that had developed in the last twenty-four hours. Musallim, Bin Ashara, and Ali Salim now lounged around the fire while the boys worked. They no longer talked to us, frustrated by our poor Arabic and too embarrassed to attempt any English. Instead, a loud Arabic conversation ensued, too fast for any of us to follow. I felt like an outsider in camp. Touarish went to the pickup and returned with a bag of pop cans. The water in our *gerbers* no longer seemed so precious. How much longer could we fight this? It felt like a losing battle.

After eating, Jamie, Leigh, and I retreated to discuss the situation once again. Could we prevent the expedition from becoming nothing more than a "car camping" trip across Arabia? There appeared to be no simple answer. On the surface, so many of the principles we fought for must have seemed ridiculous to the Bedu. When we were tired after a long day in the saddle, we refused to ride in the truck. Bin Ashara and Musallim would jump in gladly and hand the camels' reins to another. When handed a pop we often choose instead to drink foul-smelling water from the *gerbers*. When others kindly offered to help us arrange our loads and saddles, we preferred to do it ourselves. And now, when they had come to cook us a warm meal, we preferred that they leave. Maybe it made no sense to them. Were we discovering that the days of traditional travel in the Arabian deserts were truly gone forever? I struggled to find meaning in our journey, and what was left of it. We had travelled 250 kilometres (155 miles) so far, less than a quarter of the total distance, a lot still lay ahead. That night I slept atop a nearby rise, apart from the group. Our spirit as a travelling team had broken as quickly as it had formed.

After feigning ignorance of our concerns the night before, Touarish and Salim Ali seemed to understand the next morning. After prayer and tea, they drove off with promises that we would not see them again until we arrived in Mugshin. We rode all morning across rolling gravel flats. In the distance the great dunes tantalized us, appearing in muted colours of grey and red. Rare clouds threw intermittent shadows across their twisting forms, highlighting sharp ridges and delicate patterns created by the wind.

The gravel plains abounded with hardy green shrubs. Their long spindly roots, a good source of firewood, often lay exposed, snaking across the sands. We saw few signs of tribulus or callagonum, esteemed by the Bedu as the best desert grazing for the camels, particularly when they were thirsty. Gone also were the fields of *quassis*, a hardy sedge, now almost non-existent after years of drought. Frustratingly, the most common shrub, a form of salt-bush, caused the camels to have diarrhea and other stomach upsets, so I tried to discourage Crazy Dancer from grazing as we rode. But as the day wore on, more and more often I could sense his eyes searching the ground below. Approaching a small bush, he would drop his neck and, as we passed by, uproot it with a mighty pull. Continuing, he would slowly chew the head of leaves and twigs as the spindly roots hung bouncing from his mouth.

Travelling with twelve fully loaded camels made it difficult to break for lunch. Unless we only stopped very briefly, we needed to drop all the loads from the pack camels. Otherwise they might roll on the ground to scratch themselves, and the loads could get damaged – even more wor-risome, one of our *gerbers* could burst or be punctured. Also, as soon as we dismounted, the temperature seemed to soar: not only did we lose the light breeze generated by the camel's gait, but we were closer to the hot sand. Temperature differences between the saddle and the ground varied by as much as ten degrees Celsius (18° F), and in this heat we had to unload and hobble each protesting camel carefully. The entire proce-dure would take half an hour. While we ate and napped during the hottest part of the day, the camels would drift off in their search for grazing. Rounding them up, retightening the saddles, and replacing all the loads would take almost an hour. Often, it seemed much easier just to keep going. If it was not blisteringly hot, we would ride all day, snacking on scraps of dried meat from our saddlebags. But as the summer season approached, and each day grew hotter, the camels would began to lag and falter in the midday heat, and we were forced to stop more often.

Ahead of us on the plains a lone *graf* tree offered the only shade for as far as the eye could see. It seemed a natural place to stop for lunch. Although it appeared close, it was more than an hour before we finally arrived under its spreading branches. The tree looked like an umbrella, for the lower branches had been nibbled in a perfectly straight graze line, and Swad, our big bull, was the only camel able to raise his head high enough to reach the fluttering leaves. The effort did not appear to be worth the reward. Once his blankets had been removed and his saddle loosened, Swad drifted off to lie with the other camels among the wilting salt bushes.

A large, dead lizard, more than half a metre (2 ft.) from head to tail, lay in the thick bed of twig-and-bark litter beneath the tree. Its hollow shell was a further sign of the bad drought the land was facing. Ali Salim explained that lizards are usually the last animals to die, since they are able to scavenge small insects and eat the scraps others leave behind.

Bin Ashara started a small fire. Soon he passed around glasses of sweet, black tea. The hot liquid was surprisingly refreshing and, as we sat sipping, I watched Bin Ashara add another stick in the fire. He did not casually lay it right over the whole fire, as I would have done. Rather, he carefully placed it to butt into a small circle of burning embers at the centre. The Bedu always slowly feed sticks into a fire, burning them only from one end, rather than creating the teepee or log-house constructions common in the West. I had seen the same thing while guiding in Belize, and now wondered why this habit had formed in these places. Was it because in both regions they predominantly use hardwoods that burn hot and thus do not need a large inferno? Or could it be that both cultures cooked on fires at home, often with pots supported by three rocks or bricks. Perhaps simple geometry, in conjunction with the need to carefully control the fire's heat, had created this habit. Or was it a general philosophy of conservation? Canada is blessed with an abundance of forests. Still, wood was hardly in short supply in tropical Belize, and amazingly we never had any problem finding enough here in the desert. This was largely due to the fact that nothing rotted in the parched environment, and whatever grew during the infrequent rains remained dry and intact for decades after.

My reverie was interrupted when someone pulled two oranges from a saddlebag, leftovers from our stop in Shisur. After sharing these, we all lay back in the shade and slept on the uncomfortable clutter of twigs. I awoke a few hours later to find Bin Ashara already stirring, and we began the tiring job of collecting the wandering camels and reloading them. The heat seemed to sap every last ounce of our initiative.

Riding on, we all retreated into our own worlds. Wandering thoughts would take us far away, only to be rudely reawakened by the ever-present heat and saddle pain. As afternoon slipped into twilight I kept turning to look for Leigh. Labian had been dropping farther and farther behind the group each day, despite Leigh's constant exhortations. I feared Leigh may have given up, his spirits already floundering, resigning himself to the will of his camel. I could no longer see him anywhere behind us, and the sun had just dropped below the horizon.

Ali Salim, riding far out in front, soon stopped, just as the very last

rays of light were leaving the sky. Exhausted, I slipped quietly off my
camel and drank the last drops from my water bottle. We unloaded and
hobbled our camels by feel in the dark. Jamie and I kept yelling for
Leigh, who was somewhere behind us. We were able to dig out our
headlamps, and shone them as beacons in the direction from which we
had come. Finally Labian's massive form lumbered into sight. Leigh
dropped easily from her saddle, apparently none the worse for having
been left behind, enjoying his moments alone.

Day after day passed with the same routine. Four days after leaving
Shisur, we arrived at the lonely police post of Qitabit. Here a few lone
buildings and a dilapidated camel pen were all that marked the Omani
presence near the southern Saudi Arabian border. The three men stationed there emerged to greet us, and invited us into a portable trailer
to eat. We must have smelled and looked awful, but we eagerly accepted.
We collapsed on the carpeted floor, and soon a tiny Indian cook
appeared with a platter of saffron rice topped with roasted chicken. My
eyes bulged greedily at the sight of the new food, for we had eaten dried
camel or boiled goat every day for more than six weeks. Musallim shot
a look of disdain towards the cook and quietly grumbled "*Lahem zain.
Dajaj mafi zain* (Meat good. Chicken no good)." I could hardly believe
my ears. When I later caught Musallim pulling large pieces from the
roasted breast, I smiled and raised an eyebrow at him.

The Bedu are riddled with contradictions. In some regards they are
completely inflexible, refusing any change to their ways. A good example
is the absolute horror with which they regarded me if I considered eating
a date while drinking tea. Dates were reserved strictly for coffee; only
*khobz* should be eaten with tea. Anything else would have been bar-
barous. If I followed this simple adage, they assured me I would stay
healthy. Break it and I may suffer terrible stomach upsets or worse.
Another strong belief was that only *lahem* (meat) and *gamel halib* (camel

milk) could help make a man grow strong. Nearly all other foods were eyed with contempt. Yet while holding fast to these old traditional beliefs, they simultaneously carry a cellphone in their *dishdasha* pockets and protest at the suggestion of travelling anywhere without a truck.

After eating, we all used a small makeshift shower outside to rinse the sand and dust from ourselves. In the hot, dry wind our handwashed clothes dried instantly. As the three of us huddled around our laptop working on an update for the education program, I was amazed to see Manaa's pickup pull up outside. He had estimated we should pass by Qitabit today, and had driven from Thumbrait across dusty tracks to get here. He quickly assured us he was only staying briefly, but had wanted to check on us and the Bedu. Inside the trailer Jamie, Leigh, and I chatted with him about the 140 kilometres (87 miles) we had ridden from Shisur and the remaining 75 kilometres (47 miles) to Mugshin. We were all pleased to be operating without support, and wanted to ensure this would continue in the more difficult sands that lay beyond Mugshin. So far we had been in the Bedu's backyard, but I sensed their apprehension about the lands beyond. Leigh suggested that, if the Bedu had not travelled in the big sands, then perhaps Manaa should look for a more experienced Rashid guide in Mugshin who could join us, but Manaa assured us our Bedu knew the land perfectly. It was very hard to get a straight answer; Manaa was so eager to please that he would answer positively to any question. Our predicament was further complicated by the pride of the Bait Kathir, who naturally could never ask another tribe for help, especially the Rashid, who Thesiger praised in *Arabian Sands* at the Bait Kathir's expense.

Leigh was once again frustrated. He was sceptical of Manaa's motivations, suspecting him of using the expedition to expand his own reputation and influence within the tribe, while not caring about our concerns. "I am a lawyer. I am paid to be cynical," he noted. I was not in the mood for listening to this. After we left Qitabit, I found myself slowly swaying on Crazy Dancer in the late-afternoon light. The growing tensions and disappointments that had simmered below the surface

during the last weeks finally felt overwhelming. It seemed as if nothing
I did satisfied Leigh. I could no longer put on a brave face. Singing riding
songs to myself more than to Crazy Dancer, I could feel warm tears
slowly flow down my sunburnt cheeks. I felt much better afterwards,
and in the silent, contemplative respite that follows an emotional storm,
I opened my eyes and looked all around, appreciating the enormity and
beauty that surrounded our slowly plodding caravan. As we ground
onwards, late afternoon slowly gave way to twilight.

Today, as every day, an unusual fringe of reddish purple ringed the
entire horizon just after sunset, a last reminder of the sun's glory. I had
never seen anything similar in my travels. As we rode into the night I
wondered if this was due to some atmospheric effect of fine dust in the
air. Ahead of us Ali Salim slowed, and I felt relieved to be finished the long
ride, but as Jamie and I prepared to dismount, Musallim signalled us to
stay on. Bin Ashara wanted to ride farther. It would be better riding for
both us and the camels in the cool evening air, he noted. First, however,
the Bedu had to attend to their evening prayers. Facing east towards
Mecca, Musallim and Ali Salim took their places behind Bin Ashara. The
three Bedu bowed their heads in unison. Both Musallim and Bin Ashara
took turns leading the prayers on the journey, a role usually, but not nec-
essarily, falling to the most elderly or respected figure.

"*Allaaaaahu Akbar* (God is great)!" Bin Ashara's warm voice echoed
across the unending desert wastes. Cool evening breezes had already
rushed in, bringing relief from the previous heat of the day. The others
joined him in prayer. Beneath us the camels stirred gently. The Bedu
knelt, and then prostrated themselves in unison, pressing their foreheads
against the sand. Their silhouetted forms were unmistakable, a sight seen
across the deserts of Arabia for the last fourteen hundred years.

The faith and discipline of the Bedu was humbling. Not once during
the three months we spent together did a single man ever miss a call to
prayer. Five times a day they faced Mecca and prostrated themselves in
*salat* (prayer). Every day they rose before dawn, despite cold and fatigue;
every day they dismounted at noon, during the height of heat. They

carefully washed their hands and feet each time, and although sand is permissible for doing this, water is preferable. It was better to go thirsty than be disrespectful. The Koran dictates a set number of *rakah* (a defined ritual of prayer and prostration) during each of the five daily prayers. By tradition it is accepted that travellers suffering the hardships of the road can reduce their prayer commitments, from seventeen *rakah* a day to eleven. These *rakah*, each a complete prayer routine itself, are divided between the day's five prayer times. When we had visitors at camp, those following the travellers' schedule carefully separated from the others, and the two groups would independently line up, so as to not disturb the other's routine.

Now the Bedu before us lifted their heads and turned them ritualistically from side to side, uttering "Peace be upon you, and the mercy of God," before once again lowering themselves and pressing their foreheads to the gravel. "Oh God, Thee do we serve and to Thee do we fly, and we are quick in the hope of Thy mercy and we fear Thy punishment. For surely Thy punishment overtakes the unbeliever."

With the prayer over the Bedu rejoined us, distinctive patches of light sand pressed against the dark skin of their foreheads and noses. These they rarely brushed off, and the mark of honour could often be seen lingering for hours.

As we moved on, now in darkness, the herd rode close together. Crazy Dancer, who had required encouragement all day to keep up, now pressed into the dark forms ahead. If he accidentally dropped behind, even a few metres, he would immediately rush forward, afraid of losing the others. Leigh rode behind me in the dark, and we chatted to pass the time. It helped take our minds off the gnawing pain we were experiencing. At one point I was sure I could take it no longer. I excavated through the depths of my saddlebag and retrieved two small coffee candies I had tucked away at Shisur. I leaned back carefully in the dark and passed one to Leigh. He laughed as he hungrily tore open the package. Very sensitive to caffeine, Leigh usually would have never considered having a coffee candy this late in the evening. Now they were an immense relief as on into the night we rode. It was pitch black around us; the waning moon had not yet risen. To the north a faint glow on the horizon indicated a distant oil camp near the Saudi Arabian border.

It was impossible to gauge the terrain we were riding over. Intermittent drops and rises would cause the camels to stumble unexpectedly, challenging both our balance and our nerves. After what seemed like an eternity, Bin Ashara slowed and the camels jostled together in a crowd.

"*Aweez grhalas? Canadi tabaan?* (You want to stop? Canadians tired?)" he asked.

I looked at Leigh and Jamie. We were wrecked, but we did not want to show it. I shook my head.

"Are the Bedu tired?" I asked.

"*La* (No)."

I was not sure why the Bedu wanted to continue pressing further. With a snap of his stick Bin Ashara urged his camel forward, and we were off again in a tight, jostling line. Every fifteen minutes the Bedu would ask if the Canadians wanted to stop. We would reply that it was their decision, they knew the country best, and we would ride until the Bedu considered it was time to stop. A small game of machismo had developed.

Finally, no one could take it any longer, and we pulled over. We were all completely exhausted, and we dropped from the camels, semiconsciously removing their saddles in the darkness. A small fire was lit as Ali Salim double-checked every hobble. We silently ate *khobz* cooked the day before. By the dancing firelight I could see all twelve of our camels quietly couched nearby, happily chewing their cud. Beyond them was complete darkness. We sipped a pot of sweet tea before falling asleep where we lay.

The next morning we rose to find we had entered a sea of gently rising and falling ridges. The desert surface here was moon-like. Our footprints were sharp and defined, sinking almost an inch deep in the loose dust and sand that uniformly coated the underlying gravel surface. We left camp early, planning to arrive at the oasis of Montessar by noon. I found myself riding beside Jamie. As we absent-mindedly steered our camels through the winding gravel rises, we laughed and exchanged glances from beneath our *masars*, talking of home, family, friends, and future plans.

The landscape unfolded slowly before us. Subtle rises would give way to new vistas as we passed, but everything was exposed gradually, due to the great distances and our slow rate of travel. What at first appeared as a canyon emerging from behind a ridge would change to a great open basin, and finally reveal itself as a wind-formed crater. I watched for hour after hour as new landscapes emerged from behind the subtle rise and fall of the desert.

At last we spotted the oasis of Montessar. Palms graced the horizon, their green an inviting change in the world of brown. As we drew near, intermittent grasses began to spring forth from the sands, and soon complete fields rustled in the noon breezes. Long before we reached the oasis, the sound of birdsong floated on the air. Brightly coloured migrants, passing on their way from Africa, flew in magnificent flocks. They darted to and fro, thousands of tiny birds turning in perfect unison.

A large concrete trough lay on the outskirts of the palm thickets. It was continuously filled with water that was slowly bubbling to the surface from an underground pipe. Overflow from the trough formed a small stream, ending nearby in a pond fringed with reeds. The shiny dark water made my heart sing, but sadly its strong sulphurous smell immediately ended any thoughts I had of a rinse-off. I noticed a thick grey and black blotchy residue formed along the banks of the tiny stream, and floating in its waters. I assumed it was some precipitate of dissolved salts in the underground water.

The camels jostled around the trough, but were hesitant to drink. We sang drinking songs to encourage them, and softly tugged downwards on their halters. Slowly, one after another, they sniffed and then drank the foul-smelling water. As I stood beside Crazy Dancer, I stroked his shoulders and thick neck, picking out ticks buried beneath his coat. I pulled out a fat grey tick, the size of a grape. As I turned it in my hand its tiny brown legs reached out ineffectively from a blood-gorged body. Tossing it into the trough, I was pleased to see it sink helplessly to the bottom. Experimenting with one of the smaller, spider-like ticks, I was less pleased to see that it floated on the surface, and to my horror began drifting downstream towards the other camels. I was unable to retrieve it with my stick, and it undoubtedly went on to a new home on another camel. The herd began to drift away after drinking their fill, but I assumed we would stop for our midday break in this paradise. I was disappointed when I realized that the Bedu planned to press on. Reluctantly we mounted and left the oasis behind.

At Montessar we had entered an almost imperceptible depression in the surrounding gravel flats. It was a wide, shallow trunk *wadi*, formed from the confluence of several major drainages emptying the northern slopes of the coastal mountains. Thesiger had known it as Wadi Umm al-Hait ("Mother of Life"), and he reported that twenty-five years of unbroken drought had left it devastated. Modern maps identify the parched drainage as Wadi Mugshin, and our Bedu knew it by that name.

The *wadi* still bore the marks of terrible drought. No longer could we see the salt bushes and sedges that had marked the previous days' riding. Instead, sun-bleached twigs and twisting roots lay scattered, half-buried in drifting sand. We entered a devastated stand of sprawling trees, a graveyard of splintered black skeletons standing dead and wasted in the baked gravel. A few hardy trees survived, but their sun-ravaged canopies offered little shade. Sand, blown from the huge dunes visible on the horizon, had begun to bury them. We rode into a sea of small crescent dunes. The steep faces, only a few metres in height, faced south, away from the winds that were building them. At first we wove a winding route through the maze, but soon grew tired of the slow progress. We found we could ride the camels straight up and over with little effort, and we resumed a straighter line.

As we followed the shallow depression, which was more than a kilometre wide, I tried to imagine it brimming with water. It would have
been more like a lake than a river. Such a huge volume of water in this
arid land seemed unbelievable, so I asked Bin Ashara, who was riding
beside me, if he had ever seen water in Wadi Mugshin. He cocked his
head back and thought.

"*Yimkin gabl khams-o-eshrin . . . la . . . arbin sanat* (Perhaps before
twenty-five . . . no . . . forty years). *Ana arbaa* (I was four)." The water
had been about half a metre deep, he indicated with his riding stick. It
must have been a massive flood.

We stopped an hour later, at the height of the afternoon heat, huddling in the shade of a scraggy tree. Why had we not stopped in the paradise of the oasis an hour before? I shook my head. Did Bedu have
absolutely no sense of aesthetics or forward planning, or did they love
the desert, feeling more comfortable here in the arid wastes than
amongst the cool, green refuge of the oasis? I never did learn the answer.
I wondered the same thing many evenings, as we would pass beautiful
areas – flat, with soft sand and many trees – only to camp shortly after
in a rocky hollow that was windswept and cramped. Did they not have
our instinct to look for a beautiful campsite?

That evening offered a change, however, because we camped atop
the largest dune we had yet seen. The site was perfect. A healthy stand of
trees dotted its crest and lee side. A large wind-scoop offered a perfect
cooking and sleeping shelter. We rode the camels right to the top, which
rose ten metres (32 ft.) above the gravel bed of the *wadi*. The large dunes
to the north were growing ever closer. They rose directly out of the flats
stretching beyond the *wadi*. The small dunes we were riding through
here in the *wadi* were only satellites of the massive sand ocean to our
north. Leigh estimated Mugshin lay only eighteen kilometres (11 miles)
to the east. *Inshalla*, we would be there before midday tomorrow. After
two days' rest, we would head north, into the ocean of sand.

# CHAPTER NINE

# Crisis at Mugshin

He protested. "Why do you speak like this, Umbarak? Listen to me! Have I not promised to take you across the Sands? I, Sultan. What do you want with the Rashid anyway? You know the Bait Kathir – old friends – your companions of last year. Did we fail you then? By God Umbarak, why do you doubt us now."

– Wilfred Thesiger, *Arabian Sands*

$\mathcal{T}$he tiny settlement of Mugshin straddles the border of two worlds. The red dunes rising on the horizon mark the beginning of the Empty Quarter, a sea of sand that runs continuously north to the Arabian Gulf. To the south lies the parched, flat land that we had just crossed, an uninterrupted series of gravel plains stretching back like an outstretched hand, its fingers pointing towards the southern coastal mountains near Salala and the Hadramaut in eastern Yemen. Between the thick fingers lay the great *wadis* that drain the distant ranges. By the time they reach Mugshin their courses are wide and shallow, the energy of even the largest floods being nearly spent. Here the waters dissipate; the floods slow, spread over the land, and are absorbed. Wadi Mugshin is the largest of these, a great trunk drainage, formed by the confluence of five major tributaries. Here at the settlement of the same name, Wadi

Mugshin is immensely wide, its shallow bed spanning several kilometres.

Despite the long droughts, a permanent water table remains below the ground. Near the town of Mugshin this water table surfaces, forming a small, salty pond. A nearby well provides access to the sweeter water lying below. The palm-fringed oasis has been a nomadic gathering point for centuries, the only permanent water in this massive tract of desert. It has also been the scene of countless battles, a natural target for passing raiders. In 1942 the Sultan of Oman, Said bin Tamour, ordered a fort erected beside the ponds. The small, white, clay brick building was built for strategic reasons, not to protect the water source, but rather to fly the Omani flag. When British planes flew over later that year to aid in the establishment of international borders in southern Arabia, it was clear to those observing from above how far north the sultan's rule reached.

In 1987 Oman established a government outpost at Mugshin. At the same time rows of semi-detached homes were constructed on the plateau south of the *wadi*. These subsidized dwellings were built to help stem the flow of local nomads to Oman's growing, large cities, and the Bedu who moved in brought with them many of their old ways. Goat pens built of corrugated aluminum have been built against the back doors of many homes, and livestock roam the enclosed yards. Camels can be seen everywhere, tethered to gates and drainpipes.

It was almost noon on February 17 when we emerged from the groves of *graf* trees and palms lining the far bank of Wadi Mugshin, and gazed across to the distant settlement. It was here, among one of these stands of trees, that fifty years earlier Thesiger's party had dragged Mashin, an older man travelling with them. His leg had been broken when he fell from a spooked camel. Many of the men in Thesiger's party were relatives of Mashin, and on their honour they could not leave him alone. If word spread that he was here defenceless, those with blood feuds against him would travel for weeks to kill him. A passerby might murder him only to steal his dagger. Still, a large number of the party could continue, but now even they refused to go further. This marked the start of problems Thesiger would face while trying to organize a group to accompany him across the big sands. The Bait Kathir, who until this point had assured him they would lead him through the dunes, now declared it impossible. Thesiger was delayed in Mugshin for nine days, and eventually gathered a team of four, two Rashid and two Bait Kathir tribesman, with whom he made his historic crossing. But similar to Bertram Thomas, who was forced to turn back here on his first attempt to cross the Empty Quarter almost twenty years before him, Thesiger very nearly never left Mugshin. We did not appreciate the weight of these omens as we approached the dusty town.

We had been riding all morning and the heat was now blazing down on us at full force. The eighteen kilometres (11 miles) had dragged on insufferably, and the tendons and ligaments in both my knees were protesting with every jarring step of the camel. Ahead of us stretched the *wadi*, several kilometres wide, its dry gravel bed spotted with brush. High on the opposite bank a water tower marked the settlement. We dropped down a steep sandy bank and entered a series of winding trails that ran across the flats towards the village. Soon we saw the characteristic dust raised by a racing vehicle rising from the flats ahead. Our arrival was expected, and the locals were already on their way to investigate. As we rode farther and farther out into the hot basin, I turned to look behind. Finally Leigh and Labian appeared at the crest of the bank, and followed our tracks down. Only a few more kilometres and Labian could be retired to serve as a pack camel. *Inshalla*, we could find a new and faster camel here for Leigh to ride.

A large cement trough had been built just west of town, providing water for the local herds. The sulphurous liquid spilled over one end, forming a small trickle that ran into a field of green grass below. As at Montessar, the tiny flow was thick with grey precipitate. It ran across our path, its winding course no thicker than a fire hose, but this was enough to spook the camels, who balked and jumped at the strange sight. No amount of encouragement from the saddle could get them across. Eventually we had to dismount, and with one person dragging

on the halter and another using a camel stick from behind, we marched
them over one at a time. Few showed any interest in drinking.

Abandoned camel pens marked the outskirts of town. Ali Salim
found one that seemed reasonably intact, and we herded all twelve
camels in. After removing the loads and saddles we gave them a fresh
bale of hay. A number of men gathered to greet us, and soon our Bedu
disappeared to visit friends and family in town. The *wali* kindly offered
Jamie, Leigh, and me a house to stay in during our rest stop. The semi-
furnished bungalow, hidden in the enclave of the government compound, provided a welcome respite as we dozed inside in the cool shade.

Manaa arrived later that afternoon. He had come to sell Labian and
buy us a new camel, as well as for a final check on the herd and the
Bedu before the trials that could lie ahead. We met at the home of
Ghranem bin Mohammed al-Toof, the brother of our friend Sheikh
Salem in Thumbrait, who hosted a lavish dinner. A large meal of fresh
goat and rice was served to the crowd, many of whom I did not recognize. We ate our fill and more, finding it impossible to refuse the constant press of hospitality. As we relaxed on cushions around the front
room after the feast, I began to realize many plans were being made for
parties and activities during our stay in Mugshin. Bait Kathir sheikhs
from around the country were arriving. Someone had called the television. Everyone wanted to be on film, partaking in dances or riding our
camels. I could only catch snippets of the conversation, but still I was
worried. We had planned only on a brief rest, and I knew what was
scheduled for one day could easily grow to take up three or four. Already
I suspected we would be delayed. I wondered what effect this might have
on Leigh's obvious frustration.

At our insistence, we met with Manaa and the Bedu early the next
morning. Manaa had suggested that everyone take a holiday, but before
they did I wanted to make sure that we agreed on a plan for the journey
northwards. Bin Ashara announced he was in a hurry to leave by car for
a trip back to Salala. He needed to have the army reservist stamp in his
passport updated before he crossed the border from Oman into Saudi

Arabia. I was annoyed that this had not been done before we started the expedition. The Islamic weekend began the next morning, and all government offices would be closed for two days. Bin Ashara's trip could take longer than expected. No amount of discussion seemed to impart our frustration to Manaa or the other Bedu.

"Mr. Saleh," they kept repeating, "please, by God, there is no problem, he can go now. *Inshalla*, he will get his stamp quickly, and when he comes back, we will start."

"But that is a problem," I would reply. "Maybe he is gone for three or four days. The hot season is coming. We have to keep moving." But they only looked at me with puzzled expressions.

"Daily days (every day) you worry," Manaa smiled. "*Inshalla*, he will return quickly."

I relented. I was making no headway.

Over the main floor of the bungalow, we spread a mass of maps covering our proposed route northwards from Mugshin. Many of the local Bedu had joined us, and soon everyone had a finger pointed at some place on the map. As we tried to discuss possible routes with Manaa, the others chatted noisily among themselves. I kept hearing the word *siyara* (truck) in the background, and I grew more annoyed. We had been clear about this issue with Manaa and the other Bedu from the very start, months before the expedition started. We had been in the country forty days now. We were trying to complete the journey without trucks following us every step of the way. Why did we have to revisit this issue at every opportunity? The unsupported leg from Shisur to Mugshin had been a success. Why not continue in this manner?

I asked Manaa why the Bedu always wanted a truck, and all the other discussions simultaneously stopped as everyone listened.

"The Sands are very difficult," Manaa explained. "The camels can make only twenty kilometres (12 miles) a day; before you made forty, maybe more. The land you just crossed, the Bedu know very well. They know every rock and every tree. This land is new. Maybe they will get lost?"

I suggested we consider taking a local Bedu who knew the Sands.

"Oh no, that is not necessary. *Inshalla*, we will be all right. We are Bedu, we know the desert."

"Have Bin Ashara or Musallim ever travelled there?"

"No."

"But we will be all right without a truck?" I asked rhetorically. The gathered crowd muttered indignantly. Could I not yet see we needed a truck? It was rude of me to press Manaa they thought.

"I think it is better you take a truck, Saleh." Manaa hastened to quiet the murmur.

"Is there anyone in Mugshin who can join us who has travelled the Sands?"

"We don't need anyone. They will know the way. Trust me, Saleh."

The arguments became circular. We were getting absolutely nowhere. More and more people dropped by the house – and of course joined in the discussion. Everyone told us we could not make it. We were crazy. We were asking the Bedu to face an unfair challenge. I felt like pulling my hair out. I thought what had been unfair was Manaa's assurance six months ago that it would be no problem if we didn't want a truck. But it was too late to communicate that.

In my broken Arabic I tried to explain that we had come for adventure and challenge. We knew we could cross the desert with vehicles. Others had done that. We hoped to live and travel as the Bedu of old had, on our own, alone in the desert with only our camels and ourselves. I appealed to their sense of history and pride.

Somewhere my meaning became confused. Bin Ashara and Musallim became irate. The word "adventure" to them meant "danger." Were we asking them to accompany us on a journey that was as dangerous as possible? To seek snake bites? To get lost in the desert? Even young Ali Salim, usually easy-going, looked angered, caught up in the excitement of the meeting. I tried to explain – yet again – that we were not trying to court danger, but we also did not want "the soft side" that they often

*Above: Bedu of southern Oman. The nomads of Arabia have faced massive changes in the last sixty years. With the discovery of oil, wealth has rushed into the region, and now the Bedu's culture is rapidly disappearing. Sheikh Mabhoot bin Said bin Salim (upper right), who as a boy of thirteen travelled with Thesiger up Wadi Ghadun, has experienced the upheaval first-hand.*

*Previous page: Descending into Wadi Ghadun, a deep canyon that we followed north for over 150 kilometres (90 miles), towards the sands of the Empty Quarter.*

*Above: The meat of a slaughtered camel is hung over an acacia tree to dry in the desert winds. Packed into two burlap sacks, the uncooked, unsalted meat helped sustain us for the entire journey.*

*Below: Bin Ashara (left) and Ali Salim riding in the sands beyond Mugshin. Note that Ali is seated on his heels, a precarious position all the Bedu favoured, but one that we found almost impossible.*

*Above: The view from Crazy Dancer's saddle, three metres (10 ft.) off the ground.*

*Opposite: Looking back towards the end of our caravan as we work our way across a gravel flat, footprints stretching off towards the horizon. Note the gerbers (goatskin bags) on the second pack animal.*

*Above: A camel stands silouhetted against the rising sun, shrouded in rare early-morning fog.*

*Opposite: Riding through the massive dunes fields of eastern Saudi Arabia.*

*Last page: Jamie atop a dune near the United Arab Emirates border. In the background lies a vast area of* sabkha, *or salt flats.*

proposed. It seemed to be too late. They were all indignant, Musallim especially. I had pushed too far.

After almost three hours, we could reach no resolution. I was exhausted. The effort to understand the quick Arabic translation and all the surrounding yelling had worn me out. We were no closer to deciding upon a route or making a contingency resupply plan. Jamie had tried to work through the frantic discussions with me, and we lay dejected on the maps spread all over the floor. Leigh also was not pleased with the meeting, but did not say much. His only comment was that the expedition had become a joke. Bin Ashara left town to get his passport stamped, and both Musallim and Ali Salim decided to accompany him. Manaa drove them all as far as Thumbrait, where he would look for a replacement for tired Labian.

We puttered away the remainder of the day, but a dark cloud had descended on our moods. Leigh was very quiet and reserved, missing dinners with the locals, and rarely talking. The next day offered no improvement. Neither Bin Ashara nor Manaa returned to Mugshin. Late that evening, while Jamie and I sat cleaning and sorting our camera gear, Leigh approached us, breaking his silence. To our dismay, he told us that he was seriously considering leaving the trip. It was not the physical discomfort that bothered him, rather the lack of control we had with the Bedu. The constant uncertainty in our plans and the complete unaccountability of the Bedu were driving him crazy, and he suggested perhaps he was not as much of a team player as he had originally thought. Leigh hated the unknown aspects of the journey, which no longer held much meaning for him. He had decided that, if things did not change, he would rather spend his time at home.

I had known Leigh was struggling. During the last few days both Jamie and I had tried to give him room, hoping he could find some resolution, but I had never suspected his angst was this extreme, and I was shocked at the thought he might depart. My initial instinct was to encourage him to stay and see the journey through. Jamie pointed out that, if he went home, he would always wonder what it would have been like to stick it out. It would be a question that would last his lifetime. Even if he found the trip insufferable, we were now only a month away from completing our journey. Couldn't he last just that little longer? In the grand scheme of things it was not really that much more.

Inside I realized I felt torn. I knew it would be a great loss for our team if Leigh left. No matter the outcome of our journey, we would have failed on some level; the three of us would not have completed the journey together. On the other hand, there was a part of me that wished Leigh would just leave. He seemed to have brought very little positive energy to the trip since we began, and his negative mood had spiralled downhill the whole time.

We sat around the table talking late into the night. There was no animosity or hard feelings. We just tried to make sense of a difficult situation. In the end Leigh agreed not to decide just yet; he would give the journey a probationary period. By the time we reached the border crossing at Butabol, a week's ride beyond Mugshin, he would make up his mind. I was still not sure what outcome I hoped for.

ربع الخالي

To make the deteriorating matters worse, the next morning, February 20, we received news that Manaa and the other Bedu would not return to Mugshin that day. We had already waited four days, two more than in our initial schedule, and there was no end of delays in sight. Leigh said nothing, but I feared this may have been the last straw. We knew something had to be done, and after much discussion we decided to drive to Thumbrait and deliver Manaa an ultimatum. Dressed in Western clothes for the first time since arriving in Thumbrait to begin training over five weeks earlier, we set out in a borrowed Land Cruiser. During the drive, we discussed our strategy. Since I spoke the most Arabic, I would bear the brunt of the negotiations. Jamie felt I needed to be very firm, and not afraid of getting angry. It was a good point, and I took it to heart. By nature I had a more gentle leadership style, which was becoming increasingly frustrating to the others since we saw few results. We briefly considered abandoning the Bedu altogether and travelling alone, but in the process we would have lost everything that the journey was about. Our goal at the meeting was to regain some control of the expedition.

Inside, I worried it was a battle we could never win; it went against the very nature of the men we travelled with. We had to work with them, not confront them, but I tried not to feel defeated before we started. I owed Jamie and Leigh my best effort.

We found Manaa when we reached Thumbrait, and secluded ourselves in a back room of the roadside restaurant. I tried forcefully yet clearly to outline why we were not happy. I explained that the five-day stop in Mugshin was not *mafi mushkilla* (no problem), as the Bedu thought. It was a *mushkilla* (problem), a *mushkilla kabir* (big problem). Before we reached Mugshin, Musallim had warned us daily that the hot season was coming soon, and we had to hurry. Together with the Bedu we had planned for a maximum two-day stop, and now Jamie, Leigh, and I had been waiting, doing nothing, for five days. From now on we would make the decisions, and work with the Bedu to make sure they were good and fair. Jamie jumped in, adding in no uncertain terms why the trip had been a failure so far. I was glad he did. It was not in my nature to get so angry, and I was happy for his input. If this plan failed, I wanted everyone to have given it their best shot. Leigh seemed genuinely pleased with the outcome when we finished. Although it felt like we had made progress, I wondered to myself if anything had really changed.

At the meeting we carefully went over the maps with Manaa, and laid out a plan for the next seven days. The team would head north for two days through uncertain sands to the tiny Bedu camp at Ramlat Mugshin. Thesiger had travelled from there directly on to Liwa, but we would be forced to parallel the Saudi Arabian border northeast until the border post at Butabol, the only point our visas could be checked, which lay approximately five days beyond. Everything made sense; finally we had a plan.

When we had started the journey almost a month earlier, we had left one of the camels behind in Thumbrait. Purple Knees, who was the prize of the herd Manaa had bought in the Emirates, had developed an infection behind the calluses of his front knees on the drive back from the U.A.E. His name arose from the purple aerosol disinfectant that the Bedu sprayed on his injuries. However, the infection never healed properly, and when we started the journey, Manaa decided that he needed still more rest. To replace him Manaa had bought a feisty camel, Bin Saeban, from a local widow, who would use the money to go on the *Haj* (pilgrimage). Now Purple Knees's infection had healed, and we returned to our training camp outside Thumbrait one last time. Purple Knees was loaded in the back of a pickup as a replacement for Labian.

Hastily we returned to Mugshin and made preparations to leave the next morning. Our personal gear had been ready and waiting for days. Manaa unlocked the shed where we stowed all our saddles and group gear. Jamie and Leigh emptied the dirty burlap food bags, cleaning all the containers and resupplying them with sugar, coffee, flour, rice, and tea. Ali Salim and I used a hose to fill all eight *gerbers* with fresh water, and delicately placed the near-bursting skins between camel blankets on the floor.

When the call to evening prayer echoed down the deserted tracks of Mugshin it seemed too early. I was already tired, and there was much more to do. The stress of the few last days, the division in our team, the general unhappiness, and our lack of progress had all worn heavily on us. Now, on the eve of our departure, I was happy to be moving again, but felt a lingering concern. Something was not quite right. When I finally retired to the army cot in our bungalow, I tossed and turned. A sadness tinged my sleep, and, when I awoke, I was not rested.

We had agreed to eat breakfast with the Bedu at six o'clock that morning, planning to leave by six-thirty. When the Bedu had still not arrived by seven o'clock, I knew I had better go and find them. I discovered the group comfortably sitting sipping coffee in Ghranem al-Toof's house, the site of our dinner the first night in Mugshin. They smiled, happy to see me, and asked me to stay for coffee and dates. I indicated that our departure time had long since come and gone, but they didn't seem to remember that plan. "Do not worry, we will be riding again soon," Bin Ashara told me. I sat briefly to join them for tea; it helped my nerves. Finally, by eight o'clock, they were ready.

When we arrived at the camel pen, a small crowd had already gathered to see us off. Slowly I saddled Crazy Dancer, the familiar routine putting both him and me at ease. One of the other camels had bitten his right ear, and it barely remained in place, attached only by a thin strip of flesh. I was happy the whole ear had not come off. I tried to clean the wound with salt and water, but Dancer preferred that I not touch the area, and made that very clear.

I noticed Labian galloping across the gravel flats outside the pens with Ali Salim bouncing nonchalantly on his bare back. At the end of the stretch Ali slowed Labian, and in one smooth movement swung a leg forward over the hump. He dropped softly to the ground and led the tall camel to a group of men who were gathered around Manaa. Labian was up for sale, and Ali had just performed a demonstration ride.

Further down the row of pens, Bin Ashara was inspecting a temperamental camel. One of her forelegs had been lassoed. While Bin Ashara stealthily approached her with a halter in hand, the frothing beast bucked and jumped wildly. At one point she sprang into the air, all four legs flying spastically off the ground in a display of her anger. Snapping and bellowing, she continually backed away from Bin Ashara. Finally, just as the Bedu's soothing whispers appeared to have calmed her, a young boy inexplicably whipped her on the behind. The frightening scene started over again. I was aghast when I learned Manaa was considering trading Labian for this berserk animal. A fierce-spirited, unbroken pack camel trying to break free of the caravan all day would upset the entire herd. We had enough problems with our own camels; we definitely did not need any more.

I found Manaa and implored him not to take the young female camel. "*Mafi mushkilla*," he replied. "Trust me, Saleh. She is a very strong camel."

So I could see!

"Her name is Bin Sahma. *Sahma* means 'beautiful.' Look at the shape of her hump. Long after the others are tired and starting to die she will keep walking. She is very strong."

The decision was already made. I had to put my faith in the Bedu, but I also knew I did not want the new camel tied anywhere near Crazy Dancer in the caravan!

I was making my final preparations to leave, slipping two full water bottles into my saddlebags, when Manaa approached me once again. He had come with a younger man that I had seen during one of our dinners in town.

"Saleh, you are my good friend," he began. "Daily days we have talked about how the journey will now be difficult. Last night I talked to many people from my family. This man knows the Sands. The way we planned to Ramlat Mugshin is very difficult; it will take many days. Instead there is a track heading north. This will be much faster and easier. From there you can cross the Sands directly to Butabol. I think this way is better. I have already talked to Bin Ashara and Musallim."

As he said this he pointed over my shoulder and I turned to look. Our three Bedu were already several hundred metres out of camp, leaving in the opposite direction to what we had planned. At the back of the caravan I could see the new wild camel bolting from side to side. Crazy Dancer was straining on his rope to join the departing group. I looked at Jamie, who was standing beside me, and we shrugged our shoulders. Only twelve hours after we had made out best effort to regain some leadership of the journey, every single aspect of the plan we arranged with the Bedu had changed.

We walked from town side by side with our four camels trailing behind us. Amazingly we did not feel discouraged. This appeared to be par for the course. Even Sir Wilfred had faced similar difficulties here at Mugshin.

# CHAPTER TEN

# In the Big Sands

> I looked round, seeking instinctively for some escape. There was no
> limit to my vision. Somewhere in the ultimate distance the sands
> merged into the sky, but in that infinity of space I could see no living
> thing, not even a withered plant to give me hope.
>
> — Wilfred Thesiger, *Arabian Sands*

We finally caught up to the Bedu, who had opened a substantial lead
after leaving Mugshin before us. The rutted track we followed out of
town slowly faded, and we headed north across rolling gravel plains.
Cresting each successive rise, I watched the red dunes on the horizon
ahead draw ever closer. After five days of rest at Mugshin the camels
were energetic, and constantly rearranged their order in line, surging
ahead and dropping back again. As I rode I was pleased to note my legs
had to strain to stretch around Crazy Dancer's distended belly. It was an
indication that he had drunk his fill before we left, and I knew he would
need it in the days to come.

As time passed, Leigh slowly dropped behind again. It seemed too
cruel a twist of fate. Why was his camel always the slow one? We had
discussed this before. Was it how he rode? Was he too heavy? He was
certainly much larger than the diminutive Bedu, but not much heavier

than Jamie or I. I wondered if his mood was picked up by his camel, or vice versa? Our camels had been travelling for more than three weeks, and were in good shape. *Inshalla*, Leigh's new camel, Purple Knees, just needed a few days to become accustomed to the daily effort.

The Bedu were ahead, chatting happily amongst themselves. They always seemed to ride just a bit faster, and despite watching them closely, I could never understand why. We could trot to catch up, but, as soon as our camels returned to a walking stride, they would begin to slowly fall behind. Even when we traded camels, the Bedu still rode faster on ours. Perhaps it was our weight; after all, we were nearly double their size. As the morning passed they continued to pull ever farther ahead.

I was riding with Jamie as we entered a long windswept roll between two sandy rises. Ahead of us the tracks of the Bedu disappeared around the corner. We decided to stop and wait for Leigh. He had long since dropped from sight, and we were concerned – mostly for his mood. We knew it could be very frustrating to constantly encourage a camel to keep up while the others surged effortlessly ahead. It was a lonely existence at the back. Jamie jumped down, taking the opportunity to relieve his bladder. I remained on top of Crazy Dancer, since the effort of dismounting in the heat seemed too great. Our four camels huddled closely together and silently waited.

Soon Leigh's bobbing head rose over the small dune behind us. After taking a quick break himself, Leigh and Jamie remounted their camels. Mr. T. rose immediately, but Purple Knees remained where he was, turning his head to roar in protest. Leigh flicked the reins, clicked his tongue, and slapped half-heartedly with his stick. Nothing could persuade the massive camel to stand. Jamie and I encouraged Leigh to be more firm, but I couldn't blame him for being timid. It was frightening to give the camel you are sitting on a hard whip. Leigh tried again. Nothing. The camel chewed its cud. Leigh sat expressionless. Somewhere behind the dune ahead, our Bedu rode farther and farther away, likely not yet having turned to look for us. The sun beat down. Jamie dismounted and heaved on Purple Knees's halter. I circled behind, riding as close as I could to Purple Knees, who still refused to budge.

Finally Leigh stood up and got off. With a mighty swing he flung his camel stick and muttered words of disgust. If there had been any way he could have left the expedition at that instant, I am sure he would have. Luckily we were in the middle of nowhere. Leigh grabbed Purple Knees's halter. The camel now stood, and Leigh led him on, labouring through the deep sand, as Jamie and I rode slowly beside him. We were all completely at a loss as to what to do next. This was obviously not a long-term solution; Leigh would soon falter in the terrible heat. I jumped down, and persuaded Leigh that we should give it one more try. Bravely he mounted and dug in with his heels from the saddle, I pulled forward on the halter, and Jamie rode up directly behind. Purple Knees roared with his lips pulled back, revealing rows of yellow teeth. Regurgitated cud spilled from his mouth. The smell of his awful breath assaulted me as I heaved on the reins, but slowly the camel lumbered to his knees.

Together we rode around the dune and out onto another large plain. It was terribly hot, and no one felt much like talking. To my amazement Leigh's camel had no problem keeping up. We had been worried he was exhausted from the short ride, but it now appeared he was just being stubborn. Ahead of us the Bedu had stopped under a large tree for lunch.

By the time the sun's rays had turned gold in the late afternoon, we had still not reached the Sands. In the rolling gravel foothills we arrived at a deserted Bedu encampment. Barbed wire and twisted wooden stakes marked the borders of former camel pens. An atrocious collection of garbage was strewn everywhere. In the sun-bleached piles I could see an old transistor radio, countless milk tins, a box-spring mattress, and torn cardboard boxes. Mixed in with the modern garbage were signs of the old life: an ancient brass coffee pot, with its characteristic long, pointed spout, and a hand-crafted bowl woven from palm fronds, traditionally used to collect camel's milk. As we picked a path through the camp I watched carefully for broken glass, not wanting to risk cutting the sensitive feet of our camels. Beyond the clearing lay a cement trough filled with stagnant green water. After dropping their loads, the camels almost stampeded in their haste to drink.

Bin Ashara discovered that one of the cedar spikes securing the frame of his saddle had cracked and broken sometime during the day. As coffee and tea boiled on the fire, Ali Salim helped Bin Ashara roam the compound looking for repair material to salvage from the debris. Jamie, Leigh, and I worked with Musallim to hobble all the camels and then securely tethered them to nearby trees and shrubs. Later that evening we bathed by the trough. The water was refreshing, and we did not know when we might be able to rinse again.

Hours after I had drifted asleep by the fire, I was startled awake by the sound of camels. I sat up and, in the darkness, I could vaguely make out of a mass of milling forms across the clearing. Bin Ashara suddenly leaped from under his blankets and dashed towards them yelling and waving a stick. A large herd of free-ranging camels had stumbled across us while heading for the water at the nearby trough. Camels can be gregarious, but also have a defined social order within the herd. Now the two herds were simultaneously greeting and challenging each other, and our camels were in danger, as they were tethered and helpless. Our two large bulls struggled against their restraints, frothing at the mouth. Musallim loaded a shell into the chamber of his gun, ready to scare away the intruders with a blast. We stoked the fire, which threw only a small ring of light out into the black desert. Bin Ashara returned, but did not get back into his blankets. Instead he sat up, remaining watchful. The passing herd did not leave, but instead lingered among the trees just beyond the light of our flickering fire. Occasionally one would cry out with a mournful sound, further exciting our camels. Sometime late at night they disappeared into the darkness, but we all had a long night and a fitful sleep.

In the morning a thick fog blanketed our camp, which the rising sun lit with warm hues of orange and yellow, silhouetting the camels. I had never seen a daybreak like this in the desert, and wondered where the moisture could have come from. As we saddled and loaded the camels, Musallim noticed the rear saddle strap on the large bull, Swad, had slipped forward. It is important that the strap lie behind the drooping triangular flap of the camel's penis sheath, otherwise it can prevent the animal from urinating. Musallim called me over to help, and indicated that I should hold the camel's halter down to prevent him from rising. As he handed me the reins, Musallim quietly mumbled "*Ghralee balek* (Be careful)." I barely heard him. I held the halter as tightly as I could, directly under Swad's massive jaw, noting with surprise the care Musallim took slowly approaching Swad's rear quarter. I had never seen him tentative around the camels before. He poked and prodded the strap from a distance with his camel stick, and then lightly kicked the couched camel on its rear legs, hoping Swad would reposition himself in a manner that allowed for better access. Ali Salim came to help Musallim, and together they delicately tugged on the strap with the crooks of their sticks.

Suddenly, Swad swung his head and caught my forearm in his massive mouth. I jerked back instinctively, and before he could bite down hard on my arm it slipped from his grasp, uninjured apart from two long bruises where his canine teeth had run from my elbow to my wrist. "*Hamdulilla*," the Bedu whispered, shaking their heads. I concurred. Camels' jaws are terribly powerful, and stories of crushed bones and dismembered limbs are not uncommon. We had become complacent, and the incident was a reminder that we could not for an instant lower our guard.

## ربع الخالي

By early afternoon we started leaving the gravel plains behind. Ahead of us towered the Sands. Reaching hypnotically towards us was a series of small crescent dunes, each less than a metre (3 ft.) in height. Insignificant in the face of the towering wall behind, these signalled the continual movement of the desert, the slow colonization of these flats by wind-borne sand. Weaving through the small rises, we arrived at the base of the first massive dune. To our left, a winding buttress led upward towards a pass on the high summit ridge above. We followed its course. The camels strained together, but uttered no sound of complaint. Ali Salim carefully picked a route with a steady gradient, minimizing their work. On steep sections we had to lean far forward in our saddles and hold on to the camels' manes. I turned to look behind as we rose higher. The gravel plains stretched as far as the eye could see.

A faint breeze whispered over the high dune as we arrived at the top, bringing a welcome relief from the heat. We broke for midday. The scorching sand burned the delicate sides and tops of our sandalled feet as we searched for wood, which was more sparsely scattered than ever. We were forced to run short distances and then stop, quickly burying our feet in the cooler sand that lay below. Leigh rigged an old headwrap between a tripod and a large bush in an effort to create some shade. All six of us fit underneath, jammed together like a human jigsaw. The thermometer read over fifty degrees Celsius (120°F) in the shade. I was happy sipping on my water bottle, but the Bedu craved a hot drink, even in this heat, and Musallim lit a fire to brew tea. The radiant heat close beside us seemed almost unnoticeable in comparison to that of the sun and the hot sand. Lying down, I could look out on the delicate forms of the wind-blown sand around us. The massive dune was itself covered by a series of smaller dunes in an endlessly repeating pattern.

As the afternoon lingered on, the Bedu showed no sign of rousing from beneath the small patch of shade. Again something felt wrong, but I could not put my finger on it. When Bin Ashara left to search for more firewood, I began to suspect they planned to stop here for the day, and asked Musallim if we were going to continue. He only shook his head.

After Bin Ashara returned, we tried to determine why we had stopped. No clear answer was forthcoming, but eventually it emerged that the Bedu wanted to talk with Manaa before continuing. They were defensive, but it appeared that they were unsure of the route, and afraid of getting lost in the big sands. We could easily see where we were on the map, and the route onward seemed challenging but straightforward. Manaa had mentioned nothing to me about seeing us again before the border at Butabol, but the Bedu would not budge until they had talked to him once again and assumed he would follow our tracks at least this far before turning east to follow the four-wheel track leading towards the coast and then back to Butabol. *Inshalla*, he might drive by today or tomorrow. *Allah karim* (God is merciful). We argued, but their minds were already set. With nothing to do, we waited. All of us were frustrated. Leigh's mood was beyond sour.

Several hours later I was out shooting photographs in the fading light, when, in the distance below, I saw headlights racing across the flats. We signalled with a flashlight, and the truck turned its course directly towards us. Five minutes later Manaa arrived. Jamie and Leigh wanted to call his bluff and threaten to cancel the trip if nothing changed. Tired and frustrated, but not willing to follow through with the ultimatum, I instead sat with Manaa. He promised once again the vehicle would leave us for good and head directly towards Butabol. Along the way it would leave several bales of hay. The grazing was too poor to support our camels. I would have preferred no support at all, but I could not judge the camels and land well enough to argue. We rehashed the issues, pored over the maps, and consulted with Bin Ashara to ensure he agreed. The plan seemed logical; we would try once again.

صحراء

The next morning we watered the camels from the two hundred-litre (50 gal.) drum carried on the pickup. Then we walked down the steep backside of the dune, and rode out onto a great gravel flat. A few minutes later the truck roared by heading north, and I hoped it was the last we would see of it for some time. As he passed, Manaa yelled from his window that something looked wrong with Jamie's camel, Mr. T. Although none of us could detect a limp in his gait, Mr. T. was not his usual self, and throughout the morning he stayed near the back of the pack.

The terrain now consisted of alternating dune chains and flats. The mountainous dune chains ran roughly east to west, directly across our route, and appeared to stretch from one horizon to the other. Our map showed that many of them ran for over a hundred kilometres. They rose hundreds of metres above the valley floors, in some places gradually rolling and in others drastically steep. Between the dunes were mirror-flat expanses of gravel and baked mud. There was markedly less life here than on the steppes we crossed while travelling to Mugshin. Only a few hardy bushes dotted the desiccated land. We tried to maintain our northward bearing, but were forced to meander as we searched for breaks in the dunes' imposing faces. The temperature rose quickly once again, and by mid-morning it was insufferably hot. I had felt dizzy at breakfast, and had added a dash of rehydration powder to my water bottles. The hot, salty liquid tasted foul, but my dizziness had returned, and I forced myself to drink some more.

Riding provided endless time for contemplation. Weeks earlier, when I first confronted the long days of monotony and discomfort, I had found my mind drifting to thoughts of home. Never before had I so clearly been able to recall every female I had ever known, briefly met, or even hoped to meet. Then abruptly, after only three days, thoughts of women ended. Food had overtaken them on the scale of importance, and I dreamed of vegetables, crisp baby carrots – but even that only lasted a day, and was followed by the simplicity of a cool, clear glass of water. In the end even dreams of water faded, and the pull of home no longer intruded. Never before had I so completely lived the moment. I was conscious only of our group, the camels, and the journey. Around us I sensed the desert, lingering hypnotically in the periphery of both my thoughts and vision.

As the temperature continued to rise, Mr. T. began to drop farther and farther back. I tried to wait with Crazy Dancer, but he disliked being left behind and often fought to catch the others. Jamie and I rode in silence. It was too hot to talk. Mr. T.'s pace dropped to a slow shuttle, and he was noticeably favouring a rear leg, but we had no option but to continue. Luckily the Bedu had stopped just ahead, on the opposite side of a large salt plain. The white crust reflected the sun cruelly; both my eyes and head ached. The few hundred metres between us seemed to last an eternity. Finally we limped up to the grove of dry bushes where Musallim and the others waited. The Bedu said nothing, for the heat was draining them as well. Their camels were already tied to nearby bushes, and they slowly wandered about collecting firewood. Leigh explained that Bin Ashara was preparing to brand Mr. T.

Branding, or *wasm*, is common among Arabia's nomads. It is used as medicine on both themselves and their camels. Nearly all the Bedu we met had a scar from a childhood branding. Most common was a circular mark directly between the eyes, where it was believed to release the evil spirits that cause headaches. When I inquired further, many pulled up their sleeves and robes, exposing brands on their shoulders and thighs. Camels are branded for two reasons, identification and healing. Crazy Dancer had two brands directly over his right jaw. When I asked Manaa why this would have been done, he told me it was either because he wasn't eating enough, or because he used to grind his teeth.

The thought of a fire in this heat was unimaginable. I didn't even have the energy to rustle through my saddlebags in the search for water. Every movement seemed to create more heat than it was worth. I just wanted to stand still. Even lying down on the baking ground would be too hot. Soon a small fire was going. Musallim and Bin Ashara crouched to inspect Mr. T. They carefully probed his flank, using both single fingers and then the knuckles of their fists. They did this while Mr. T. was couched, and then they stood him up and repeated the procedure. They slowly walked him in circles, quietly murmuring as they watched his tentative stride. Finally they agreed on a point a foot behind his right elbow, on top of a thick muscle overlaying his forward ribs. Bin Ashara went to his saddlebags, and returned with his 7.62-mm rifle. He slowly unscrewed the long metal cleaning rod and buried one end in the fire.

The other end he covered in sand, so it wouldn't become too hot to handle. Ali Salim tied Mr. T. down, and Jamie came to comfort him.

Jamie and I looked at each other. I knew he must feel terrible – both that Mr. T. was hurt and that he would now suffer a branding. I tried to imagine how I would have felt if it had been Crazy Dancer they were going to brand. I know I would have wondered if it would do any good. A brand just did not seem like good medicine, especially on this raging hot day.

Bin Ashara checked the cleaning rod; its end was now red-hot. He gave a slight nod to Ali, who pulled Mr. T.'s head back to the opposite side, preventing him from rising or seeing the branding. Bin Ashara grabbed the poker with a wrap of cloth from his *dishdasha* and sprinted from the fire. Carefully aligning the rod, he pressed the red-hot metal against Mr. T.'s forward flank. The fur flashed away in flames, and below the hide crackled. Thick grey smoke poured from the spot. Bin Ashara spun the rod and pressed again. Another great plume of smoke swirled upwards. Bin Ashara returned to the fire and replaced the poker in the flames. He repeated the process three more times. Throughout the branding Mr. T. never once bellowed in protest. I could not tell how painful it had been for him. He was left with a new T-shaped brand, this one having three distinctive downward strokes underneath the cross bar. When the procedure was finally finished, Jamie stayed beside him, gently stroking his muzzle.

Ali Salim brewed a pot of tea, and we drank the hot, clear liquid while crouched around the glowing embers. The sun was so bright that removing our sunglasses almost blinded us. Although the fire was close, I could not notice its heat. This was the hottest day so far. We didn't think to pull our thermometer out, but in the shade of a saddlebag the daily high read over fifty degrees Celsius. There was no shade here, and after fifteen minutes we slowly prepared to leave. With his saddle removed and only a light halter holding him, Mr. T. was tied behind Crazy Dancer, where I tried to keep an eye on him. Amazingly, his limp was almost gone, and by evening he had returned to normal. Jamie rode a thin grey camel who had previously carried a load of water, her two *gerbers* now empty. The opposite of Mr. T., she pranced lightly with high choppy steps, leaving Leigh and me far behind. Jamie would never ride Mr. T. again, although he would prove to be a strong pack camel for the duration of our journey.

By four o'clock we arrived on the shoulder of a dune where Manaa had dropped a single bale of hay. I felt I could not ride another minute. I was very tired and dizzy, the loss of electrolytes associated with dehydration, I assumed. I had already finished the two litres (half a gallon) of water I had mixed with flavoured crystals at lunch, and Musallim shot me a dirty look as I stooped to refill a bottle from a *gerber*. The Bedu wanted to continue, so we let the camels each eat a small handful of the hay, and strapped the rest on the bull's back. We camped later that evening in a silent valley, finally stopping on the low ramparts of a great dune chain. The shallow sand slopes offered only meagre grazing for the hungry camels.

Every night, we excavated shallow pits in the sand and settled to sleep in our bags and blankets near the dying fire – and every morning we arose to find an amazing array of delicate tracks traced around us in the fine, flour-like sand. Many were made by dung beetles – usually buried in the sand for much of the day – while on their nightly searches for camel droppings. Deeper imprints with smooth centres told the story of those who had been lucky enough to find a treasure, roll it away with their back feet, and then bury it under the sand, creating a small mound. Other tracks were made by the ticks that constantly fell from our camels. We could see where their fat bodies had dropped and scurried great distances before they also buried themselves. Most alarming was the realization we had come to a few nights earlier. A large scorpion had been frightened from its hiding place under a small shrub near the fire. Only after it scurried away across the sand and disappeared into the darkness did we realize that many of the tracks we had seen circling our bags each night were identical to those it had left. Luckily we had not yet had any nocturnal visitors in our sleeping bags.

## ربع الخالي

Each day the *sabkha* (salt flats) grew wider, and the dunes higher. Our route was twisting and convoluted. Once, after riding forty long kilometres (25 miles) we checked the map and discovered we had progressed only twenty kilometres (12 miles) in a straight line. Each day the heat grew worse, and more debilitating. By noon of the fourth day the camels refused to go farther. Atop a small sand plateau between two massive dunes, we stopped to let them rest. There they collapsed, and offered no protest as we unsaddled them in the suffocating heat. Jamie and Leigh again erected a small shelter, made from a headwrap, and all of us crowded underneath. Musallim, intent on having hot tea – for reasons that eluded me – lit a fire beside us. I lay face down under the headwrap, happy finally to be still. Leigh's digital thermometer read fifty-two-point-one degrees Celsius (126°F) in the shade. We picked half-heartedly at sandy pieces of dry camel meat. The effort to chew the hard jerky seemed too demanding. I lay back down. My eyes burned even when they were closed, and I slept only fitfully.

We began to resaddle after three in the afternoon. The camels had not drifted during the long break, which was a bad sign. Usually they wander off despite their hobbles to search for grazing. Many lay prostrate in the sand where we had dismounted. As we organized the loads, Jamie did a quick inventory of our water supply. He estimated there were only two full *gerbers*, or 30 litres (7.9 gal) left, a fraction of what I thought we had. At our current rate we would finish that in a day, and there were at least two full days' riding ahead of us until we would reach another well. It would be very tight, but we could probably stretch our supplies just far enough. There was no room for error.

As we mounted our camels I felt stupid and angry at myself. How could we have been so careless? It had been difficult with six different users to properly monitor or ration the water, but that was no excuse. Our water was so obviously vital, it was unimaginable how irresponsible we seemed to have been. I became acutely aware of how vulnerable we were. If our water ran out in this heat, we would be incapacitated in a day, and die shortly thereafter. Should anything happen to our camels, there was no way we could walk out of this land under our own power. We would do much better simply to stop, cease all unnecessary exertions, and radio for help. Deep in this featureless terrain, our lives depended utterly on our camels. The dangers of the desert are subtle, but severe – and they had sneaked up on us.

As these thoughts passed through my head, I instinctively checked my saddlebags. I had two full litres of water. I knew they were there, but still I felt compelled to check the bottles, to verify that they were indeed full. I decided to save them for the evening, to savour the liquid as I lay resting in my sleeping bag, recovering from the day. I had drunk a litre (0.26 gal.) at lunch, and the worst of the heat had already passed. But even as I made this decision, aware as I was of our finite water supply, I began to experience thirst as I never had before. My mind seemed drawn to a dry scratching forming in my throat. I could not help but think how a little sip would help. I cast my attention elsewhere, and tried to chat with Bin Ashara, who rode by my side. He only looked at me detachedly but did not say much, also suffering in the heat. I sang the "Huron Carol" quietly to myself, and thought of geese flying over a snow-blanketed landscape. I thought of water again.

I had flavoured my water with lemon-lime crystals at lunch, just enough to take the edge off the rotting leather taste supplied by the *gerber*. Maybe just one little sip would be all right. It certainly would help the dust in my throat. I battled the urge for an hour. I had never known thirst in this way before; I tried to quantify it, and examine it; describe it; face it head-on rather than being scared. It seemed a thirst of the mind, not of the body, a longing for water I simply could not have.

No distraction could take my mind off my desire to drink. I reached down and felt the bottles through my saddlebags. I imagined I could hear the water sloshing, and could stand it no longer. I capitulated and took one small sip, but it was hardly enough. I had only just replaced the bottle when I reached for it again. This time even a gulp seemed to have no impact on my consuming thirst. Hearing a familiar clink beside me, I turned to look. Bin Ashara had just taken a sip from his canteen. I watched him replace the cap. He moved slowly, looking drawn and worn. His eyes were not as lively as they usually were. We nodded at each other, and both turned to look at the flats stretching out in front of us. We rode for another four hours. When we finally stopped that evening, I had finished both of the bottles I had sworn I would try to save. I felt ashamed.

We slowly hobbled the camels. Most were so exhausted that they simply lay down in the sand after being unloaded. We had a few scraps of meat to eat, and Ali Salim dug out the remains of our dates. Cooking either rice or *khobz* was out of the question. Both required too much water. As we prepared to bed down for the night I decided to recheck our vital water supplies. The eight *gerbers* had been carefully piled between camel blankets away from the fire. None were completely full. Two were empty, and the rest contained varying amounts of water. Carefully estimating the water remaining in each, I found there were almost three full skins or 45 litres (12 gal) in total. *Hamdulilla*, our situation was much better than we thought. We each filled a bottle. I added a solution of electrolyte salts to mine and placed it beside my sleeping bag. I woke often, fighting a nagging dehydration, and rejoiced every time I did, realizing that I could take a sip from my bottle. The foul *gerber* water never tasted so refreshing.

I awoke to the sound of a vehicle speeding across the flats below us. The night was black, and the vehicle's headlights appeared as two bouncing points in the distance. I knew substantial smuggling traffic moved through these remote areas, although we had seen no recent signs of it. Trucks laden with illegal workers travelled from Yemen through Oman to the U.A.E., returning with guns and spare automobile parts. Bin Ashara and Musallim both jumped up. They always slept with their loaded guns by their heads, and now they stood and watched the headlights pass. Musallim fired a shot in the air. The truck slowed and turned to point directly at us. Although it had stopped more than a kilometre away, both Bin Ashara and Musallim now had their guns shouldered, watching intently. I wondered where I would dive if a gunfight broke out. Sadly, the only protection I could think of were the thick bodies of the nearby camels.

After what seemed like ages, two shots rang from the truck – a traditional salutation of peace. The truck drove towards us. It was Manaa, with Touarish and Salim Ali; they had grown worried and come to look for us in the desert. I appreciated their concern, but once again lamented our loss of solitude. However, at three-thirty in the morning, I decided we could discuss it the next day. Despite the late hour, desert hospitality dictated that we should light a fire and prepare food. Huddled in blankets, we sat eating handfuls of hot rice, boiled with a ration of our dried meat.

صحراء

The pickup had a drum of fresh water aboard, and in the morning we watered the devastated herd. Many were now so weak that they had not risen from where they had dropped the night before. It was amazing how they had deteriorated. The camels had all drunk only four days earlier, but I doubted they could have continued more than a day further. I marvelled at the apparent decline in camel endurance over the last fifty years. Thesiger's party had gone sixteen days at one point, and nomads grazing in the cool of winter had been known to travel for fifty days between wells.

Bin Ashara and Musallim looked over the milling herd as we prepared and packed the loads. Mr. T. was still not fit to ride, and the small camel to which Jamie had transferred was tiring under his weight. Purple Knees seemed to be deteriorating as well. He was thin, lethargic, and very unfriendly. The big camel we had all felt so empathetic towards after his initial knee problems did not seem to be meshing well with the herd. He was an ornery loner, and appeared to be growing thinner daily. Leigh was transferred to the big bull Swad, and Jamie would ride Tynoona, one of the initially wild camels. *Hamdulilla*, Crazy Dancer still maintained his good health, I thought silently.

Because of the shift, Bin Ashara would ride the strong pack camel Bin Sabien. Just saddling her was a battle; she would rise and try to escape at every opportunity. Bin Ashara, only a tiny man working beside the massive camel, was soon forced to cinch both her forelegs closed. As she continued to fight, he tied her halter to her tail, wrapping Bin Sabien's head back against her body, and preventing her from standing. It was a frightfully intimidating scene as the strong-willed camel, now effectively tied in a knot, continued to squirm, snap, and roar. Bin Ashara calmly continued to work around her, mounting the saddle pieces. At one point Bin Sabien managed to nip Bin Ashara's arm, despite his quick and deft movements. Without pausing, Bin Ashara reached down, shovelled a large handful of sand into the open mouth that was preparing to bite again, wrapped a rope over the writhing head, tightly strapped her mouth shut, and then stood on her head as he calmly finished adjusting the saddle. There was not an ounce of callousness in Bin Ashara's actions. He respected the camels greatly, and treated them with the most love of any of our Bedu. But, given an inch, the camels would take a mile, and Bin Ashara was unflinchingly firm in the face of their temper tantrums.

On the desolate *sabkha* flats our caravan stretched out. I watched in amazement as, far ahead, Bin Ashara fought to control his camel. Bin Sabien's mood had not improved as the day progressed. She now dashed to and fro across the plains, raising clouds of dust in her fits of bucking, trying desperately to throw Bin Ashara off. He sat perched only on his knees. Three times I watched Bin Ashara dismount and tighten her halter, only to bravely remount again and face the same struggle. Bin Ashara's physical endurance, dexterity, and patience were astounding. In camp that evening I quietly asked him how he felt. First checking that the others were out of earshot, he admitted that he was sore and tired. I offered him some anti-inflammatories to help ease the pain, which he gladly took.

ربع الخالي

Late the next day, February 27, after another blisteringly long ride, we arrived at the remote Omani border-patrol outpost of Butabol. Rounding the corner of a massive sand buttress, we saw the fortified buildings shimmering in the distance, tucked into a receding corner of a long flat, starkly out of place in the otherwise monotonous desolation. The only access to the outpost is by winding desert tracks, and the journey from Muscat takes two full days, although it is only four hundred kilometres (250 miles). As we approached the compound, a dishevelled black dog rushed out to greet us, barking at the camels. He quickly retreated as the herd ignored him and drew closer. A beautiful garden grew against one wall of the fort, fed by the station's waste water. Colourful birds darted between the small trees and bushes. Their songs were so loud and distinct, that I grew aware of the silence we lived with in the desert. The lush green, the tiny flowers, the birds, the colours, just this tiny splash in the sea of brown was comforting.

We were all tired. The heat and worries of the last week had been demanding on us, on the Bedu, and on the camels. We were planning to take a one-day rest here before crossing the border to Saudi Arabia, and I eagerly anticipated the break. A group of soldiers emerged from the gates to greet us, and although they knew we were coming, they still stared with disbelief at our ragged team. We were led into the compound, where a large volleyball court occupied the centre of the grounds, and concrete barracks lined the perimeter. From a distant room I could hear a television, and the muffled sounds of Asian MTV. We were invited to sit on a thick carpet in the shade of the officer's mess. Coffee and dates had been laid out, but I preferred the cool water available from an ancient refrigerator by the gate. Jamie and Leigh drifted to sleep as the Arabic conversation swirled around us, and I felt myself fading.

Later, when the crowd dispersed, we rinsed off in the wash hall. As I was brushing my tangled hair, Bin Ashara called me aside. He told me he had received a message through the border police that Manaa was waiting for us in Arda, only thirty kilometres (20 miles) away across the border in Saudi Arabia. Bin Ashara wanted to ride tomorrow, and have a rest day there, instead. I knew this was not what we had planned, but Bin Ashara was insistent, which was unusual. I chatted with Jamie and Leigh. None of us were keen to saddle up and leave the next day; the thought of lying amongst the trees and birds in the lush compound had already weakened us. But it was only one more day, so we agreed to push on.

The track between the two border posts of Butabol and Arda wound through stunning orange dunes. We skirted huge fins of sand, their sharp edges rising in curving lines to summits far above us. A steady wind was building, and billowing plumes of sand blew from the dune crests, like spindrift snow from a mountain ridge. On the sheltered leeward faces, swirling gusts lifted a fine layer of sand. The suspended grains danced across the flat surfaces in mesmerizing patterns, fluid sheets shifting in unison, drawn across the windswept faces.

Crossing the border between Oman and Saudi Arabia seemed sadly anticlimactic. There was a small concrete post set in the sand, and a bronze plaque on top was inscribed with the names of the two nations. The boundary had little significance in the desert, for the land contin- ued on unchanged ahead. I thought about all the effort it had taken to gain permission to enter Saudi Arabia. All the negotiations, the overseas trips, and the couriered letters. It had been a year-long effort. Jamie, who was riding just behind me, yelled out in celebration. He, as much as anyone, knew what had been involved in reaching this point. We marked the moment together and yelled ahead to Leigh as the almost unnoticeable border passed by. Beside us the Bedu chatted ceaselessly, unaware of the change.

After several hours a chaotic mess of industrial garbage, half covered by the drifting sands, indicated we were nearing "civilization." Rounding a final bend we could see the buildings of Saudi Arabia's most remote border post wavering like a mirage in the distance. Before us stretched a final white salt flat. But the Bedu had turned and were heading away, up the valley. I could not figure out where they were going. Staring out on the flat I eventually saw the imperceptible lines of a wire fence, hidden amongst the shimmering heat waves. Somewhere out there on the flats a military runway blocked our path, and we were forced to ride around the obstacle. It took another hour to arrive at the buildings that had originally appeared only minutes away.

Arda looked like a ghost town. Derelict frames of ancient trucks dotted the periphery. Drifting sand covered piles of trash, and sprouted with tendrils of desert grass. Beyond the compound lay a small pond, dug directly out of the baked gravel. The water was a by-product of nearby oil production. Our camels rushed forward to the sparkling waters, and we had to stop them from plunging their heads in to drink. Bin Ashara tested the water by mouth, which had a terrible stench of sulphur, and he reported that it was too saline. It would make the camels sick. A few men finally emerged from behind the barbed wire of the police barracks. They offered us water from their large storage tanks, and the camels drank greedily from a trough.

A small compound with living quarters for the Bedu workers at the site lay to one side of the outpost. Why they had been separated from the rest of the staff I did not discover. Bin Ashara and Musallim had friends here, extended family who offered us food and shelter. We stayed that night on the floor of a portable trailer. Manaa arrived later with Chris Beale, who had come to ensure the border crossing went smoothly. They had spent the day driving north to scout sections of our proposed route, and now they wanted to discuss its feasibility with us. We decided to let it wait till the morning. We all needed sleep. As we huddled down in our blankets, I asked Manaa if he had sent word for us to meet him here?

"*La*," he replied. "I thought you would rest in Butabol. It is much nicer there."

CHAPTER ELEVEN

# Sandstorm

A rush of wind heated by the burning desert floor does more than parch the lips and redden the eyes. It desiccates the whole body, destroying its capacity to cool itself. Experienced a short time, it is misery; for a long time, it brings death to men and camels.

— W. Polk and W. Mares, *Passing Brave*

*F*rom Arda our plan was to veer northwest towards Liwa, the oasis which Thesiger had reached to complete his first crossing of the Empty Quarter. On route to Liwa we would have to traverse a range of dunes made famous by Thesiger in *Arabian Sands*, the immense Uruq a Shaiba. We did not know what Manaa and Chris had in mind when they said they wanted to meet us to discuss our options, but I suspected that they had discovered a more direct route heading directly north towards the United Arab Emirates border at Umm a Zamel. We had been pushed around enough by the Bedu and our support staff during the expedition. I went into our meeting with Manaa and Chris that morning closed to any changes on our predetermined route northwards.

I sat listening impassively as first Manaa, and then Chris, detailed the options. Towards Liwa the entire route was sand, very loose, deep sand that would slow our camels to less than half their regular pace, they claimed. The only well on the route was too sulphurous for even the camels to drink. The area had seen a terrible drought, and there was no grazing anywhere. The alternate route to Umm a Zamel also passed through the massive dunes, but was more direct. There was more hard gravel and *sabkha* that way, meaning we could reach the U.A.E. border in ten days. They doubted that we could ever reach Liwa, and if we did it would take at least thirty days. Now summer was coming fast, they warned.

Our Bedu sat listening, nodding in agreement. Chris, who had earlier insisted that the stretch to Liwa was simple, now backed Manaa, saying it was impossible. A local Bedu raised his eyebrows and added, "*Umm a Zamel, zain; Liwa, ghralas* (Umm a Zamel, good; Liwa, finished)." He meant we would die. There was little doubt what the mood was of those around the fire, though Manaa agreed that it was up to us, and he would support whatever decision we made. However, he added, if we chose to stick with our original route towards Liwa, he thought the only solution would be to hire an eighteen-wheel water tanker to follow us on the route, watering the camels each day.

As the arguments and reasons poured over us like unwelcome rain, I sat detached, realizing that we could no longer stem this tide. We had come to Arabia with a romanticized vision of desert travel, of an unsupported pilgrimage across this great land. We had been blessed with an experience of unrivalled proportions, we had witnessed endless vignettes, poignant beyond words. We had learned – about the desert, the camels, the Bedu, and ourselves. But our vision had remained elusive. I realized it may have disappeared forever, passed to a bygone era. We theoretically could insist on taking the route to the Liwa, but if the Bedu did not share in our desire for adventure, we would never find it, no matter what route we were on. Perhaps the problem lay in our expectations; maybe we were asking for too much.

I was suspicious of many of the arguments presented against the longer route, but that didn't really matter. Maybe the camels couldn't drink from the well, and maybe they could. Maybe the sand was loose and difficult. We had been warned of similar difficulties with the sands lying ahead when we were in Mugshin. The locals and our Bedu alike vehemently insisted our progress would drop from the forty kilometres (25 miles) per day we averaged after Shisur to less than twenty kilometres (12 miles) a day when we entered the Sands. Yet the reverse had been true: despite the terrible heat and soft sand we had averaged fifty kilometres (30 miles) a day! The tiny reasons piled like bricks against us were not the issue. If the desire was not in Manaa and the Bedu's hearts, travelling the longer route to Liwa would only bring out the very worst in our journey. I feared we would become a travelling roadshow, hay and water supplied as we endured the "meaningless penance" of the ride. There was no challenge, no daring, no adventure there.

Jamie, Leigh, and I retreated to a remote trailer to discuss our options. As we left the fire, in one breath the Bedu assured us they would support us whatever the decision we made, but in the other warned us to be reasonable.

Leigh had no doubt the choice was clear. We should head to Umm a Zamel and onwards to the coast at Abu Dhabi. Jamie was resolute. He would rather fail in an attempt to travel to Liwa than succeed on the new route. I was somewhere in between, but my resolve had broken. I agreed with Leigh. I could see no benefit in going to Liwa. The entourage of support trucks that would undoubtedly follow if we chose to take the longer route dispelled any magic it once held. I hoped we could salvage the adventure by travelling alone and unsupported straight northwards.

The discussion became terribly heated. Arguments for both routes could be made to appear eminently sensible. We were concerned for the camels. Was it fair to take them into the difficult sands towards Liwa? But as soon as that was voiced by one, the hypocrisy was pointed out by others. We had pushed the camels already. I myself had even once speculated that they enjoyed the work, suggesting it gave them a sense of purpose or pride. What about the Bedu? Was it fair to force them to accompany us on the longer route? But was it fair for them to force our hand now? We had planned the expedition from the start, and had raised the money with which we now paid them. We spiralled downwards.

We were filming the discussion, and this made us all conscious of the position we took and its portrayal. I suggested we shut the camera off, but that was immediately vetoed. Jamie suggested a vote. What else was there to do? The outcome was obvious. We emerged to discuss our non-unanimous resolution with the Bedu.

The three of us had never been so low. Jamie sat in the truck, half-heartedly writing in his journal. Leigh stayed inside the trailer. My heart felt torn in half. Most of all I despaired that the journey we all cared so passionately about now seemed to be coming to naught. I chatted with Jamie through the truck window. He said he was the one who lost the vote; he should be the one feeling bad. I suppose he was right, but no one had won or lost. How I wished we had taken the time – however long it took – to come to a decision by consensus, rather than by the divisive vote. I felt I had let Jamie down, but I knew I would vote the same way again if pressed.

Throughout the afternoon the winds built, until the small compound was blasted by drifting sand. The air took on an ominous brownish tinge, and the sun was blotted from view, appearing only as a faint glowing orb through the thick dust. It seemed like pathetic fallacy: nature definitely mirrored our mood. The Bedu in the encampment donned protective hats and goggles, looking like a collection of characters from *Mad Max*. They warned us that this wind would last for twelve days, which was why it was called the *Eitnashar* (twelve). We should beware.

# صحراء

The next morning the winds had dropped, offering a respite. Inside the trailer where we slept, small drifts had formed by the windows and doors; the fine sand had blown through the smallest cracks. The pile of gear we left outside was almost completely buried. I brushed Crazy

Dancer's coat, trying to remove the encrusted layers of sand from his fur. We despondently loaded the camels and left across the *sabkha*, heading north towards Umm a Zamel. Sporadic gusts carried occasional sand-devil twisters racing across the flats.

By ten-thirty that morning the wind had begun to build again, carrying with it an ever-increasing amount of sand and dust. The sun again faded, and visibility dropped. I strained to catch glimpses of the camels ahead through lulls in the wind. Our tracks were getting filled in quickly, and we fought to ensure we could always see the riders both ahead and behind. I rewrapped my *masar*, carefully covering both my mouth and ears. I left only a slim crack for my eyes. Even with this protection, my mouth soon filled with blowing sand. My teeth grated together like sandpaper with every bump of the camel. Jamie rode beside me, and looking up I saw his lips were covered in a thick paste of lip balm and sand grains. He yelled, but I found it hard to hear what he said. I tried to clean the sand from my ears, but only succeeded in pushing it in deeper.

Leigh was close behind us, and we rode on together, revelling in the exhilaration of the turmoil. The raw power was stunning. This was a face of the desert we had not seen before. There is something very basic and elemental about a storm. It has the same universal appeal as staring out over the ocean, or huddling by the embers of a fire. Perhaps it runs far back in our psyche; generations of our ancestors have been moved by the same sights. We leaned into the swirling dust and wind, straining to follow Musallim. How ironic it seemed that only a hardship like this could remove our lingering tensions.

ربع الخالي

By three-thirty, progress in the maelstrom had become impossible. We were in danger of losing each other. After cresting a rolling pass, we stopped to camp in a sheltered wind-scoop, notched between two high dunes. The Bedu dropped everything on the ground as they removed it from the camels. Their rifles were the only pieces of gear that they treated with any respect or dignity. The speed of sand accumulation and drifting was astounding; I watched a thick rope become covered in before my eyes. Jamie, Leigh, and I fought a battle against time to retrieve all the equipment before it was lost, piling our saddles and bags carefully under camel blankets.

The Bedu soon buried themselves in blankets. It was impossible to do much else. Even wearing a pair of goggles, I could feel the fine sand swirling behind the lenses. Sand grains grated behind my eyelids with every blink. Trying to clean our eyes was out of the question, since our hands themselves were useless, covered by a thin layer of fine sand. I tried to drink from my water bottle, but sand blew in despite my efforts to seal the opening with my hand. The water had become a grainy soup. I couldn't even rinse out my mouth, which was full of sand. Eating was also out of the question. I did not dare open a duffel bag.

Rather than sitting around, Jamie and I headed off to climb the large dune on whose flanks we were camped. We struggled upwards through loose sand, following a winding ridge towards the summit. In places the turbulent air was thick with sand, and I could feel its added force in the wind. Elsewhere only a thin film floated over the dune's flat surfaces. These flows hit the ridge line at great speed and were launched into the air, forming massive brown plumes. The wind tore at our feet, and sand eroded out around them. After forty-five minutes we reached the top, leaving much of the maelstrom behind. Huge clouds of dust and sand swirled by below us, others rushed up to engulf us, obscuring our view like mist on a mountain summit. Through breaks in the dark sky, we could make out the valley up which we had travelled, and beyond that more chains of dunes stretching into the distance. We sat and drank in the power swirling around us.

From the summit the sand dropped away in all directions. We found the steepest face we could and ran straight down towards our camp below, tumbling through the deep sands. On the descent we noticed six of our camels had strayed from camp, and we circled wide to herd them back. As we arrived at the valley floor, a distant rumble caught our attention. We listened, and as we did I felt an almost imperceptible drop of rain hit my sunburnt foot. And then around us in the sand tiny craters appeared, as more heavy drops began to land. Without warning a squall-line hit; the sky turned black and the wind began to scream like a jet engine. The dunes seemed to tear apart before our eyes. Massive plumes launched from the ridges high above, curling back in swirling eddies to enshroud us. The camels turned from the wind and dropped to their knees. Jamie and I struggled to stand up, leaning into the blast for balance.

Then it started to rain in earnest. After a ten-year drought, huge drops began pounding the sand surface. Carried almost horizontally by the gusts, the rain hit us head-on. The front of my *dishdasha* was instantly soaked, while the back remained perfectly dry. We fought our way towards camp, where the others were staring in disbelief. I could only discern dim outlines through my goggles, which were smeared with sand and water.

As quickly as it came, it was gone – the rain, the wind, and the storm. A wonderful silence enveloped us. The landscape was transformed. In the dampness the dunes had assumed an even richer hue of red. The air was clear and cool, and the rains had settled all the dust. The Bedu sang and danced.

"*Hamdulilla, hamdulilla*," Musallim shouted, grinning impishly. The tranquillity lingered on into the evening. Our small party gathered quietly together by the smouldering remains of our fire, alone in the great emptiness of the desert.

Tired, we settled into our bags and blankets around the fire. I was covered in wet sand, which was all through my hair, beard, and clothes. Since trying to brush it away did not seem to work, I chose to ignore it. If I did not move, I could not feel it scratching me. During the night the rains returned. A heavy drizzle settled in, soon soaking through our overbags and blankets. I lay on the dark, wet sand, listening to rain drops beat down on the canvas I had pulled over my head. It seemed incredible after the heat we had endured that we now lay here, chilly and wet, waiting for dawn to break and the sun to warm us. Before morning the clouds passed, and once again we rose to a silent world. We could not saddle and load the camels until their coats dried, so while we waited Ali Salim fried a large pot of salted meat and fat over the fire.

# صحراء

As we rode in the quiet, clear morning, the true *sabkha* began to appear. The plains we had crossed up till now had been mostly gravel and dried mud. From here onwards they changed drastically in nature. Their baked surface, a hardened mixture of salt and sand, resembled ice suddenly frozen in the throes of spring break-up. Jagged edges and pointed shards reached up from the jumble, jingling as they broke underfoot. The *sabkha* had formed as a result of continual flood-and-evaporation cycles. The waters, rich in salt and other dissolved compounds, had left behind a caustic white residue, in places forming crystals, elsewhere mixing with sand to form the rock-hard flats.

This *sabkha* posed a threat to our camels. Bin Ashara picked up a tiny shard and demonstrated how each step would shave a small shred off the camel's foot pad. By the time they had walked a few kilometres, their entire protective callus would be gone, leaving the camel lame and unable to continue, destined to die out on the hot flats. We were forced to follow low, stretching drifts of sand reaching far out from the dunes, or to search for the tracks of vehicles whose weight had flattened the sharp edges.

These *sabkha* flats marked the edge of the legendary Umm as Samim ("Mother of Poison"), where the Empty Quarter's central dune ranges give way to a sea of quicksand, stretching three hundred kilometres (185 miles) across. The Umm as Samim is the product of three major *wadis* which empty Oman's eastern coastal mountains into a large shallow inland depression. Thousands of years of repeated flooding washed down piles of organic matter from the mountains, and the slowly decaying detritus mixed with damp salt and sand to create a bog. A thin sun-hardened crust formed after each successive flooding, trapping the moisture of the quagmire below. Faint dustings of windblown gypsum leave the quicksands indistinguishable from the surrounding *sabkha*. It is a dangerous land. Throughout history the local nomads have known that anyone breaking through the thin crust would became mired in the mud, and efforts to escape only worked them deeper.

Very few ventured out into the Umm as Samim, carefully following faint and often secret paths which traversed the sporadic regions of firm ground. Raiding parties had tried to escape through the maze, only to be swallowed up. When Thesiger passed by the opposite, eastern edge in 1949, he became the first European to see the quicksands. His Bedu recounted stories of entire caravans becoming lost and disappearing, men and camels alike.

The *sabkha* flats across which we now worked our way were extended fingers of the Umm as Samim, long since dried and hardened. As we rode, I noted places where the surface had broken and heaved, revealing a crust more than twenty centimetres (8 in.) thick, covering dry ground underneath. I gazed out to the east as we rode. Somewhere on the horizon the unending flats turned imperceptibly to quicksand. Farther out, the once-secret and faint tracks which marked the only routes of safe passage through the bogs had been overrun by the deep wheel ruts of heavy oil exploration and production equipment.

Here the sand dunes ran almost parallel to our course, and we spent long hours following their edges, saving the camels' foot pads while looking for occasional point to cross. Despite the challenging terrain we continued to cover good distances, riding up to ten hours each day and averaging fifty kilometres. On our fourth day beyond Arda we stopped a few kilometres short of what appeared to be a Saudi Arabian police post shown on our map. It began to rain lightly later that evening, and we buried ourselves in our sleeping bags without eating much.

Late at night a Saudi border-patrol vehicle pulled up. It had followed our tracks, and arrived with a platter of rice topped with boiled chicken.

The fresh supplies were welcome, as the camel meat we had dried a month earlier was now decidedly tough, very sandy, and home to a multitude of small beetles. We rose to welcome our guests, and, huddled around the fire, happily ate handfuls of the warm food. The kind men did not stay long, and after they left we cleaned our greasy hands in the sand and returned to our bedrolls. As we had noted early on in the journey, the Western concept of time has little place in Arabia. We ate when food was there, rising to greet visitors and prepare coffee no matter what the hour. The simplicity of our travel was so appealing. We needed very little, carried everything with us, and lay down to sleep in the sand whenever we needed to break.

In the morning the loading of the camels went quickly and without incident. After winding through an extended section of low dunes, we saw the Saudi border post ahead, a massive distribution of garbage and old industrial equipment strewn across a small *sabkha* flat. As we approached, a sickly looking camel and several mangy dogs ran out to greet us. I wondered if they were begging to join our caravan, and leave this sad place behind. I would have welcomed them, but Crazy Dancer growled and snapped his teeth. I supposed they would have to stay.

Past the police post, which lay in the middle of absolutely nowhere, we approached a massive dune blocking our path, and followed tire tracks that led into a winding wind-scoop. The route progressively narrowed and rose. Soon we were in a twisting canyon of sand. High wind-smoothed walls rose above, carved by years of swirling winds. The gully ended abruptly in an impossibly steep face. Bin Ashara rode straight at it, and started up. I leaned forward and held on to Crazy Dancer's neck as he too began to struggle up the steep slope. Incredibly, all twelve camels persevered, and, as we emerged onto the dune's rolling crest, the view was stunning. The sand chain on which we stood was more than a kilometre wide, and several hundred metres high. As we looked down its crest, it appeared to stretch infinitely in both directions. The wide, flat top was itself covered in a sea of smaller dunes of rich golden yellow. On the far side, our route dropped sharply towards another huge *sabkha* flat. The camels charged down the incline, and I could barely hold Crazy Dancer in control. I was forced to reach behind with one hand and grasp his tail to prevent myself from sliding forward over his hump.

The winds returned again that evening, filling the air with sand. We dropped many of the loads haphazardly, and the next morning I shuddered at the sight. Littered around camp, tattered corners of our blankets and saddles, caked in sand, poked through the flat surface of the new dunes, like the buried skeleton of a dinosaur. Amazingly we were able to find everything and dig it up.

As I prepared to saddle Crazy Dancer, I grabbed a half-buried blanket and shook the sand away. A painful sting rocketed up my leg from my foot. I looked down in surprise. A translucent yellow scorpion writhed in the sand beside me. It had fallen from its hiding place in the blanket and landed on the top of my foot, which it stung. I was shocked. I tried to quickly assess the situation, and reassured myself that none of the Arabian scorpions were lethal – at least not for adults. After calling the others over and showing them the fat, grotesquely prehistoric creature, I returned to saddling my camel, though Leigh wisely urged me to sit for a moment. I hadn't realized how shocked I felt, and I needed a few minutes to calm down. The sharp pain, similar to a bad wasp or bee sting, started to spread up my leg, through my calf and hamstring. I was concerned about how I would feel if it spread into my abdomen, but the pain soon receded back to my foot again. I convinced the others I would prefer to ride on than stay idly sitting about. After I took a large dose of ibuprofen, we continued loading, and were soon riding.

In the contemplative silence of the saddle, I assessed my foot. The pain was still sharp, but it seemed to vary. At times I imagined it had frozen solid and was now painfully defrosting. Later it seemed to be burning hot, as if covered in boiling liquid. Still later, I could imagine a small hacksaw cutting back and forth between the two toes where I had been stung. In this self-absorbed state I realized that the pain actually must have been quite bad. The giveaway was that, with the dosage of ibuprofen I had ingested, my normally intolerable saddle felt like a comfortable leather couch.

More and more tufts of tall sedges and desert grasses appeared as we continued north. There had been very little at the start of the journey, but now, as we approached the border with the U.A.E., sparse fields sprang up. Without breaking stride, Crazy Dancer would dart and weave, dropping his great neck to snatch mouthfuls of the succulent grass. At first I fought this behaviour, conditioned by our days among the diarrhea-causing salt bushes, but soon I realized my error and began steering him towards the clumps of grass, hoping to provide him with all the nourishment possible. At this point in the journey, every little bit helped, and I desperately wanted Crazy Dancer to remain healthy till the end. With my foot still throbbing from the scorpion sting, I rode on, absent-mindedly tapping Crazy Dancer with my stick.

Late in the afternoon Crazy Dancer stooped for a mouthful of grass, but suddenly decided it would be easier to eat if he were kneeling. He dropped to his front knees, and I was vaulted over his hump, landing directly on his head, driving it into the clump of grass. Crazy Dancer was as surprised as I was. As I rolled off to one side, winded but laughing, I looked back: his large dark eyes gazed inquisitively into mine. There was no anger or frustration at the sudden blow. I could have sworn he was concerned for me. As Leigh and Jamie caught up, also laughing, I jumped on and we continued.

Two more days of travel winding through the largest dunes yet brought us close to the U.A.E. border post at Umm a Zamel. We had traversed only a tiny portion of Saudi Arabia. As I looked at the route we had travelled on the map, I thought how ironic were the incredible efforts we had undergone to gain permission to enter the country. But they had been absolutely vital. Had we not been able to enter the Kingdom of Saudi Arabia we would have had to detour far to the east, around the quicksands of the Umm as Samim, and in the process leave the sands of the Empty Quarter. Instead, we had the great privilege of entering this region that few men have seen, the heart of the Empty Quarter, where dunes of the great desert swell to their most impressive heights in an astounding series of *uruqs* (chains). The toughest land was behind us. Now only 300 kilometres (185 miles) of rolling dunes lay between us and the coast.

# CHAPTER TWELVE

# The Coast at Last

Love of the desert seems at first to be against all reason; but the instinct of healthy man must be for it, and once known it draws him back forever.

— Gerald Du Gaury

Kilometres ahead of us a high steel fence stretched across the salt flats, marking the border between the Kingdom of Saudi Arabia and the United Arab Emirates. The border was a man-made abstraction, running in a perfectly straight line across *sabkha* and over dunes, irrespective of the land. Patrols for both countries operate around the clock on the graded tracks that run along either side of the tall fence. As we approached the impenetrable barrier, we swung to the right, heading towards the nearest port, the border crossing at Umm a Zamel.

An hour later we crested a large dune and looked out across a shallow valley ahead. Beyond we saw what appeared to be a medieval castle rising from the sand in the distance, surrounded by a lush plantation of trees. The impressive building was a new high-security prison, which had been built adjoining the border outpost. In this remote desert, I supposed a convict's hope of escape was dulled by the prospect of a quick recapture or an unpleasant death amongst the dunes.

I approached the border riding beside Bin Ashara and Musallim. The track we were following was funnelled between two high fences, and the route blocked by a red-and-white barrier. In the shade of an inspection hut, a group of prison guards and border officers sat playing cards. They seemed reluctant to rise, even as twelve camels approached their station. Eventually a small man jumped up and raised the road barrier, which was counter-balanced by a large boulder perched precariously on the opposite end, and we rode into the United Arab Emirates. Although it was only noon, we stopped just past the gate at the end of the plantation. A trough of fresh water allowed the camels to drink, and after quenching their thirst they stared hungrily at the lush trees growing on the other side of the fence. That evening we dined on a terrific feast inside the prison walls. From the small courtyard where we sat, we could hear occasional yells and screams echoing down the cement halls of the buildings around us.

One of my eyes had become irritated in the last few days. I seemed to have a grain of sand stuck in it, but despite Jamie's best efforts nothing could be found. Just the night before, as we had prepared to go to sleep, Jamie had carefully coated the affected eye in a thick ointment. While settling in by the fire and pulling my blankets up around my neck, I had accidentally flung a pile of sand from a corner of the blanket into my open eye, and it became mired in the ointment, which only aggravated the problem. Now the prison doctor, who ate across from me, noticed my discomfort. He kindly took me to his office, where he rinsed my eye and treated it with a lubricating wash. Later, as I lay awake in my sleeping bag, I realized that, when my eye was open, the pain was gone, but as soon as I closed it, the eye felt as if it were full of sand grains, which scratched with every movement. It must have been a mild case of sunblindness. Using duct tape, we created glare shields on the arms of my sunglasses, and after a few days the pain subsided.

ربع الخالي

*Jamie and Leigh ride ahead as we approach a lone graf tree in the golden dunes of the United Arab Emirates.*

*Above: Jamie pressing on into a building sandstorm.*

*Previous page: The caravan rides through a pass atop one of the mountainous dunes.*

*Below: At the height of the storm, the air was thick with sand, and dune ridges disintegrated before our eyes. Moments after this photo was taken, a squall line hit, with strong gusts that knocked even the camels to their knees.*

*Above: The storm passed quickly and the brief rains turned the surrounding dunes around a rich shade of red.*

*Below: The team nears civilization, only 150 kilometres (90 miles) from the coast of the Arabian Gulf. After thirty-eight days in the desert, we came across this remote gravel road, with three rows of irrigated trees running down each side.*

*Arriving on the beach in Abu Dhabi (left to right, me, Jamie, and Leigh)*

*His Highness Sheikh Zayed bin Sultan al-Nahyan, the president of the United Arab Emirates, greeting Leigh.*

*The end of the journey. Jamie, me, and Leigh riding on the final day.*

*Left: Saying goodbye to Crazy Dancer, my loyal companion for over forty days, was one of the hardest moments of the journey.*

*Below: Visiting Sir Wilfred Thesiger in London, more than fifty years after his historic journey. From left to right, Me, Sir Wilfred, Jamie, and Leigh.*

*Following page: Jamie leads Crazy Dancer and Mr. T. across the great gravel plains near Mugshin.*

Early the next morning we received a call from Stuart McDowall, the Canadian ambassador in Abu Dhabi. I had worked with Mr. McDowall before the trip while arranging visas, and now he relayed the exciting news that His Highness Sheikh Zayed, the president of the United Arab Emirates, had requested we attend an audience with him. The embassy, not knowing when we would arrive, had agreed to a meeting at his Al Wathba palace on March 13, six days from now. With more than three hundred kilometres (185 miles) left to travel before we reached the coast, this would require us to average sixty kilometres (37 miles) a day, an almost impossible pace. On a few occasions we had ridden more than fifty kilometres, but we were always exhausted the next day. I discussed our options with Jamie and Leigh. It would be a great honour to meet His Highness, but we did not want to set an unrealistic goal. If we could not arrive on time, we could arrange to be driven to see Sheikh Zayed and then complete the journey afterwards, but none of us were particularly keen on this. We all agreed we would prefer to finish the journey first, and celebrate after.

As we discussed our options, the Bedu caught wind of the possible visit and leaped into action. Previously they had seemed happy to pass the day relaxing in the shade of the plantation's flowering trees. Now, with visions of meeting His Highness and receiving magnificent gifts driving them on, they began to saddle the camels in an unstoppable rush. Jamie, Leigh, and I decided we would try. We would see how the next few days unfolded, and if we were unable to arrive on time, we would decide what to do then.

That afternoon we became mired in sands north of Umm a Zamel. An apparent shortcut led us into a series of dead-end *sabkha* flats and impassable high dune ridges. Frustrations escalated as we rode late into the evening, travelling more than forty-seven kilometres (29 miles) during the day, but cutting only twenty-five (15 miles) from our distance to the coast. It was not a good start. That evening we pored over the maps and GPS co-ordinates, hoping to cut a straighter course the next day.

The next morning we left the *sabkha* flats behind for good, and entered a sea of yellow dunes. Their rounded shapes were covered with soft sand, as if a great snowfall had blanketed the land. The small irregular dunes, no more than six metres (20 ft.) high, presented very difficult riding. There was no easy way through the maze, and we had to ride up, down, and over all the obstructions. The lead camels would gallop down the steep drops, dragging the pack camels behind. Then the team had to be vigorously encouraged to climb up the adjacent rises, since the animals preferred instead to graze in the small basins between. As we crested each successive dune I scanned the horizon, but the yellow, rolling swells stretched on endlessly in every direction.

The riding was exhilarating, but completely exhausting. Navigating through the dunes required all the riding skills we had gained on the trip. We coaxed the camels up narrow ridges, the sand sliding away on both sides. On the summits, with a click of the tongue and a gentle tap of our cane we dropped over ledges so impossibly steep that we had to grab the back of our saddles to avoid tumbling over the hump. The camels would gallop down, and we all bounced mercilessly in our saddles. My legs ached from gripping Crazy Dancer, my bottom felt worn and bruised, and both knees screamed in protest. Jamie was riding beside me. We laughed and cried simultaneously. The pain paled in comparison to the joy of riding and the stark beauty of the desolate region.

We eventually arrived at an unused track, where at one time a grader had ploughed straight through the dunes. The track was now covered in the same soft, yellow sand as the dunes, and looked like a magical winter road hidden under a layer of deep snow. Although we would travel for four more days through these desolate lands, our spell in the untouched core of the desert was quickly ending. We were nearing civilization: we would travel by graded track or gravel road for the remaining two hundred kilometres. We followed the untracked path until long after the sun had set, eventually collapsing exhausted in a hollow amongst the small dunes. We had travelled sixty-seven kilometres (42 miles) in one day.

Each day more vegetation appeared as we rode closer to the coast. Little difference would have been discernible to an uninitiated eye, but after so long in the barrens, we looked on each new burst of green as an encouraging sign of our progress. Sporadic *graf* trees stood alone, rooted only in sand, their branches spreading like willows. The troughs between the dunes were lined with desert shrubs and tufts of sedge. The small dunes we passed through now rode atop much larger chains, a steady rise and fall of the land which ran across our travel. The gradual swells in the land took hours to climb. As we slowly approached the top of each undulating crest, I would imagine that from the high vantage, we could look out across the sands to the Arabian Gulf, now tantalizingly close. But the view was always the same, an unending sea of sand stretching to the horizon in every direction. Still, each new crest brought with it the same hope. At some I caught an almost imperceptible freshness in the air, a subtle note of the ocean, faint but unmistakable.

The next day at lunch we reached a wide graded road of crushed stone. Three rows of trees were planted in the sand along each side. Chain-link fences enclosed the road, prevented roaming camels from devouring the precious greenery. Miles of hose ran through the plantations, and small holes by each tree provided irrigation in the dry sand. It was part of the government's project of reclaiming or beautifying the land. Thousands of kilometres of plantation have been created bordering the roads that stretch out like tentacles from Abu Dhabi and Dubai. Driving between the two cities one can hardly see the desert at all for the thick plantations of palms lining the highway. Here some one hundred and fifty kilometres (95 miles) from the crowded coast, I wondered how many people saw this massive project.

We followed the gravel road, and the camels tried to nibble on the seedling trees whenever we rested. As the sun set, we found a break in the fence and stopped amongst the nearby dunes. Almost immediately, a Land Cruiser arrived with our first visitors. How did they know we were here? They brought a small goat in the back seat, and it appeared as if our diet of dried meat was coming to an end. Manaa found our camp later that evening. He had been in Abu Dhabi making preparations for our arrival, and had scouted possible routes to the city. If we could ride fifty kilometres tomorrow, we would arrive on the outskirts of Abu Dhabi, making our final day only a short ride to the coast. He had not been able to drive all of the route, so he had estimated the distance based on a shortcut we would take! My memories of previous shortcuts made me cringe, but our poor maps of the U.A.E. offered no further information. The swampy coastal flats change constantly, and if any of their surfaces were wet and soft we might have to take lengthy detours.

After a quick breakfast we set off for the long ride. I occupied myself by playing with a GPS unit. Monitoring our speed on the camels, I noted that, in the cool of the morning they travelled six kilometres per hour (3.5 mph) at a walking pace. When the herd bunched together and became excited, they would break into a trot of eight kilometres per hour (5 mph). Our progress resembled the action of a Slinky. The camels would come together and begin trotting, which led to their spreading out and slowing, a process that was repeated over and over throughout the day.

Jamie and I decided to gallop our camels for a stretch. In the chaos of trying to navigate the sands and read my bouncing GPS, the maximum rate I was ever able to focus on was twenty-one kilometres per hour (13 mph). We slowed, enjoying the thrill of the gallop and the wind on our face. It took no encouragement for the Bedu to gallop. Spurred on by our charge, they raced past, singing loudly and waving their sticks high above their heads. Leigh joined the chase, and soon we were all caught up in the giddiness, singing and galloping across the sand. As the morning passed and the heat rose, I watched the pace slowly drop, until by noon we rarely exceeded five kilometres per hour (3 mph).

As the afternoon wore on it became apparent that we were nowhere near Abu Dhabi. Manaa had not returned from his scouting foray, and there was little to do but maintain our enthusiasm and continue riding. We had finally run out of food. All we had left was a handful of dates. Even our tea leaves had been finished at breakfast. We passed the time discussing Bin Ashara's shocking revelation that his main reason for wanting to visit North America was to find a large, second wife; one hundred and fifty kilograms (330 lb.) would do, two hundred kilograms (440 lb.) was his goal! Jamie, Leigh, and I almost fell off our camels laughing. Why so large? we asked. Bin Ashara shrugged; he had heard rumours of people so large, and he was simply curious.

After riding almost ten hours in the hot sun I was amazed how little I had drunk. At the beginning of our journey, I often finished both of my water bottles before noon. I would refill them at lunch and drink another two litres (0.5 gal.) before reaching camp in the evening. In the height of the heat I had been consuming between eight to ten litres (2.1-2.6 gal.) of water a day. Now, reaching into my saddlebags, I discovered I had drunk less than half a litre (0.1 gal.) since breakfast. Our bodies had slowly adapted to the heat.

When Manaa finally reappeared by five o'clock, the sun hung low in the sky, an orange sphere illuminating the low dust over the desert. His news was not good. We still had at least thirty kilometres (20 miles) to go, which was in itself the length of a reasonable day's ride. We already ached from the long hours in the saddle, and we had long since exceeded the recommended daily allowance of ibuprofen to ease the aches and pains. Musallim, Bin Ashara, and Ali Salim decided they had ridden enough for one day. Touarish and Salim Ali, who had arrived with Manaa, took their reins and prepared to form a long caravan. Manaa suggested we dismount and drive with him to Abu Dhabi. We would hear nothing of it. Despite the notable discomfort in my butt, I was enjoying the day. I laughed with Manaa as I explained we had come to ride, not drive, across the Empty Quarter.

"Saleh, be reasonable. Just a one-hour break," Manna pleaded.

I laughed. "Ya, Manaa, I know the Bedu are very tired, but today the Canadians feel very strong. We will keep going. *Mafi mushkilla.*"

Touarish had already started off at a trot with Salim Ali right behind. Manaa shook his head as I released Crazy Dancer's reins, and he instantly charged after the departing group. Leigh, Jamie, and I rode close together. The day had been exhausting, but it no longer seemed to matter. We were so close to the end. We joked and laughed about our plans for the city, what we would eat in the days ahead. Soon I could hear Manaa returning in the truck.

"Please take a break, my friends," he begged. We smiled at him. Nothing was going to stop us now.

"Ya, Manaa, what would people say if they found out we drove?" I joked.

"*Mafi mushkilla*. I can take care of that. No one will ever know." His concern was touching, and his reasoning humorously flawed. Over the course of the trip he had always cared for us deeply, the father wolf. He was exasperated. "You Canadians make me very angry. Hungry or angry? I do not know which is the right word, angry I think, you make me very angry." He laughed and turned away.

His voice slowly faded into the distance behind us. Moments later his pickup sped by one last time, and we were alone in the coolness of the approaching night.

ربع الخالي

The evening was tremendous. As in the first warm nights of summer, the air was a perfect temperature. The salty taste of the sea hung tantalizingly around us, like a faint note in a wine you think is there, but are never quite sure exists. Its promise of comfort and completion drove us on. In the darkness I rode beside Jamie, one moment sharing laughter, the next almost in tears as the grating pain in our knees and bottoms became unbearable. Somewhere in the darkness we slowly drifted apart. I rode alone. Hour after hour passed. I sensed the herd ahead of me, and a few riders behind me. I was alone with my thoughts on this last night of the trip. I felt the power of Crazy Dancer's back rippling beneath my legs with every step. I whispered his name, and he grunted, swivelling his ears back to hear if I had more to say. How could I tell him how much I had come to care for him? He swivelled his ears forward again, never breaking stride. Step after step he continued. I wondered how long he could keep it up. He seemed even stronger now in the cool air than he had twelve hours before.

At ten-thirty that night we finally reached the last dune of the great desert. We had ridden since seven o'clock in the morning and had travelled eighty-three kilometres (51 miles). Before us in the darkness stretched a plain of salt flats, and beyond that shimmered the lights of Abu Dhabi. The sweet scent of the Arabian Gulf washed over us.

News of our arrival had spread through the local Bedu community and a crowd was gathering. Mercedeses, Lincolns, and Land Cruisers were parked near a blazing fire. Radios blared familiar Western tunes, and blinding headlights continually swung off the nearby road to join the party. Men dressed in immaculate white *dishdashas* floated around the sand, some chatting by the fire, others holding hands – as is the custom with Arab men – and wandering through the crowd.

The commotion brought home to us that we were leaving the desert for good. I slowed, remaining hidden in the shadows to the side, craving the quiet of the desert, stealing one last moment alone with Crazy Dancer. The noise was making him nervous. I carefully removed his blankets, packing them in the saddlebag, wrapping it tight with a halter strap. This was a routine I had followed every night of our trip. A small group gathered around me. I shook a few hands and smiled.

I prepared to tie Crazy Dancer's hobble and handed the reins to a young boy who was silently watching close by. After living amongst the desert Bedu for two months, I had assumed any child would be accustomed to camels, and likely an expert rider himself. But this child dropped the rope, darting behind me in fright to hide from Crazy Dancer's inquisitive look. As I took his hand and led him back to the halter, I felt saddened, yet privileged to be part of the strange moment. I, a Canadian, was introducing this young Arab to camels, a defining part of his heritage. Fifty years ago it would have been inconceivable. So quickly have some skills been lost.

Great platters of rice and goat appeared, and we gathered to eat. Jamie disappeared in a truck to find his wife, Barbara, who had arrived in Abu Dhabi by plane that day. For the first time in three months Leigh and I ate alone. Surprisingly, I was not ravenous after the long day.

It was late when we finally wrapped ourselves in our bedrolls, and lay staring up at the dark sky. We were between two worlds. Already the lights of the nearby city stole the stars from half of the night sky. The distant sound of traffic muted the sounds of our camels quietly stirring in the nearby sand. The comforts of home that we had dreamed of for so long didn't seem important any longer. The suffering, privations, and discomfort of the journey seemed to pale in comparison to the beauty of the land we were leaving and the simplicity of life we had been touched by there. Now that we stood on its doorstep, the desert was calling us back. I knew I would miss the quiet nights, the simple unadorned life, and the camaraderie of our team, alone in the vast space of the dunes. Tonight was our last night in the desert, and I treasured every moment of it – the coolness of the night sand, the gentle breezes. Crazy Dancer sat somewhere amidst the herd, slowly chewing his cud. I called out, and he replied with a quiet grunt. I dreaded having to say goodbye to him. Tomorrow we would ride together one last time.

The next morning we saddled quickly and prepared to leave. A shocking mess was strewn around the fire: cases of pop and bottled water had been indiscriminately scattered everywhere. These city Arabs obviously had no better trash habits than their desert cousins. We half-heartedly tried to tidy up, collecting box after box of empties. The Bedu admonished us to forget about it as they waited, already on their camels.

"*Haboob, haboob* (Wind, wind)!" Bin Ashara yelled back, explaining how the mess would disappear if we left it.

Leigh had driven ahead with Manaa to scout filming locations near the beach. Jamie and I rode side by side, behind the three Bedu, who were out in front. We joined an asphalt road running towards the city. There was a quiet sense of anticipation, almost like a Christmas morning. In the silence we rode on, knowing how soon it would be shattered. A flooded *sabkha* flat appeared beside us before we realized it was there. Jamie and I stared at the water, which sparkled beautifully in the early morning sun. Shorebirds ran in the shallows, bobbing for tiny prawns. We breathed in the cool air deeply, sharing our last quiet moment of the trip.

Jamie had been a very good friend from the first day we had met three years before. Since both of us had ambitious and purposeful personalities, we had at times locked horns. Before the trip started I knew there was no one else with whom I would rather share a major expedition. Jamie is reliable, responsible, and strong, but so are many others. What sets James apart is his ability to find fun and joy in the mundane, and to appreciate the extraordinary often hidden amongst the expedition's inevitable frustrations. In setting out we had agreed that the most important goal of the trip was to finish better friends than we started. Otherwise, despite any other success, the expedition would be a failure. There were still many simmering emotional issues, leading back to even before we landed in Arabia, but I trusted time would help make these clear. Our friendship had strengthened. We had succeeded in our goal.

As we turned the last corner rounding the shallow salt-water reservoir, a major highway ran ahead of us, congested with traffic speeding in both directions. This would be one of our most difficult obstacles of the trip, and I worried about how we would navigate it. Leigh rejoined us near the highway, untying Swad from behind Musallim and remounting. Two police cars were waiting for us at the junction, and others soon joined them. As we rode down the shoulder, a constant stream of speeding trucks and cars whizzed by, many honking in apparent recognition. The Canadian embassy staff arrived, and someone showed us a newspaper. Our story was on the front page. A brigade of television and newspaper reporters found us, jumping from their cars to ask a question, and then speeding ahead to repeat the process. We continued,

skirting massive construction projects on the outskirts of the burgeoning city. At underpasses and bridges the police completely stopped the
traffic on the country's largest highway while our caravan of camels
lumbered by. We steadily ground on towards the heart of Abu Dhabi.

The day was intolerably hot, and it was worsened by riding over the
road's black asphalt surface. We were concerned about the camels' feet,
and veered off onto the gravel shoulders whenever possible. Around us
the cacophony of the city grew. Brakes squealed, engines roared, neon
signs flashed, and the air was thick with pollution. The camels ignored
everything, and rode on as if they were in the open desert. Crazy
Dancer never once balked or pulled on the reins. I was amazed, and
proud of him.

After hours of travelling along the motorway we eventually neared
the island on which Abu Dhabi is built. A curving bridge led over
sparkling blue waters to a palm-lined boulevard on the far side. Here
our route to the water was blocked by a divider of cast concrete too high
for the camels to cross; it appeared to run on interminably. We continued on down the road, looking for a way to the other side, and the
waters that awaited.

Suddenly we saw a small break in the barrier, and we slowly turned
our camels around the last bend, ahead of a long line of traffic patiently
waiting behind one of our police escorts. I began to feel the weight of the
moment as we converged on the small beach. We dismounted for the last
time, and lined up hand-in-hand with our Bedu companions. Our
camels seemed to sense the poignancy of the occasion, and stood quietly
watching in a tight circle. After slowly counting to three in Arabic, all six
of us stepped forward into the warm and salty waters of the Gulf. We
laughed, hugged, and brushed noses. Leigh threw Ali Salim farther out
into the blue waters, but had to dash in and retrieve him when we realized he could not swim. Bin Ashara doused his soiled headdress. The
Clarke brothers embraced. Time stood still. Although the water was not
in fact our true goal – that had been the journey itself – still the importance of the moment was not diminished. Emotion swept over us.

# CHAPTER THIRTEEN

## "Going into Exile"

We embraced for the last time. I said "Go in peace," and they
answered together, "Remain in the safe keeping of God, Umbarak."
. . . As the plane climbed over town and swung out above the sea, I
knew how it felt to go into exile.

> – Wilfred Thesiger, the last sentences of *Arabian Sands*

The journey may have been over, but our duties were only just beginning in Abu Dhabi. The local authorities had planned a full itinerary for
us. Still dripping with salt water, we loaded three of our camels into a
trailer and drove downtown for a photo session. Reporters hovered
around asking thousands of questions. I felt overwhelmed, having just
finished the journey; without time to reflect, I could offer few insights
beyond the obvious.

The local Bait Kathir community had organized a ceremonial
welcome at the Abu Dhabi fairgrounds. We arrived on our camels, and
were greeted by a team of Arabian horses and colourful riders. Although
these were probably some of the best Arabians in the world, I was acutely
aware of how strange and ungainly they looked to me. Somewhere in the
desert I had fallen in love with the long, graceful stride of the camel.
How strange the little horses looked with their squat bodies and short
legs. Worst of all was their prancing gait; they appeared very high-strung.

A group ran forward to greet us, and requested we stop outside the gates. We did, and soon the team of Arabian horses began racing in circles around our nervous herd. The camels fidgeted; some bucked. Swad became uncontrollably excited, and Leigh decided to dismount. As he swung his legs over the hump, Swad twisted violently away. I turned to watch with concern as, amid the mass of jostling camels, Leigh hung upside down, caught in the reins. Luckily he worked his way free and landed unceremoniously on his head.

With the display over, we were invited into a large wooden pavilion, where a circle of plush pillows awaited. Crowding in amongst more than one hundred local sheikhs and dignitaries, we drank cup after cup of the familiar cardamom-flavoured coffee. We were tired and weak from the events of the day, and the evening passed by in a blur. By the time we finally escaped at ten o'clock we had still not eaten anything solid since breakfast. At the hotel, I peeled off my salty *dishdasha* and collapsed in the soft bed, but my sleep would not last long. Early the next morning we were to meet officers from His Highness Sheikh Zayed's Protocol Office in preparation for our visit to the palace.

ربع الخالي

His Highness Sheikh Zayed bin Sultan al-Nahyan is an icon of the Arab world. He has been instrumental in the shaping and development of the United Arab Emirates. In 1971, when the country was formed, Sheikh Zayed was elected as the first president, and he has remained in office through five consecutive terms. Few leaders in modern history have successfully managed such significant change to their nation as Sheikh Zayed. He became the ruler of Abu Dhabi in 1966, when it was one of seven separate emirates (Sheikhdoms), all poor and undeveloped. Their flagging economies had never recovered from the collapse of the pearl market in the mid-thirties. Shortly before oil production began to flourish in the Gulf, Great Britain announced its intention of withdrawing from the region, then known as the Trucial States. Sheikh

Zayed rallied the seven separate emirates, forming a strong federation, which he has seen through dramatic growth and economic expansion. Today Abu Dhabi and Dubai are immaculate modern cities, where towering skyscrapers mingle with oases of green parkland and boulevards.

Sheikh Zayed's policies have always focussed on improving the lives of his people, and it is almost impossible to capture in words their respect for, and devotion to, their beloved ruler. His photograph can be seen everywhere – in hotel lobbies, on street signs, in offices. Most interesting are the cardboard cutouts that have a likeness of His Highness printed on one side. Nearly half the cars driving through downtown Abu Dhabi, from taxicabs to Mercedes, have the image of Sheikh Zayed smiling from the back seat, an imaginary passenger.

For us to be invited for an audience with the sheikh was an incredible privilege. Certainly our embassy was shocked. They had been trying for more than two years to gain an audience with His Highness, yet their calls were rarely returned. On the day of our arrival an amazed Under-Secretary confided to me that the embassy had received over twenty calls from the palace that very day to verify plans for our visit. It was unheard of, he said. I was honoured, and knew the sheikh's interest in our journey had deep roots.

Sheikh Zayed grew up in the desert. He was well known in his youth for his abilities to ride a camel, shoot a rifle, and fight. He values the lessons a harsh life has taught generations of his people, and worries now that many grow soft living in the cities. Fifty years before our arrival, Wilfred Thesiger visited Sheikh Zayed after his second crossing of the Empty Quarter. The two friends have met many times since.

Waking bleary-eyed from a deep sleep, on the morning of our audience, we threw on clean *dishdashas* and hurried down to meet the protocol officers in the hotel lobby. I stared longingly at the lavish buffet, the piles of fresh fruit and warm croissants, the steaming hotplates. Sadly, there was time to grab only a quick bite before leaving to gather at a camel racetrack outside the Al Wathba palace. Our Bedu were already there when we arrived, and they had transported our camels with them. We were to be escorted on our ride to the palace by a ceremonial team of the Royal Camel Guard, and their massive camels were lined up by a nearby fence. When I had first arrived in Arabia I never dreamed that I would one day be able to tell one camel from another, let alone a good one at a glance, yet I knew immediately that these camels were outstanding. Their coats were a uniform gold colour, thick and healthy. They stood a foot taller than our anemic-looking herd, and their massive muscles rippled with slow twitches as they waited patiently.

The Bedu's excitement and anticipation was unbridled. Everyone had on a freshly pressed *dishdasha*, heavily scented with *al-aut*, a strong, oaky Arabian fragrance. They ran about, checking and rechecking the saddles, ensuring everything was just right. I felt happy for them, and was touched by their enthusiasm. I joked with them, promising to tell His Highness that they wore a lot of perfume because they had not yet had a shower. Musallim scowled and frowned. Joking like this was wrong, he insisted. Touarish and Salim Ali, our two young drivers, became the most worried. They kept returning to demand that I be serious when talking with the sheikh, before rushing off to check their saddles once again.

The news of our invitation to meet the sheikh had reverberated through the extended Bedu community, and now we faced hordes of new friends wishing to accompany us as members of our party. The day before, we had arranged for several members of the Canadian embassy to accompany us, and I wanted to recognize the local Bait Kathir as well. The problem had snowballed beyond belief, and now I stood with Manaa studying an enormous list of men who were campaigning to join our audience. Most I had never heard of. Many kept grabbing me and explaining in detail why they should be there. Finally I had to leave it to Manaa, since he knew the customs, and what would be acceptable; as long as our whole team was together I was happy. In the end more than fifty additional people followed our small team of six.

At a signal from the protocol officers we mounted and rode with the Royal Camel Guard in a great pack towards the palace. All the camels were terribly excited; my forearms ached as I relentlessly fought Crazy Dancer for control. He wanted nothing more than to run to the front of the pack, and jostle with the big camels for superiority. It would be our last ride together. The large camels of the Royal Guard held their heads high, ignoring our upstart herd. A long, paved road led to the palace, and once through the gates we followed a cobblestone boulevard, barricaded on both sides by high walls. Finally we turned a corner and were led into a small courtyard by a group of professional-looking soldiers. We dismounted and couched our camels on a sandy shoulder. The tension was high as we waited in the hot sun. Armed guards swarmed about talking into hidden microphones on their lapels, securing the area.

Soon silence fell over the courtyard, and a parade of cars appeared at the gate. Several of Sheikh Zayed's sons arrived first. Though they were not recognizable to us, our Bedu companions looked on in awe at the powerful and influential men. At last the car carrying His Highness arrived. As it stopped in front of our group, a rear door swung open. Military officials from the other cars swarmed to help, and through the confusion I caught a glimpse of a stocky man slowly emerging. He wore dark glasses and sturdy boots, and although short and stooping slightly with age, he had a commanding presence. Eyeing our group, he announced something in Arabic. The men around him smiled and laughed. Beside me Manaa grinned and whispered a translation in my ear, "Where are the Canadians? I see only Bedu here!"

We lined up to shake hands, each of us having a brief chance to exchange greetings through an interpreter. I could not help but notice Sheikh Zayed's hands. They were thick and strong, marked by years of sun and heavy work. They did not appear to be the hands of a head of state. Musallim read a poem he had been carefully composing during the last days of our ride and, although I missed the meaning, the crowd applauded vigorously. Sheikh Zayed asked to keep a copy, and Musallim handed it to him, beaming. After we had all been introduced, I assumed the meeting was over, and was thrilled to find the entire group had been invited inside.

We left our herd in the care of the Royal Guard and were chauffeured out of the compound and up a large marble ramp to the main palace buildings. The meeting room was immense. Large windows filled one wall, overlooking the city of Abu Dhabi, which lay in the distance. Long rows of couches lined both sides of the hall, already filled with ministers of the government and senior army officers. At the centre, two couches remained open, one for His Excellency and the other for our team.

Jamie, Leigh, and I sat to the sheikh's left, and through his interpreter, who sat opposite us both, we shared details of our trip. The sheikh listened attentively and asked us many questions. What did we learn from the journey? Was it too tough for us? Did we enjoy it? How were the camels? Did we now eat with our hands? With the last question he reached forward and scooped a large fingerful of *haluva* (a pistachio-flavoured confection, served in the U.A.E. as a jelly) from a bowl I had been eyeing. My hunger from the desert was still strong, and I was only too glad to follow suit. The sheikh nodded with approval as Jamie, Leigh, and I took handful after handful of the sweet jelly.

"Many people visit His Highness, but very few eat like Bedu," the interpreter explained.

Our ambassador, who had joined us for the visit, leaned forward and scooped a small portion of *haluva* with a spoon that had been politely placed beside the bowl. Sheikh Zayed laughed and noted, "This man has not lived in the desert." We all enjoyed a moment's silence as servants brought coffee in tall brass pots.

His Highness related stories of his struggles while forming the country, when he brought the proud and free nomads under his leadership. Despite their immense respect for him, many refused to believe that a central government could ever bring good to the land. One Bait Kathir sheikh had declared that camels would grow flat backs before the seven emirates along the coast ever united to form a country.

"The man has still not been to see me in thirty years," said Sheikh Zayed. "He was a good friend, but he is proud; and of course, camels still have humps!"

He recalled how, with the introduction of the motor car, many of the Bedu in the land had come to him complaining that the value of their camel herds were being destroyed. His Highness urged them to be patient. God would not desert them. Through Sheikh Zayed's heavy support and encouragement, camel racing has attained prestigious status in the country. Now the value of the once almost worthless herds has skyrocketed.

The sheikh shared his belief that one has to suffer hardship and challenge to become a full person. He was worried that the harsh ways of the desert were becoming only a memory for many of the people in the region. Comfort is not a bad thing, His Highness explained, but one must understand suffering to be able to fully appreciate what we have now in this country. The changes had been great, he admitted, and he had done all he could to help his people.

The time passed quickly. Our meeting stretched well beyond what was scheduled, and two parties awaiting an audience were backed up in the antechamber. Eventually, we felt that we could take up no more of His Highness's time, and sadly tore ourselves away. We had been with him for nearly two and a half hours. Unaware of the significance of this, we returned to the camels. It was only later our ambassador explained that visiting heads of state are typically given twenty minutes to half an hour! Even more important to us was the news that returned from the Bedu. Their sources in the palace reported that Sheikh Zayed enjoyed our meeting, and had not been seen so happy in years.

## ربع الخالي

The last and most difficult part of the day still remained; we had to say goodbye to our camels, because we would now leave them behind at the palace as a gift for His Highness. We had all experienced very different relationships with our camels. I was the only one lucky enough to have ridden the same camel for the entire journey. Leigh had ridden four, and was not particularly fond of any of them. He bypassed the opportunity to bid farewell. Jamie and I drove back to collect our saddles as keepsakes and, most importantly, to visit one last time.

I had grown close to Crazy Dancer on the journey, coming to know him better than I ever thought possible. He had reciprocated with a growing trust. My debt to him was immeasurable. He had borne me across the desert with enduring patience. Every morning he quietly suffered my clumsy saddling attempts, and each night quietly waited while I hobbled him. I always saved him a few dates from each meal, and he would eat these delicately from my hand, then sniff my other hand, and look behind my back, searching for more. When I inspected him for ticks, he learned he could distract me with a friendly nuzzle. Day after day we had ridden together, and our bond had grown. I had spent more time with Crazy Dancer than with anyone else on the journey. His presence and silent comfort had supported me during the emotional strains of the expedition.

I slowly removed his saddle for the last time, fashioning a halter out of nylon rope with which to tie him. I had packed a last handful of dates from a container in the pickup. Bringing them over I crouched by his head.

Camels' eyes often water when they are tired or scared, and Crazy Dancer had cried the first day he arrived in our Thumbrait camp, over two months before. I had watched thick tears soak the fur under his eyes, and become caked with windblown sand. At that time I could not even touch his nose without his pulling back. Over the course of the journey I never imagined I would clean the dark tear-streaks; they had been there throughout. As I sat with him now, gently stroking his brow and whispering, I began absent-mindedly to roll the matted fur between my fingers and clean the remains of the sandy tears from his cheeks. It was the unconscious completion of a circle. Crazy

Dancer stared silently at me with his big brown eyes. Now it was my turn to cry.

It seemed such a loss. Everything we had developed – the understanding we had gained, the teamwork we had enjoyed  was finished. Never again would his ears turn quickly back as I whispered his name. Never again would my strange clicks bring him instantly to a trot.

I knew I was going in circles, getting nowhere but more upset. It was time to leave. I looked over at Jamie who was taking a picture of Mr. T., and decided not to disturb him. I went to sit in the pickup, and soon Jamie came, too. Losing the battle to fight back tears, I drove off quickly. As hard as I tried not to, I kept looking back.

We returned to the hotel, and I could already feel the desert slipping away. Only days before I had felt totally comfortable in my *dishdasha* and *masar*. Now I started to feel self-conscious about the questioning stares of Western tourists and Arabs alike. I changed to trousers, but the Bedu looked on with distaste when I visited them in their suite.

Sheikh Zayed had extended tremendous hospitality to our team by offering us rooms at a hotel in Abu Dhabi, but the Bedu did not want separate rooms, preferring to sleep close together. The solution the protocol office found was to offer them the presidential suite, which occupied the entire top floor of the Intercontinental Hotel. Manaa told me they slept huddled together in blankets on the floor of the main meeting hall. On our last day I asked them when they would leave to go home to their families. Manaa shrugged his shoulders. "Saleh, I do not know. Maybe in one month, maybe in one week, maybe in one day. We will leave when the sheikh asks us to leave. Until then this is our home. It is in the hands of God."

There were no tears as we packed our bags into waiting cars, ready to be driven to the airport. I felt a great loss, but the Bedu seemed already to be thinking of something else far away. No moment of farewell, however poignant, can ever do justice to the grand experience of a journey or time shared together. It just cannot be distilled into a word or deed. Perhaps, like the large campfire gathering in the desert, where no one ever said goodbye, it was easier just to walk away. As we brushed noses, I wondered when I would see our Bedu companions again. Later that night, as I walked up the steps to our waiting Airbus 330, I paused, turning to look back out over the tarmac of the Dubai airport.

This was goodbye. Perhaps the Bedu way of life would survive in small measure, despite Thesiger's predictions. Certainly it would never be the same as it once was. Much was already lost. I knew, should I ever return, that Arabia would never again hold for me the treasure that I had just experienced. After one last deep breath I turned, and ducking under the door, entered the waiting plane.

The English countryside, blooming in the full glory of spring, passed by the cab windows as if it were the backdrop on a old movie scene. The change was too sudden, too abrupt, to digest. My mind was elsewhere. As we raced up the long lane, Sir Wilfred stood waiting by the door of his country home. His eyes shone and he walked forward to greet us as we emerged from the cab, sunburned and bearded.

"*Salaam aleykum,*" he said, surprising me. Although I knew he could speak Arabic I had never heard him do so before.

"*Aleykum a salaam,*" we all replied, gripping his hand.

"*Keif halek?*" he asked.

"*Hamdulilla.*"

We gathered around an outdoor table to share stories and look at photographs. As we talked, Sir Wilfred reached forward to pick up a picture that had been taken on the beach at Salala just as we prepared to depart. With a shaking hand he gently traced the camels and their saddles, identical to the equipment he himself had used fifty years before.

"You are all making me feel terribly homesick," he said with a faint smile, his voice tinged with sadness.

On a tiny video monitor we replayed a few moments from our journey: the camels crossing the great orange dunes; our companions singing around the campfire; the well at Ma Shadid that he had visited. We did not want to impose on his patience, so we stopped after a few minutes and prepared to pack the video away. Sir Wilfred quietly asked if it would be all right to look at "another bit with the camels." He leaned forward and watched intently as uncut scenes of our caravan played, the massive beasts labouring over dune crests and swaying with a majestic gait on the flats. A tear formed in one eye, and, as the tape finished, he shook his head. "For those few minutes I was right there with you, riding every step of the way," he muttered. "In fifty years I have never seen anything so fine."

The stories and memories enlivened Sir Wilfred. Now, sitting in the comfort of a large chair, he began to recite Arabic: "*Daem allah di kollo, / beniadem ya doom, / Ossrah fakhura, / waal gamel hayen el yom.*

" 'God endures, mankind doesn't last,' " he said. "I don't know why that popped into my head. It was a riding song Bin Kabina used to sing every night before we went to sleep. You have reminded me of it for some reason."

We discussed with Sir Wilfred the changes we had seen, the difficulties we had faced, and how in some ways we felt we had failed. He looked at us surprised. "Indeed, not at all. Rather think of what you have achieved. It would not have been easy, and I suspected you would meet a lot of difficulties." After a pause he added, "It is probably the last chance it will ever be done. Ten years from now no Bedu will want to do it."

Sir Wilfred's approval meant a great deal. I felt honoured to be able to give something back to him, to share our stories and show our pictures, to touch so deeply the cantankerous and often pessimistic explorer. As we had driven out to the estate I had reflected on how Sir Wilfred's time in Arabia had marked his life. It had been his defining moment, and they were, he declared, "the happiest five years of my life." In the ensuing decades he had passed those adventures on to millions through his writing, yet no one had ever shared a similar experience. Although I knew our journey paled a hundred times over when compared to Sir Wilfred's incredible exploits, I realized we offered a connection to the desert, to the men, to the experience, that no one in fifty years had previously been able to supply.

We finally tore ourselves away; it was time for Sir Wilfred's afternoon medicine and preparations for our flight home. From the door he stood and waved as the cab drove off down the lane. I turned for one last look.

# EPILOGUE

*Ya Rub al Khali wasat kalbi tarabaat,*
(Oh Empty Quarter, you grip the centre of my heart,)
*Hobek tarabaa fi fouadi houssounah,*
(Your love holds my soul in her fortress,)
*Wallahi ouhebak wa aftakher ma tasanaat,*
(I swear that I love you with great pride,)
*Hobak fatan zawad al azar fetounah,*
(A love stronger than any other,)
*Haythou anaka al morabi wa wassatak taraarat,*
(For you are the place of my birth, the home where I grew,)
*Wa mar bay elay ehtadanet be houdounah.*
(And the land which holds me in its soul.)

*– a poem by Manaa bin Mohammed bin Musallim al-Musali al-Kathiri*
(Manaa wrote this more than twenty years ago. It is now widely sung across southern Oman. He proudly taught us the verse the day we arrived in Thumbrait.)

*W*e landed in Canada on March 18, two days after our visit to Sir Wilfred. From the window of the airplane the frozen ground and drifting snow appeared oddly foreign and unwelcoming. While it does not take long to assimilate back into one's own culture, inside, things were only just starting to settle. We had been branded by our time in the desert, although I did not realize how deeply until we returned home to familiar surroundings.

At a reception that evening I found I myself sitting on the floor, even though others around me were in chairs. I had worn sandals, but quickly

215

dispensed with them, being more comfortable barefoot. Mingling with guests, I unthinkingly ate the messy food with my hands. Later that night, when a friend's husband dropped me off at home, I instinctively drew him towards me to brush noses as we shook hands. With a mortified look he pulled away and squirmed to avoid me, fearing I was trying to kiss him.

Almost all the habits of daily life amongst the Bedu slipped quickly away. The last vestige remained the poetic words *Hamdulilla* and *Inshalla*, which I still use regularly. These hold for me a memory of the Bedu's humble acceptance of life's events. The literal translations carry with them many connotations here in the West, and there is no equivalent phrase or enunciation of feeling that I can find in English.

Shortly after we left Abu Dhabi the Bedu returned to their homes in Oman: Bin Ashara to his camp near Qitabit, Musallim to his home in Salala, and Ali Salim to Thumbrait. Being eighteen, Ali was ready to be married, and he told us, *Inshalla*, his mother may have arranged for a bride while he was away travelling in the desert. Astoundingly, I am able to remain in contact with Manaa through his interpreter, Sami's, e-mail, and regularly receive news and stories from Dhofar.

By the time we arrived home, Jamie, Leigh, and I had spent eighty days together, almost never apart. Words were unnecessary: we always seemed to know what the others were thinking, and exactly what needed to be done. We had accepted each other for our differences, which had been clearly revealed in the intense and emotional arena of an expedition. Our individual experiences on the journey had been very different. We began to follow our own paths.

Jamie left for a trek in Nepal, and a week later I flew north to spend the summer guiding on Arctic rivers. Despite the distance, we stayed in touch. Our friendship had weathered intense disagreements, and emerged strengthened. We still brush noses whenever we meet − the Bedu greeting a reminder of the desert experience woven into our past.

Leigh returned to a consuming corporate career. The journey had not been easy on him, physically or emotionally, but as I sat chatting beside him on the flight back, there had been a smile in his eyes, a lightness of being, that had not been there a year earlier. The journey had helped him see the value of the life he had in Canada, he told me, and now it was time for him to face some of those challenges anew. Apart from a few phone messages, we hardly spoke for months. This was not because of anger or any difference of opinion. We had become more deeply connected on the expedition than I initially realized, although Leigh remained enigmatic to me. My greatest sadness was that I had been unable to lead a trip that fulfilled him. I had failed in my efforts to oversee the Bedu effectively, and this had caused Leigh enormous consternation. Somehow it seemed symbolic that we each reflected on the experience alone.

Two years before we had started with nothing more than an idea – an idea we were told would be impossible. We had followed a fascinating journey, even before arriving in the desert. Through the planning and organization of the expedition our eyes had been opened to new horizons; the geography and history of Arabia, the culture and traditions of the nomads; a new language and religion; confusing diplomatic protocols; courting and maintaining relationships with sponsors; initiating an education program that enrolled twenty-two thousand children from nineteen countries around the world.

Preparing for the journey we had entered metaphorically uncharted territory. No one had travelled across the Empty Quarter by camel in more than fifty years; there was no one to turn to for advice, no recent examples to follow. We had created, or more correctly recreated. During the process we had been swamped with a dizzying number of phone calls, meetings, and e-mails, yet every moment had been a joy. There was the focus and passion in our daily lives that comes from having a dream or great goal. Flying to Arabia, all the clamour dropped behind. In the desert I had surrendered completely, immersing myself in life with the Bedu, purposely cutting my own ties to the outside. They had been three glorious months. And the entire experience – from its beginning in an

idea, through the planning and organizing, to its final completion –
stood as a validation of the belief that, with dedication and persistence,
no goal is too large.

Still, despite the apparent success of the expedition, I initially felt
little pride or sense of achievement when I returned home. Rather, I was
sad somewhere deep inside, but I could not understand why. I struggled
with what our expedition had meant. It seemed we had failed, and I was
not sure how. Was it that we did not find the adventure we sought? Had
we been so blinded by expectations that we did not embrace the experience we actually found?

Our challenges had not been the same as Thesiger's, fifty years earlier.
The unknowns we had faced were different. The vast desert had been
mapped, the unadministered tribesmen living on its borders had
settled. We carried a satellite phone, and, had all our *gerbers* leaked and
our camels gone lame, we likely could have been rescued. Our obstacles
were less romantic. We fought instead to attain exceedingly difficult
diplomatic permissions. We faced a continual struggle with the Bedu
over the expedition's ethics, ironically fighting for authenticity in a traditional nomadic journey.

*Arabian Sands*, a powerful and emotional tribute to the Bedu and Sir
Wilfred's life amongst them, is set against his crushing prediction that
"the Bedu with whom I lived and traveled . . . [are] doomed. If anyone
goes there now searching for the life I led, they will not find it."

Although much of the past still remains – the Bedu's pride, their ideals
of freedom and manliness, their honour and integrity, even their love of
endless conversation – there is no disputing that the once "illiterate
herdsmen" have changed irrevocably, and a way of life has almost completely passed. Arabia's nomads have been swept into our modern world
by the enormous upheavals that have gripped their land.

No culture is ever static. All civilizations, great and small alike,
evolve, flourish, and one day fade. Are we justified in mourning the loss
of another civilization? None of the Bedu we encountered would have
traded in their pickup or cellphone for a return to the old ways and an

uncertain life in the desert, where every night brought with it the threat of raiders, and every day brought the danger of thirst. With the rapid growth of technology have come advances that all of mankind should share: the eradication of plagues and disease, access to education, the sharing of information and knowledge, a general easing of life's rigours. It is irresponsible to suggest that a remote culture should remain in the past, denied modern advances, only to present a sideshow for Western travellers.

But these advances have not been without a cost. And the changes to the Bedu highlight a greater challenge facing us all, the spread of a generic world culture, a shocking loss of diversity, a growing sameness. Sadly, in a global economy ruled by material and economic forces, the immeasurable value of this kaleidoscope of languages, rituals, and beliefs is diminished. And as these unique cultures are absorbed by the planetary juggernaut, we all suffer an intangible loss.

Our increased presence in remote places bears with it a responsibility. We cannot stem the tide of change, but must work with it. By taking a sincere interest, both at home and abroad, in the differences that make us unique, we can help maintain our global diversity, and renew pride and interest in foreign cultures as they meet our Western goliath, and thus help them face the rapid changes – to evolve, and not simply be assimilated or extinguished.

صحراء

And so the Bedu today remain, as they were in Thesiger's time, riddled with contradictions and threatened by change. Perhaps one day Manaa's sons will make a great journey in the desert, as he told us was his wish. If so, they will learn some of their father's great skills, taught to Manaa by his father before him. And maybe they in turn will one day teach their own children, helping the spirit of their forefathers, and the land they once roamed, to survive.

*Inshalla.*

# GLOSSARY

*ata allah:* "God's gift," a term commonly used in Arabia to refer to a camel

*aleykum as salaam:* "with you be peace," the response to *salaam alaykum*, Arabia's traditional greeting

*bedu:* bedouin

*bin:* son of

*dishdasha:* traditional Arabic gown

*gerber:* a goatskin used to carry water

*graf:* a common desert tree

*hadut:* the primary piece of a camel's saddle, a wedge-shaped piece of cedar padded with a mat of woven palm fronds

*hamdullila:* "praise be to god"

*harif:* the rainy season of southern Oman, part of the Indian monsoon

*inshalla:* "god willing"

*jebel:* mountain

*Keif halek?:* "How is life?" "How are you?"

*khobz:* unleavened bread, a mixture of flour and water baked in hot sand under a fire

*masar:* headdress

*mafi mushkilla:* "no problem"

*mafi zain:* "no good"

*Ramadan:* the ninth month of the Muslim year, when strict fasting is observed from sunrise to sunset

*Rub al-Khali:* "The Empty Quarter," southern Arabia's massive sand desert

*sabkha:* salt flats found between dunes

*salaam aleykum:* "peace be with you," the traditional greeting throughout Arabia

*salat:* pray

*Umm as Samim:* "Mother of Poison," a massive sea of *sabkha* and quicksand

*wadi:* a dry river course, worn through millennia of intermittent flooding

*wasir:* a skirt-like undergarment worn by the bedu

# SELECTED BIBLIOGRAPHY

Asher, Michael. *Thesiger: A Biography*. London: Viking, 1994.

Banner, N. P. *Jeff Davis' Camel Corps*. Odessa, Texas: Nicholas Banner, 1994.

Bidwell, Robin. *Travellers in Arabia*. London: Hamlyn, 1976.

Boustani, Rafie, and Philippe Fargoes. *The Atlas of the Arab World*. New York: Facts on File, 1990.

Burton, Richard. *Personal Narrative of a Pilgrimage to Al-Madinah and Meccah*. London: Bell, 1898.

Carter, J. R. L. *Tribes in Oman*. London: Peninsular Publishing, 1982.

Clapp, Nicholas. *The Road to Ubar*. New York: Houghton Mifflin, 1998.

Doughty, Charles. *Travels in Arabia Deserta*. London: Jonathan Cape, 1855.

Freeth, Zahra, and Victor Winstone. *Explorers of Arabia*. London: Allen & Unwin, 1978.

Hawley, Donald. *Oman, & Its Renaissance*. London: Stacey International, 1977.

Keohane, Alan. *Bedouin: Nomads of the Desert*. London: Kyle Cathie, 1994.

Lacey, Robert. *The Kingdom*. New York: Avon Books, 1981.

Lawrence, T. E. *Seven Pillars of Wisdom*. London: Jonathan Cape, 1935.

Polk, W., and W. Mares. *Passing Brave*. New York: Ballantine Books, 1973.

Rashid, N. I., and E. I. Shaheen. *Saudi Arabia*. Joplin, Missouri: International Institute of Technology, 1995.

Thesiger, Wilfred. *Arabian Sands*. London: Longmans, 1959.

Thesiger, Wilfred. *The Life of My Choice*. New York: Norton, 1987.

Trench, Richard. *Arabian Travellers*. London: Macmillan, 1986.

# ACKNOWLEDGEMENTS

**Jamie and Leigh**
As there is no higher, or rarer, bond than a dream shared.

**NEC Technologies and Bausch & Lomb Eyecare**
For their boldness and generosity in supporting this expedition.

**The al-Musalli Family and the entire Bait Kathir Bedu tribe**
with the deepest of thanks to
Musallim bin Abdulla, Salim bin Ashara, Ali bin Salim,
and Manaa Mohammed.

**Sir Wilfred Thesiger**
and Mr. Alex Maitland
for their inspiration, advice, and friendship.

**The Canadian Department of Foreign Affairs
and International Trade**
with special acknowledgement to
H.E. Daniel Hobson, Canadian Ambassador
to the Kingdom of Saudi Arabia,
H.E. Stuart McDowall, Canadian Ambassador to the
United Arab Emirates,
Mr. Ian Shaw, Second Secretary (Riyadh),
Wanda Slip, Executive Assistant (Abu Dhabi),
Stephen Randall, Third Secretary (Dubai)

**The Kingdom of Saudi Arabia**
H.H. Prince Turki bin Sultan bin Abdul Aziz,
H.H. Prince Sultan bin Salman bin Abdul Aziz,
H.H. Prince Saud bin Naif bin Abdul Aziz

The Sultanate of Oman

**The United Arab Emirates**
H.H. Sheikh Zayed bin Sultan al-Nahyan, President of U.A.E. and
Ruler of Abu Dhabi

**Chris Beale and the staff of Heide Beale Tours, Muscat**

**For their help with this book**
Joanne Kellock, who represented me so ably; Douglas Gibson, for his
faith in both me and this book; Pat Kennedy, my editor, for her care in
the project; Peter Buck for his diligent fact-checking; Sari Ginsberg,
who brought her talented artistry to the design; and the entire staff of
McClelland & Stewart, who welcomed me in and helped me with
every step along the way.

**And the countless others who contributed their help, including**
Ian Clarke, André Lemarre, Gerald Edwards, Sandy Pearson, Karen
Harris, David Alloway, Doug Baum, Mr. David Sulzberger, Calgary
Board of Education (Frank, Cynthia, Glenn, Stephen, Joe, Terry, Jack),
Bankers Hall Health Club, ABL Photo Lab, QLC Communications,
Ellen Walsh, Ingle Health Insurance, Said bin Ali, Touarish bin Salim,
Salim bin Ali,

**and my family**
Mom, Heather, and Doug